PROMOTING PROGRESS

A RADICAL NEW AGENDA TO CREATE ABUNDANCE FOR ALL

MICHAEL MAGOON

FP
2P

Upward Press

Cataloging Publication Data

>   Michael Magoon
>   Promoting Progress / Michael Magoon

Library of Congress Control Number: 2023908018

Paperback: 978-1-958206-06-5
Hardcover: 978-1-958206-05-8

Credit and permissions are listed on the "Credits" page and are considered a continuation of the copyright page.

Published by Upward Press 2023, Boise, Idaho

**FP
2P**

Book Series

This is the second book in the *From Poverty to Progress* series about history, material progress, technological innovation, economic growth, and policy reforms. Each book in the series has a specific focus, but they all share a common progress-based perspective.

The first book in this series explains my theory on the origins and causes of progress, why it took so long for progress to get started, and how that progress has spread across the world. Each of the subsequent books focuses on either government policies to promote progress or the history of progress in a specific time and region.

"The Five Keys to Progress" and "How Progress Works" are the central unifying concepts of this book series.

Published Books

From Poverty to Progress: Understanding Humanity's Greatest Achievement
Promoting Progress: A Radical New Agenda to Create Abundance for All

Forthcoming Books

Upward Mobility: A Radical New Agenda to Uplift the Poor and Working Class (publication date: 2024)

Website for Book Series

You can find additional content related to this book series at:
frompovertytoprogress.com

With a **free** subscription to this website, you get:

- Large discounts on audiobooks and e-books
- Free book samples (E-book and audiobook)
- Access to videos and blog posts about related content
- Plus more.

Bibliography

To keep the price of this book as affordable as possible, the bibliography has been moved to the author's website.

To access this content, scan the following QR code or go to **frompovertytoprogress.com** and search for "Additional Content"

Table of Contents

INTRODUCTION

The last 30 years have seen by far the greatest material progress in human history. Since the fall of the Soviet Union, dozens of nations have moved from desperate poverty into middle-income status, and billions of people have been elevated out of poverty. Even Sub-Saharan Africa has experienced real material progress during this period.

As I documented in the first book in this series, *From Poverty to Progress*, this progress can be measured across dozens of different domains: economic growth, declining poverty, increasing life spans, declining infant mortality, improved sanitation, increasing literacy, longer schooling, declining slums, increasing nutrition, a decline in wars and violent conflicts, and increasing happiness. These trends are seen in the vast majority of nations throughout the world.

Despite this progress, those who enjoy the greatest benefits of that progress are anxious and worried about the future. Over the last ten years in wealthy Western nations, there has been a noticeable increase in pessimism about both our current situation and our long-term future. Ironically, the very people who have most benefited from progress, college-educated professionals in Western nations, have become the most pessimistic of any group.

Just as disturbingly, material progress appears to be stalling in many industrialized Western nations. As of 2022, the European economy has essentially not recovered from the economic recession of 2007. This 15-year period of essentially zero economic growth is longer than the Great Depression of the 1930s. In addition, Canada has seen virtually no economic growth since 2011.

Japan, once the Asian nation that most embodied economic dynamism, has seen very little growth since 1995. Moreover, future economic prospects in Canada, Japan and Europe do not look any better than the recent past.

Among Western nations, the United States is one of the few that has experienced robust economic growth over the last ten years. Unfortunately, recent trends as of 2022 suggest that stagnant economic growth may be spreading to the United States. Many of the causes of the apparent recession in 2022 are related to short-term factors, such as the Covid lockdowns and the Russian invasion of Ukraine. But more systemic factors are also in play.

Neither the ideological Left nor the ideological Right offer any real solutions to our current problems. Perhaps most discouraging is the fact that much of the political leadership in the West has given up on the idea of progress or completely misunderstood where it comes from. Political movements that should be promoting progress are failing to do so because of incorrect assumptions.

Many leaders on the traditional Left, for example European Social Democrats and the Democratic party in the United States, believe that progress can only come from ever-increasing government social programs to redistribute income or regulation to control corporations. With near-zero economic growth, however, this entire model is unsustainable because it relies on constantly increasing tax revenues.

The only true accomplishment of the traditional Left has been an ever-expanding central government that achieves fewer and fewer results. As of 2020, most wealthy Western nations have government expenditures that reach or exceed 50% of their total GDP. The French government accounts for 62% of the country's GDP, Italy spends 57%, Germany 51%, and the UK 50% of their respective GDPs. Even the government in the supposedly free-market United States is now spending 46% of GDP, while Japan is at 47%. Only Ireland at 29% and Switzerland at 36% have governments that spend substantially below 50% (IMF).

The traditional Left has abandoned the idea of material progress based on economic growth. They appear to believe that ever-expanding social programs to redistribute income and regulations to constrain corporations will create a better society. The traditional Left claims that things are bad, but doing more of the same will solve the problem. Failures of government redistribution in the past breed skepticism about the concept of progress and undermine confidence in the efficacy of government.

More radical ideologies on the Left are typically hostile to the idea of progress. This includes Democratic Socialists, Greens, and Critical theorists (more commonly known as "the Woke"). Many of these ideologues believe that progress is the cause of our problems, so most Leftists deliberately seek to restrain it. They believe that progress is:

- Inherently unfair because the benefits of progress are unequally distributed
- A destructive force on the natural environment
- Immoral because it is based purely on material goods
- Immoral because it relies to a large extent on self-interested decision-making by individuals
- Immoral because it further solidifies the power of the oppressors over the oppressed.

Greens believe that material progress leads to ecological collapse and cling to fanciful ideas that renewable energy and organic food will make all the difference. Critical theorists see every idea, institution, and practice as a system of oppression for people of color and other underrepresented minorities. Democratic Socialists believe in an oxymoron. You cannot radically concentrate power in the hands of a centralized government and nonetheless maintain democracy. In such circumstances, centralized power will ultimately overcome democratic governance.

Everywhere in the Western world we see the traditional Left being replaced by an anti-progress Left-wing. This means that traditional Left policies that unintentionally undermined progress are being replaced by Left-wing policies that deliberately undermine progress, particularly in the fields of energy, housing, agriculture, and the centralization of government.

Ideologies on the Right offer no real alternative, because conservatives are no more positive about the concept of progress. As Josef Schumpeter has noted, material progress works through a process of "creative destruction." As new technologies and organizations are created, they drive old technologies and organizations to extinction. This destruction affects many of the very institutions and values that conservatives hold dear.

For this reason, ideologies of the Right are skeptical of progress. They believe that the most important recent trends have been a decline of moral values, the relentless expansion of government, and the decline in religious observance, patriotism, and traditional institutions.

Most importantly, the Right has no alternative policy solutions. I believe that Conservatism is best summarized by the famous William F. Buckley Jr. quote: "A conservative is someone who stands athwart history yelling 'Stop'…" Many conservatives see Progress as a constant decline in moral standards and traditional institutions. Most conservatives look back with a rosy nostalgia at a past that, upon examination, was far less rosy than conservatives imagine.

While conservatives are correct that some change is bad, it is not true that all change is bad. The fundamental problem with Conservatism as a worldview is that it has no means to separate good change from bad change. More sophisticated conservatives, such as Edmund Burke, believed in cautious reform. But reform to what end? Reform by what means? How do conservatives know whether a specific reform is good or bad?

In practice, this has meant that conservatives oppose whatever proposal the Left has to offer at any given time. This has resulted in the Left ever so slowly winning victories, and the Right caving in to each of the arguments that had previously been made by the Left. The result is a conservative base that is bitter, skeptical of progress, and willing to follow less-than-reputable leaders.

Though conservatives (and also libertarians) oppose the practices of the Left, neither offers a coherent alternative. Supporters of both world views seem resigned to constant political defeat and focus on rallying their base during elections. Once in power, they do little to fundamentally change anything. They are opposed to everything the Left does, but they make few fundamental policy reforms once they win elections.

The entire history of material progress over the last two centuries that I documented in the first book in this series, *From Poverty to Progress*, invalidates much of the conservative viewpoint. If the world had stayed the same in 1820, as conservatives at that time believed was necessary, virtually all of mankind would be living in absolute poverty, living much shorter lives, eating less food, being educated less than one year per person, and experiencing a life of sheer physical drudgery.

The combination of hostility to progress from the Left-wing, misunderstanding of the causes of progress by the traditional Left, and skepticism of progress from the Right have undermined our collective belief in and understanding of progress. Despite what ideologues claim, it is not progress that is the problem. It is our politics, ideology, and government policy.

Unfortunately, these anti-progress viewpoints on both the Left and Right are magnified enormously by the media, social media, and interest groups. Whereas these institutions once tended towards the political center, they are now all affiliated with the ideological Left or the ideological Right. Their ideological viewpoints have corrupted the original purpose of the institutions that they dominate.

All of these institutions have learned that the best way to motivate people is with fear and hate towards the other side. To generate more revenue, viewership, votes, and political power, they have adopted a business model based on negativity and intransigence. These business models further undermine belief in progress.

Whereas politics was once constrained largely to elections and governance, it has now permeated all aspects of society. As the political parties have polarized between Left and Right, so has our society. Even families and once non-political institutions have been torn apart by ideological division. It is becoming increasingly hard for Americans to unite on any basic principles.

Some claim that all these problems prove that progress does not exist or that progress is a bad thing. At best, they claim that progress is now a thing of the past, which is no longer relevant to our current situation. The implication is that our current problems are just too large in scale to be solved by traditional methods.

I believe that the skeptics of progress are wrong, both factually and morally. Our current problems are not caused by any negative effects of progress. They are driven by politics, ideology, and failed government policies.

Progress is the single most important trend of the last century. Today, the material standard of living of humanity is far higher than it has ever been. This is not something that we should take for granted. Problems exist, just as they have always existed, but they are now less severe than ever. And the number of our problems is fewer than ever. It is merely our perceptions that magnify current problems into unsolvable crises.

Rather than abandon the concept of progress, we must learn from the ways our ancestors built progress in the first place. Our ancestors overcame problems far more difficult and complex than ours, and they did so with a much smaller base of technology and scientific knowledge. Most importantly, our ancestors gave us a toolkit for promoting progress that is still effective today, if we just give it a chance.

The fundamental problem is that neither the Left nor the Right has a concept of progress that is based on real human history. The Left compares our present condition to an ideological vision that cannot exist, while the Right compares our present condition to nostalgic memories that never existed. They are both excellent at provoking emotional reactions to mobilize supporters, but they are both bad at solving contemporary problems.

I do not believe that any existing ideology can make major contributions to maintaining progress in wealthy nations and enabling developing nations to experience greater progress. The fundamental reason is that none of them embrace human material progress as a primary goal. Far too many explicitly reject the concept of progress or are at least skeptical of it.

We need a new political perspective that is clearly differentiated from both the Left and the Right. We do not need to transform society (as the Left wants), nor do we need to preserve it in amber (as the Right wants). Instead, we need to roll back government policies that are undermining the foundations of progress.

We need a third option in the ideological center of American politics that promotes widely-shared progress and understands that this progress will largely come from society, not the government. This option cannot be based on reasonable compromises between the current positions of the Right and Left. Instead, it must offer an entirely new vision of the role of government that is both pragmatic and radical.

We need a Progress-based reform agenda focused on the following principles:

1. Promote long-term economic growth.
2. Create a prosperous working class.
3. Promote a clear pathway that enables youths from low-income families to enter the prosperous working class.
4. Focus relentlessly on results.
5. Reform the political process to make all the above possible.

I sum up goal #1 as "Promoting Progress" and goals #2 and #3 as "Promoting Upward Mobility." I will focus on goals #1, 4 and 5 in this book. In my subsequent book, *Upward Mobility: A Radical New Agenda for Uplifting the Working Class and Poor*, I will focus on the second and third goals.

Promoting long-term economic growth must be the bedrock of a Progress-based reform agenda. Economic growth gives all individuals more material resources with which to solve their own personal problems and their families' problems. Economic growth also supplies the material resources to take on improvements in education, health care, pensions, and care for the disabled, the mentally ill, and the homeless. Without economic growth, all other goals become far more difficult to accomplish because there are simply not enough resources available to achieve them.

Creating a prosperous working class is essential to ensuring that economic growth is widely shared and politically sustainable. Far too high a proportion of the benefits of our current economic growth go to the college-educated professional class. And much of that distribution is due to bad government policy.

We must implement policies that ensure that the working class receives a far greater share of the benefits of progress and that they do so by contributing to society. A prosperous working class will not achieve equality. However, in combination with economic growth, it will achieve upward mobility.

Promoting a clear pathway that enables youths from low-income families to enter that prosperous working class is also essential. With each generation, modern societies must pass on the necessary skills, habits, and values to the next generation. We cannot create a prosperous working class with no way for young people, particularly those from low-income families, to enter that class. By promoting a clear pathway into a prosperous working class, we can sustain this progress and upward mobility for generations to come.

Supporters of progress must focus relentlessly on results. A Progress-based reform agenda must never be allowed to degenerate into a dogmatic ideology that is fixated on certain policies regardless of results. While the long-term goal of promoting progress and upward mobility must be fundamental to our viewpoint, *how* we do so should always be determined by experimentation in the real world.

Like scientists looking for a cure for cancer or an entrepreneur trying to scale up a business, we must try many possible solutions and only scale one up once it has been proven effective by rigorous methodologies. The fundamental principles that I mentioned above will be very difficult to achieve. They will each require a great deal of experimentation with policy. Many proposed policies will fail to work, so they must be reformed or eliminated.

Supporters of progress cannot just dream up seemingly great policy solutions and then pass legislation. Instead, we must go into this project with a realization of how hard it is for government programs to achieve positive results in the real world.

Of course, this experimentation must avoid potential negative effects on society. In particular, we must respect basic human rights enshrined in the Constitution. Our experimentation must also be constrained by basic human decency, though admittedly this concept is hard to define. But these constraints still leave us a great deal of leeway for effective and ethical experimentation.

In the end, the actual results of a policy are far more important than the good intentions of those who implemented it. Only results matter, because it is results that affect people, not intentions.

Any reform agenda must also confront the problem of scarce resources. So much of our economy is now devoted to current government programs that there is no chance of finding additional revenues without serious negative economic consequences.

Rather than building up additional layers of government programs, a Progress-based reform agenda should focus on rolling back government policies that undermine the foundations of progress and upward mobility for the working class and poor. In particular, we should make energy, food, housing, education, health care, transportation, and consumer goods more abundant and affordable so that the working class and poor can afford to purchase those items on the marketplace without government subsidies.

Rolling back failed government policies will not only accelerate economic growth by reducing costs but doing so will also ensure that the benefits of that growth are widely shared. We should also decentralize government to promote the maximum possible amount of policy experimentation.

Finally, a Progress-based reform agenda must reform the political system. The American political system, which is polarized between liberal Democrats and conservative Republicans, leaves no space for any other perspective. Both sides are more concerned about rallying their base against the other side than about solving problems. For the good of the nation and the good of our movement, we must open up political competition to allow representation in state and federal government for ourselves and other outsiders.

FROM POVERTY TO PROGRESS

Before I propose my Progress-based reform agenda, we need to more fully explore the concept of Progress itself and why understanding it can help us solve our current problems. After decades of studying history, I have come to believe that the only way that we can make the future better is by understanding the past.

In the first book in this series, *From Poverty to Progress*, I explained how and why human progress originated, how it works and how progress gradually spread from a few small city/states in Northwest Europe to most of the world. Though we take this progress for granted, it is the single most important factor in our lives. This progress means that our lives differ radically from the standard of living of our ancestors.

A key concept in this book series is the concept of the "Five Keys to Progress." The Five Keys to Progress are the necessary preconditions to start human progress and for it to continue. When a society achieves the Five Keys to Progress, that society becomes a vast, decentralized problem-solving network that makes material life better for its citizens.

I believe that the concept of the Five Keys to Progress enables us to establish policies and practices which maintain existing progress. In other words, the concept not only helps us to understand our world and how we got here but also how to change it for the better.

The rest of this chapter briefly summarizes key concepts from my previous book that will help you to understand why I believe that the proposals made in this book will lead to greater amounts of material progress. If you have already read that book, you can skim this chapter to refresh your memory and then skip to the next chapter.

What is Progress?

I believe that the most useful definition of progress is "the sustained improvement in the material standard of living of a large group of people over a long period of time." In particular, I focus on changes to the standard of living that are rapid enough and sustained enough that one person could notice positive changes within their lifetime.

Progress within one year that is immediately erased by a regression in the next few years does not qualify as progress. Since a generation is generally considered to be 20 years, I look for relatively uninterrupted progress for at least that length of time. One sharp downturn is not enough to invalidate a decade of progress, but a downturn that lasts for decades surely means that progress did not exist during that time.

Progress is not about enriching a small portion of society. While it is possible to apply the term to changes that exclusively benefit the rich and powerful, I am far more concerned about material progress for the vast majority of citizens.

People living in Western nations today have a level of affluence far surpassing anything ever seen on planet Earth. Even the poor in Western nations have a level of affluence that is higher than all but the richest people in 1970.

All across the world, nations are being transformed from oppressive poverty to a level of affluence that was once only possible in Western nations. Japan, South Korea, China, India, Singapore, Botswana, Chile, and Puerto Rico all transformed themselves within one generation. Even in some of the poorest nations of Sub-Saharan Africa, levels of education, health, literacy, sanitation, longevity, transportation, communication, and housing are rapidly improving.

Progress is mankind's greatest achievement. It has transformed our lives in so many positive ways... But we take it for granted, deny its existence, or claim that it is actually bad.

Why Does Progress Matter?

Too many people today live in a negative feedback loop caused by cognitive biases towards pessimism and perceived threat, unrealistic views of what is possible, nostalgic memories of what life used to be like, self-imposed isolation from alternative viewpoints, and institutional self-interests that create constant crises and threats. This feedback loop creates what can only be described as an alternative reality that seems very real to people but does not exist.

I believe that the objective study of history to understand progress is a form of "therapy" for this dysfunction. We need a change of perspective to clear out the cognitive biases that make so many of us unhappy, angry, and resentful in a world full of abundance and progress.

To understand the benefits of progress, we need to shift the focus from the problems of today to the study of how our ancestors actually lived. Only by comparing today's life to the actual lives of previous generations can we fully appreciate the progress that we have experienced today.

Once we look at actual metrics comparing today's material circumstances to our ancestor's circumstances, we can see that we live in a world of progress.

Even better, learning *how* our ancestors built progress gives us a toolkit for solving most of today's problems. We can see that, in situations far worse than our own, our ancestors learned highly practical strategies for solving short-term local problems. And those that worked best were copied by others.

When we clear out our cognitive biases, we can see that life in the past was actually pretty terrible. It was full of people with the same dread and worry that we have today. It was also full of problems that were daily threats to survival that we do not have to deal with as often today.

We can learn that, though very real problems still exist, those problems are actually fewer in number and milder in severity than what previous generations had to deal with. And previous generations did not have all the technologies, skills, organizations, and scientific knowledge that we have today.

The good old days were never really that good. Utopias cannot exist in the real world. The world as portrayed by the media and politics is highly distorted and dangerously so.

Life Before Progress

Today's progress is a startling transformation compared to the way humans have lived over the past 100,000 years. In the past, humanity lived in a stable state because technological innovation only occurred very rarely.

Our ancestors lived in a world where acquiring food took up the bulk of their waking hours. Entire societies were structured around the quest to acquire enough food to survive and reproduce in their local environment. This quest was so all-encompassing that little time was left to solve other problems.

In order to innovate, people needed to live in close proximity to each other, but in order to acquire food, they needed to spread out. Therefore, the need for food was the key limiting factor in the rate of innovation.

The type of food that could be acquired was highly constrained by fundamental geographical limits. In particular, the biome (i.e. dominant vegetation) that a society inhabited and its access to domesticatable plants and animals largely determined whether agriculture based upon animal-drawn plows could evolve. Other factors such as altitude, soil type, growing season, distance from rivers and more complex societies in the Middle East placed additional constraints.

How a society acquired its food, in turn, placed powerful constraints on how rapidly the society could innovate technologies, skills, and social organizations or copy the innovations of others. Where geography made the use of animal-driven plows possible, complex Agrarian societies evolved. Where the use of animal-driven plows was not possible, humans could not evolve past less complex types of societies. Those societies had no chance of experiencing progress.

Even in geographical regions that could support Agrarian societies, two forces prevented progress. The first was that most of the food surplus went into having more babies, who then ate away much of the food surplus.

Secondly, powerful political, economic, and religious elites constructed institutions that extracted the food surplus for their own benefit. They used this extracted wealth to flaunt their social status with a lavish lifestyle, build conspicuous monuments, and construct powerful militaries capable of conquering other peoples. This extraction of wealth undermined the rate of innovation and hamstrung the potential for progress.

Because of these geographical, demographic, and political constraints, most societies of the past were trapped in poverty. There was little an individual could do other than survive and live a life almost identical to previous generations.

The Five Keys to Progress

So how did we transition from a world of poverty to a world of progress?

The single most important concept in my book series is the "Five Keys to Progress." I believe that the Five Keys to Progress is an **essential unifying concept for understanding progress**. They are so critical because they are the **necessary preconditions** for progress, and they are **actionable** in today's world. In other words, the concept not only helps to understand the world but also how to make it better.

The Five Keys to Progress enable us to cut through all of the clutter of history and modern times so that we can focus on what really matters. They enable us to answer some of history's most difficult questions, as well as provide policy solutions and practices that can make the world a better place.

Using the concept of the Five Keys to Progress, it is easier to understand:

- The historical origins of progress
- Why progress took so long to get started
- How and why progress started in Northwest Europe
- How and why progress spread to different societies over time
- Why so many poor nations were left without progress for centuries
- Which forces threaten progress today
- What policies and practices wealthy nations need to adopt to keep their progress going
- What policies and practices developing nations need to adopt to enjoy greater progress

So what are the Five Keys to Progress? To transition from poverty to progress, a society needs to acquire:

1. **A highly efficient food production and distribution system.** This enables societies to overcome geographical constraints to food production so that large numbers of people can focus on solving problems other than finding enough food to eat.

2. **Trade-based cities** packed with a large number of free citizens possessing a wide variety of skills. These people innovate new technologies, skills and social organizations and copy the innovations made by others.

3. **Decentralized political, economic, religious, and ideological power.** Of particular importance are elites being forced into transparent, non-violent competition that undermines their ability to forcibly extract wealth from the masses. This also allows citizens to freely choose among institutions based on what they have to offer to each individual and society in general.

4. **At least one high-value-added industry that exports** to the rest of the world. This injects wealth into the city or region, accelerates economic growth, and creates markets for smaller local industries and services.

5. **Widespread use of fossil fuels.** The incredible energy density

of fossil fuels injects vast amounts of useful energy into society enabling it to solve a wide variety of problems. Without this energy, life would return to the daily struggle for survival that dominated most of human history.

Each of the Five Keys to Progress is **necessary** for a society to experience progress, but **none are sufficient by themselves**. It is only in combination that they enable humanity to deliver progress.

I believe that the degree to which societies have enjoyed progress is largely determined by long-run historical factors that go back centuries or even millennia. These factors determined the extent to which societies acquired the Five Keys to Progress. For most of human history, there was no progress, because these five key factors were either completely missing or were very underdeveloped.

How Progress Works

Once a society achieves the Five Keys to Progress, that society becomes a vast, decentralized problem-solving network. Now the day-to-day behaviors of regular human beings break the chains of the poverty trap imposed by geography, demographics, and politics.

This progress comes from a self-sustaining feedback loop among the following human behaviors:

1. Technological innovation. This includes radical innovations such as the railroad, electrical grid, computers, and the internet, as well as the ongoing incremental improvement and differentiation of thousands of other existing technologies.

2. People learning new skills to support those technologies. Without these skills, technologies are not useful, a fact that is often forgotten.

3. People cooperating *within* organizations. Those people work together using a wide variety of skills and technologies to accomplish a common goal.

4. Competition *between* organizations for scarce resources. In the

past, this was usually food, while now it is usually revenue. This forces organizations to embrace new technologies, skills, and processes in order to out-compete other organizations. It also forces people within the group to cooperate more closely and enables new organizations to be founded and older organizations to fail.

5.   People copying successful technologies, skills, and organizations and then modifying them to solve different problems. This enables innovations that work to spread into new companies, new sectors of the economy, and new geographical regions. This step is critical for ensuring that progress is widely shared.

6.   Vast amounts of useful energy being injected into the system. Without energy, none of this can happen. Today, the vast majority of that energy comes from fossil fuels.

It is important to note that all of these behaviors have been in existence since the advent of modern humans hundreds of thousands of years ago. Humans have always invented new technologies, learned new skills, cooperated in organizations, competed as groups against other organizations, copied other humans, and consumed energy. It is quite likely that our hominid ancestors also behaved in ways that strongly resembled ours.

But until the Five Keys to Progress were acquired, the amount of change caused by these behaviors was so slow that they did not deliver progress – "the sustained improvement in the material standard of living of a large group of people over a long period of time." They delivered long, slow change, but no progress.

How Progress Spread Across the Globe

Human history can be viewed as a vast evolutionary process that led to the accidental discovery of the Five Keys to Progress. Once these keys were discovered, they slowly and unevenly diffused throughout the world. There were six historical breakthroughs that enabled progress to accelerate and diffuse to new parts of the globe:

1.   The emergence of Commercial societies in medieval city/states of Northern Italy that combined four of the Five Keys to Progress (productive agriculture, trade-based cities, decentralized power, and exporting industries).

2.   The diffusion of Commercial societies from Northern Italy to Flanders (modern-day Belgium) and then to the Netherlands and finally to Southeast England.

3.   The migration of Europeans to much of the rest of the world. The migration of peoples from Britain to North America was particularly important.

4.   The Industrial Revolution in Britain, which invented the fifth key to progress (widespread use of fossil fuels).

5.   The Allied victory in World War II, which ended the military threats of Nazi Germany, Imperial Japan, and Fascist Italy.

6.   The collapse of the Soviet Union in the early 1990s. This event enabled progress to spread throughout most of the world, particularly in Asia.

Today, industrial technology enables entire societies to overcome geographical constraints that had trapped them in poverty for millennia. Entire nations and sub-national groups have transformed themselves within one generation – a stunning achievement.

We Can Solve Today's Problems

Progress is the most uplifting story in human history. It has transformed poverty into prosperity, disease into health, ignorance into education, isolation into connectedness, war and violence into peace and security, slums into housing, and servitude into freedom. Quite frankly, it is the single most important force to have impacted the material existence of humanity. We must protect it in wealthy nations and expand it in developing countries.

With an awareness of the progress that previous generations have left to us, a feeling of gratitude for benefitting from their efforts, and a willingness to learn how they achieved that progress, we will be in a much better position to solve the problems of today. While today's problems seem insurmountable, we must never forget that previous generations solved far bigger problems with far fewer resources. Knowing this, we can look forward to the future with both hope and the necessary problem-solving attitude.

My hope is that this book series helps to ramp down the current level of cynicism and replace it with a new field of inquiry for understanding which factors promote progress. Just as important, I hope to spark interest in identifying which actions people need to take to enjoy the benefits of the progress that surrounds them.

PART ONE: REFORMING THE POLITICAL PROCESS

P art One of this book presents a series of reforms of the political process to make it possible for supporters of Progress to achieve political representation. Because the American political system is dominated by liberal Democrats who are either opposed to progress or do not understand its importance and conservative Republicans who prefer nostalgia for the past over progress, we must focus on political reform first. Only by reforming the political system can supporters of Progress acquire representation in the political system.

Our current political system is undermining progress because it violates many of the concepts within the Five Keys to Progress and How Progress Works. The current American political system:

- Concentrates political power into the hands of very liberal Democrats and very conservative Republicans
- Highly restricts competition between political parties
- Makes it very difficult for new parties to be formed and become competitive
- Overcentralizes power into the hands of the federal government
- Restricts the ability of local and state governments to experiment with different policies
- Makes it very difficult to identify and implement policies that actually work.

PROMOTING POLITICAL COMPETITION

The Third Key to Progress: Decentralized political, economic, religious and ideological power. Of particular importance are elites being forced into transparent, non-violent competition that undermines their ability to forcibly extract wealth from the masses. This also allows citizens to freely choose among institutions based upon what they have offer to each individual and society in general.

The bulk of this book is devoted to rolling back government policies that undermine long-term economic growth. This chapter focuses on reforming political structures that enable those policies to be implemented.

Throughout my *From Poverty to Progress* book series, I argue that transparent, non-violent competition between elites is an essential precondition for human progress. This competition undermines their ability to forcibly extract wealth from the masses and allows citizens to freely choose among institutions based upon what they have offer to each individual and society in general. Unfortunately, the terms of competition among American political elites are becoming increasingly distorted and dysfunctional.

Given the current state of the American political process, I do not believe that a Progress-based reform agenda can be implemented without first fixing those problems. Virtually all political power in America is held by the Democratic party or the Republican party. The Democratic party is controlled by left-liberal activists that are hostile to progress, while the Republican party is controlled by conservative activists that are skeptical of progress. Both are more concerned about defeating their partisan opponents than advancing the necessary reforms.

The fundamental problem is that the terms of competition between political elites has been distorted by our electoral process. Rather than healthy win-win competition that promotes good governance, we have a win-lose competition where ideologues win at the expense of the American people. Voters in the middle of the ideological spectrum are almost completely unrepresented and are growing increasingly alienated from the political system.

Of course, implementing these reforms does not guarantee that my proposed reform agenda will be implemented. Ultimately, that will be left up to the American people. But these political reforms would at least make it possible to implement a sweeping reform agenda.

This ideological polarization of American politics is the unintended outcome of many trends:

1. Complete domination of all political power by the two established parties. Independents and third parties have essentially no chance of winning elections. This is primarily caused by an electoral system that is based on plurality voting within single-member districts.

2. Declining electoral competition between Democrats and Republicans. Over 80% of Congressional seats are non-competitive with the winner known years before the election even takes place. This makes the vast majority of general elections meaningless.

3. The fact that each of the two parties selects their candidates via partisan primaries.

4. Very low turnout in partisan primaries. What little turnout there is in partisan primaries is dominated by ideological activists. These activists are overwhelmingly on the Left in the Democratic party primaries, and, they are overwhelmingly on the Right in the Republican party primaries.

5. Voters increasingly sorting themselves out geographically into "Red" states and "Blue" states.

6. The fact that Republicans in Blue states and Democrats in Red states thus get very little representation.

7. Gerrymandering to increase representation by the dominant party.

8. No real possibility for competitive third parties or Independents to emerge.

9. The media, social media, interest groups, and even non-political institutions are increasingly allying themselves with one of the dominant parties and then using their powers to vilify the other side to attract viewers, donors, and votes.

10. All of this is creating a toxic political culture that is increasingly fraying American culture and institutions.

The result of all of the above trends plus the centralization of government power at the federal level has resulted in a form of trench warfare between the two major parties. Neither of these parties represents anything close to the majority of American voters.

If the federal government were far weaker than it is today, many of these negative developments would be contained within a minority of states. In combination with an all-powerful federal government, these trends are fraying American culture and institutions. We must take steps to reverse as many of these trends as possible.

Declining Support for Major Parties

The combination of all the above trends has led to a serious decline in the support of the American people for the two major parties. In 2022, a clear majority of voters had negative views of each party; voters have 61% unfavorable versus 37% favorable views of Republicans, while Democrats have 57% unfavorable versus 41% favorable. About 27% of Americans have a negative view of both parties, almost four times the level in 1994 and 2002. This reaches 47% among Independents. Sadly, only 6% of Americans have a positive view of both parties (Pew).

More and more voters are supporting one of the parties not because they have a favorable view of that party but because they have an unfavorable view of the other party. Among Independents who lean to one party, only slightly more have a favorable opinion of their preferred party.

Independents who lean Republican have a 53% favorable versus 46% unfavorable view of the Republican party, while Independents who lean Democrat have exactly the same tepid level of support for their preferred party. Independent Leaners are also far more likely to give negative reasons for voting against a party rather than positive reasons for voting for a party (57-to-39% for Republican Leaners and 55-to-27% for Democratic Leaners).

Support for a third party is also quite high. In 2021 62% of Americans say that "a third party is needed," while just 33% think that the two major parties "do an adequate job." This is the highest support for third parties that has ever been recorded. In that same poll, 50% of Americans identified as Independents (Gallup).

Political-Industrial Complex

In their book, *The Politics Industry*, Katherine Gehl and Michael Porter compare the American political system to a dysfunctional economic monopoly. Michael Porter is one of the world's most influential business strategists. He is known for applying his competitive-forces framework to analyzing various sectors of the economy (Gehl & Porter).

Porter has long argued that business sectors can best be understood by analyzing the terms of competition of the following five forces: rivals, buyers, suppliers, threats of new entrants and threats of substitutes. While widely applied in the business and economics world, his theory has not been applied to the political world.

Katherine Gehl had the epiphany that the Porter's competitive-forces framework can also be applied to the American political system. She argues that the American political system is a duopoly where the Democratic party and the Republican party and their supporting bodies have distorted the terms of competition for their own benefit. Together, they function like a private monopoly. While healthy competition is win-win, duopolies are win-lose, with both parties winning and the American people losing. While American politics is dysfunctional from a voter perspective, the Political-Industrial complex is thriving.

Gehl and Porter's framework gives us a means for analyzing the terms of political competition in the United States. The terms of this political competition have created what Gehl calls a Political-Industrial complex that is thriving. The Political-Industrial complex consists of rivals (the two major parties), customers (voters, primary voters, donors), channels (media, social media and advertising), suppliers (potential candidates, campaign consultants, data shops and think tanks), substitutes, and new entrants.

Unlike a typical sector of the American economy, substitutes (Independents) and new entrants (new parties) are stifled. This enables the two rivals (the Democrats and Republicans) to set the rules of competition for their own benefit. All the customers, channels and suppliers are forced to choose one of the rivals to support. If someone fails to do so, it means that revenue will not flow to them. While at one time there were many non-partisan political institutions, virtually every political institution in America is now affiliated with one the two major parties.

Rather than solving problems, our political system exploits political problems to rally the base against the other side. Attacking the other party's base and distributing money to your own base are the principal means of mobilization. They simply do not want to solve problems, as this will undermine their ability to use those problems to rally the base.

While, from the perspective of the American public, our political process is broken, from the perspective of the Political-Industrial complex, it is functioning extremely well. Gehl estimates that this industry generates $100 billion in revenues each election cycle. More to the point, the winner of this competition has access to trillions of dollars in government revenue. This revenue can be used for spending programs and regulations that generate huge flows of revenues to supporters.

Ideological Partisanship Is Contagious

This form of political competition has not only caused a polarization of the two parties, but it has also caused a polarization of American society. The media, social media, interest groups, governmental agencies and non-profits are almost completely divided between the two competing ideologies. Using the latest news cycle to destroy the other side is increasingly the most important goal of previously non-partisan institutions. The original purpose of the organization, to solve a specific problem for society, has fallen by the wayside in favor of rallying the ideological base.

Whereas American media institutions once emphasized a relatively neutral and non-partisan coverage, most television and major newspapers are now highly ideological. FOX, CNN, MSNBC, the New York Times, the Washington Post and other media outlets now explicitly favor a partisan viewership. Attacking the opposing side has become a business model, used to increase ratings.

Social media companies, such as Facebook and Twitter, are increasingly moderating content in a way that censors conservatives and amplifies liberals. Interest groups who were non-partisan corporate or professional interests in the past are now much more clearly taking partisan sides. The number and influence of non-partisan think tanks has declined in favor of overtly partisan ones. Campaign consultants, fund-raisers, voter databases are now overwhelmingly partisan as well (Gehl & Porter).

It is becoming increasingly difficult to find any American institutions that do not take a side in the partisan conflict between conservative Republicans and liberal Democrats.

Polarization Is Undermining Faith In Progress

I believe that this ideological polarization is a key factor in undermining faith in progress. The material fact of human progress is very different from our perceptions, which are based on non-rational human psychology. Humans did not evolve to be happy in a world of progress and abundance. We evolved to survive and reproduce as Hunter Gatherers on the African Savanna.

To survive in harsh environments humans have evolved cognitive biases that include a very high threat instinct and a negativity bias. Any bad news, short-term loss or fear of loss can overwhelm our perception of a steady stream of improvement.

The media, social media, political activists, interest groups and political candidates have learned to harness these non-rational instincts for their own benefit. In order to win elections, they constantly bombard us with a distorted view of reality. These institutions all have a strong self-interest in dwelling on the negative and sensational, as it furthers their organizational goals.

These institutions have learned that the best way to get attention is to spike our threat instinct and negativity bias. In particular, they focus on the threat posed by the other major party and their followers. Then they follow up with a relentless drumbeat "proving" that the threat is becoming more common and more dangerous. They know that fear, anger, resentment and hate generate viewers, votes and money.

Confronted with a steady flow of sensationalistic, negative news, it is very hard for many people to believe that progress exists at all. Until we directly confront the terms of competition that drive our political institutions to promote ideological conflict over problem-solving, we will have a hard time moving towards a better society.

For this reason, I believe that a fundamental reform of the terms of competition of the American political system is essential. My hope is that my proposed reforms will have the following effects:

1. Restore faith that our current lives are not so bad, that our

political opponents are not dangerous threats, and that our ancestors gave us a toolkit for working together to solve problems.

2. Enable a Progress-based reform agenda to be implemented, which will increase future progress by promoting long-term economic growth and upward mobility for the working class and poor.

Before I explain my reform proposal, we need to get a better understanding of how and why our terms of competition have been so distorted.

Declining Electoral Competition

Healthy competition is essential for a thriving political system. The most obvious indicator of declining competition between political elites in the United States is the proportion of Congressional seats that face competitive elections. Fairvote.org, an organization dedicated to reforming our political process, has built a statistical model to predict House election outcomes based on previous voting behavior (FairVote).

In 2022, FairVote classifies only 86 of the 435 House districts as "competitive". In the remaining seats, one party almost always wins by more than 10% of the vote, even during national landslides for the opposite party. They also find only 39 seats where each party has a relatively equal chance of winning. This means that we live in a political system where over 80% of House general elections are non-competitive, and the winning party is a foregone conclusion.

Approximately 40% of all House seats are virtually guaranteed to be won by Democrats, while another 40% of all House seats are virtually guaranteed to be won by Republicans. This means that the competitive elections that are a foundation of democratic governance occur in only 20% of the seats.

FairVote also found the overall number of uncompetitive districts has increased substantially over time. As recently as 1996, only 200 House seats were uncompetitive, or less than half of all House seats. Since 2014, however, the number of uncompetitive districts has hovered between 350 and 360 seats, or about 80% of all House seats.

Similarly, in 1996, voters in 115 districts voted for different parties in the House versus the Presidency, while only 16 districts did so in 2020.

This gives incumbents in those districts a substantial amount of political power within the party. If we assume that neither party can win much over 55% of the total number of seats (or 240 seats), this means that incumbents in non-competitive districts will always control at least two-thirds of all the party seats in the House. And when that party is in the minority, it is closer to 85% of the party seats. This gives those uncompetitive seats effective control over the entire party in Congress.

The Democratic party in Congress is effectively controlled by the 40% of the districts that always vote for Democratic candidates. They have little reason to care about the other 60% of the United States. The Republican party in Congress is effectively controlled by the 40% of the districts that always vote for Republican candidates. Congresspersons from those key districts have little reason to care about the other 60% of the United States.

Because the Senate lumps together rural, suburban, and city districts, Senate elections tend to be somewhat more competitive. But Senate elections only take place every 6 years, versus every 2 years in the House.

Of course, that still leaves 20% of the House seats that are somewhat competitive, but the influence of these members is limited by party discipline. Seniority is very important in determining political influence within Congress. It is particularly important in determining committee assignments, where much of the real legislative bargaining is done.

Seniority gives a tremendous advantage to Congresspersons who are elected from non-competitive districts. Congresspersons from non-competitive districts or states can generally remain in Congress for long periods, while Congresspersons from competitive districts or states tend to get swept away by periodic "Red Waves" or "Blue Waves." The result is that most Congresspersons elected from competitive districts or states have short political careers.

Congresspersons from competitive districts or states can play a key role in blocking legislation, but they have a deeply difficult time getting through positive legislation. Without support from liberal Democrats or conservative Republicans from non-competitive districts, virtually no legislation can get passed.

Modern-day Rotten Boroughs

What we have today in America is something strikingly similar to the rotten boroughs of pre-reform Britain. Rotten boroughs were the nickname given to electoral districts that were uncompetitive and had a tiny population of voters. Rotten boroughs were typically dominated by aristocrats and the gentry, who saw the Parliamentary seat as their birthright. Drawing public attention to these rotten boroughs helped parliamentarians to finally pass the Reform Act of 1832.

Now I admit that the causes of modern-day American rotten boroughs are very different from the causes of the ones in pre-reform Britain. British rotten boroughs tended to be under-populated rural areas. American rotten boroughs represent a similar number of Americans as other more competitive districts. The problem in the United States is that the winner is effectively determined even before the general election takes place. And those who make that decision are distinctly unrepresentative of voters, even those in their own district.

Primary Problem

With the general election being meaningless in more than 80% of the House races and the majority of Senate seats, this shifts the center of electoral competition to the primaries of the dominant party. In the 40% of the House seats with virtually guaranteed Democratic victory, the Democratic primary becomes the "real" election. And the same is true of the Republican districts.

In itself, this is not necessarily a bad thing. The main problem is that primary voters are highly unrepresentative of the American public. Primaries have extremely low turnout. In 2020, for example, only 8% of voting-age citizens participated in Congressional primaries. Part of the problem is that a full 129 dominant party primaries were uncontested (Unite America).

Worse, this small number of primary voters are highly unrepresentative of citizens overall, as they are dominated by ideologues. Very liberal voters dominate the Democratic primary, while very conservative voters dominate the Republican primary. The vast majority of voters who tend more toward the center have very little influence within party primaries.

Our partisan primary system, along with single-member districts, unintentionally gives power to a very unrepresentative group of voters:

1. Voters within uncompetitive districts are already more ideological than the rest of America. By ideological, I mean either more liberal or more conservative depending upon the district or state. For example, voters in San Francisco are far more liberal than the rest of America, while voters from Wyoming are far more conservative than the rest of America.

2. Voters registered to the dominant party are already more ideological than other voters in the district. For example, registered Democrats in San Francisco are more liberal than San Francisco voters in general.

3. Primary voters are even more ideological than other voters within their party. For example, Republican primary voters in Wyoming elections are far more conservative than other Wyoming Republicans.

4. When there is no incumbent in the dominant party in that district, there tends to be a large number of candidates scrambling for the opportunity to win a safe seat that gives them a long political career. This means that the winner often earns well under 50% of the vote.

By the time voters have been filtered four times by the factors listed above, 80% of House seats are effectively elected by a tiny number of unrepresentative primary voters. And it is this group of unrepresentative voters that candidates must win the support of to maintain a career in Congress.

Typical primary voters are far more representative of the most ideological 15% of voters on each side than of the American people overall. This gives a very small proportion of a small number of voters virtual veto power over Congressional legislation.

Extremely unrepresentative primary elections put 80% of Congress under tremendous pressure to maintain the party line on every single issue. One small transgression, for instance voting for a reasonable bipartisan compromise, can lead to a more committed activist challenging them in the party primaries in the next election. Because turnout in primaries is so low, it is relatively easy for a challenger to mount a grassroots campaign against the incumbent.

For this reason, most Congresspersons do not care what typical voters in their district think. Nor do they care what the American people think. Their biggest concern is what party activists within their district think. Those are the voters who will dominate the party primaries.

It is difficult for a Republican Congressperson elected from an uncompetitive district to be too conservative for their primary voters. It is simple, however, for a single instance of support for moderate legislation to end their political career. The same goes for Democratic Congresspersons in uncompetitive districts.

Thirty years ago it was very rare for an incumbent to lose a primary election, but now it has become much more common. It has been common enough that the word "primaried" has entered the political lexicon.

It is important to note that actual incumbent losses in the primaries are still relatively rare, but even just a few instances send a powerful message: toe the party line or else. Since 80% of incumbents face no real competition in the general election, they have every incentive to avoid offending primary voters and not to care about the rest of the voting spectrum.

While turnout in individual Presidential primaries is significantly higher than for Congressional primaries, most voters never get a chance to cast a meaningful vote. Typically even competitive party primaries are decided early in the calendar when only a small fraction of all states have voted.

Using the 2020 Democratic primary as an example, for all practical purposes Joe Biden wrapped up the nomination in the February 29th South Carolina primary. Up until and including that key primary, a mere 330,064 voters from 4 states voted for the future president. The remainder of the 2020 Democratic primaries were more like a coronation than a competitive election.

This means that the future president received votes from 0.12% of the total adult population of 258 million. And this is not an unusual primary in any way. Such low overall turnout is the rule in nominating the most powerful person in the Free World.

Single-Member Districts

Having a very liberal Democratic party and a very conservative Republican party is not necessarily a problem. Other nations also have fairly ideological parties. The vast majority of those nations, however, also have more moderate parties that voters can support.

The problem is that this ideological polarization is combined with an enduring two-party system. Since the first party system was founded early in the Republic, the American political system has been dominated by two parties.

And amazingly it has been *the same two parties for more than 150 years*. The Republican party was founded in 1854, while the Democratic party goes back even further. While interpretations vary, many political scientists believe the Democratic party to be the oldest voter-based political party in the world. Some trace the founding of the Democratic party to the 1830s, while others trace the party back to Thomas Jefferson over three decades earlier.

When put in the context of the rest of American society, this is an extraordinary level of institutional endurance. It is difficult to find another example of two competing institutions that have maintained an effective duopoly in American society for more than 150 years.

Even the oldest and largest corporations in American history (Ford, General Motors, US Steel, Standard Oil, Microsoft, Apple) are young in comparison. And none of them maintained their dominance for more than a few decades.

A big part of the reason for the dominance of two parties is an electoral process based on single-member districts. Single-member districts are deliberately designed to represent the majority within a specific geographical area. The unintended outcome of such a system is a relatively stable two-party system.

Single-member districts interact with plurality voting to enhance the representation of the largest party. Plurality voting means that the candidate who wins the largest percentage of votes wins the election even if they fail to win a majority of the votes. While some states have separate run-off elections, these tend to have very low turnout so they really do not solve the problem.

Most readers might be surprised to learn that single-member districts and plurality voting are mentioned nowhere in the U.S. Constitution. The Constitution specifically designates that each state will have two Senators and the number of House seats will be determined by population, but there is no mention of electoral systems. Each state has the power to determine its electoral system. Over the last two centuries, states gradually aligned on single-member districts, more out of convenience than anything else.

Single-member districts functioned reasonably well for the vast majority of American history. Party leaders within each district effectively nominated candidates that they felt could win a majority vote within their district. For a long time, both parties had the incentive to nominate moderates who would appeal to swing voters.

American Parties Were Loose Coalitions

For most of American history, the Democrats and Republicans were not particularly ideological, at least not to the degree that they are today. This was mainly because the United States had an extraordinary amount of regional, ethnic and religious diversity. And that diversity was unevenly spread across the nation. This diversity forced both Democrats and Republicans to cobble together alliances between ethnoreligious groups to form a local political majority.

In general, the Republican party represented British and Protestant voters in the North. In the Civil War era, the Republicans added German and Scandinavian voters in the Midwest to their political coalition.

The Democrats represented White Southerners and Irish Catholics in the urban areas of the North. In the New Deal era, the Democrats then added Catholics and Jews to their political coalition. In the Civil Rights era, they added Blacks to their political coalition.

Up until the 1970s, there were many liberals and conservatives within both parties, and, more importantly, both voters and Congresspersons were liberals on some issues, while being conservative on others. Typically, Democrats and Republicans were polarized on only a few issues, while there was great diversity within each party on most other issues. Note that the terms "liberal" and "conservative" had very different meanings in the past, so I am using their modern definition.

Partisan Polarization

Since the 1970s, however, partisan polarization has gradually created political parties that agree on virtually all issues. The polarization process started with the Barry Goldwater presidential campaign of 1964 and the George McGovern presidential campaign of 1972. Both candidates lost miserably, but they each represented the future of their party.

The key institutional reform was the McGovern-Fraser Commission of 1970. After the tumultuous Democratic presidential nomination process of 1968, when a relatively moderate Hubert Humphrey won the nomination despite failing to win a single primary, anti-Vietnam activists demanded change to the nomination process.

The McGovern-Fraser Commission radically overhauled the way the Democratic party nomination process functioned, by making primaries mandatory. Soon the Republican party followed.

The McGovern-Fraser Commission effectively established the modern system of primary voters nominating their own candidates. While this may seem more democratic than the previous system, the actual functioning of party primaries handed power over to a small minority of ideological activists.

The midterm election elections of 1974 brought a new wave of liberal professional-class voters into the Democratic party. In a backlash against Watergate, many younger college-educated voters supported the Democrats for the first time. These voters were much more liberal on cultural and foreign policy issues than traditional working-class Democratic voters.

Gradually, the Democrats nominated more and more liberal candidates for the Presidential elections, and the Republicans nominated more and more conservative candidates. With each election, ideological contrarians within the party had a harder and harder time staying competitive. Eventually, they stopped trying.

This process has continued to such an extent that it is difficult to imagine a conservative or moderate candidate, like Bill Clinton, winning the Democratic presidential nomination. Nor is it easy to imagine a liberal or moderate candidate, like Susan Collins, winning the Republican presidential nomination.

As the spectrum of voters within each party's primaries changed, this had an increasingly powerful effect on Congressional elections. Each Democratic wave election (for example 1974, 1982, 2006, and 2018) tended to end the careers of many liberal and moderate Republicans, while each Republican wave election (1966, 1980, 1994, and 2010) tended to end the careers of many conservative and moderate Democrats.

By the end of the 1980s, the vast majority of elected Republicans at the federal level were conservatives. Today moderates are few and far between in both parties, and there are essentially no conservative Democrats nor liberal Republicans.

Nationalization of Politics

The very high-profile nature of modern media-based presidential elections has also had a powerful impact on lower-level races. Liberal voters, particularly in the Northeast and Pacific coast gradually left the Republican party, while conservative voters, particularly in the South, left the Democratic party. Each mismatched voter who left their party increased the power of the more ideological voters that remained, so the process fed upon itself.

Whereas American media was once dominated by local newspapers, now national newspapers, such as the New York Times and Washington Post, cable news networks and ideological internet sites dominate. National coverage of politics has created national brands for each party that are closely aligned with ideology.

Because all of these institutions are national in scope, this ideological polarization has moved down from federal politics to the local level. This process also filtered down to the state level, though the South was slower to change. The vast majority of elected Democrats at the state level are liberals, though some governors have been able to buck the trend. The same goes for state-level Republican parties. Idiosyncratic localism, such as conservative Southern Democratic state parties and liberal New England Republican state parties, are increasingly rare.

Whereas state and local politics were once far more collegial, non-partisan, and non-ideological, this is much less true today. Voters are increasingly voting for one party based on national brand, not upon local issues. Moderates within each party cannot detach themselves from the ideological brands of the national parties. Most either lose primary elections or retire.

Partisan Leadership in Congress

Ideologues are also empowered by partisan leadership in Congress. Until the 1970s, power within Congress was highly decentralized. Power was spread across a large number of committee chairmen. Because this decentralized power structure obstructed much legislation, particularly in the domain of civil rights, Democratic reformers gradually shifted power from the committee chairs to partisan leadership. Then Newt Gingrich in the 1990s further centralized power within partisan leadership to forward the official Republican party platform: the "Contract With America."

Currently, virtually all substantive legislative business must be approved by the Senate Majority Leader, the Speaker of the House, the House Majority Leaders, and their Whips. Nor can alternative legislation come up for a vote without the support of the House Minority Leader or the Senate Majority Leader and their Whips. Not surprisingly, given the need to accrue seniority to achieve such positions, these leadership roles are monopolized by Congresspersons from non-competitive districts.

Party leadership ensures that the majority within the majority party dominates Congress. By tradition, partisan leadership is determined exclusively by members of their party, so any moderates that have appeal to the other party are placed at an extreme competitive disadvantage. Even when the partisan balance is extremely close, as in 2021-22, Congressional leadership reflects majority support within the majority party, not Congress overall. And the 40% of incumbents from non-competitive districts always make up a majority within their Congressional party.

To the extent that committees still make policy decisions, party leaders control that as well. Party leaders control who gets on key committees, and going against them guarantees you will have far less influence. Individual Congresspersons do have an important influence over legislation based on their committee assignments, but it will be extremely difficult for them to get a vote on their legislation without support from partisan leadership.

Gerrymandering

Yet another source of the unrepresentative outcome of American elections is gerrymandering. Gerrymandering is the deliberate attempt to draw election districts to maximize the number of seats that one party can win. Gerrymandering is also sometimes done to maximize the likelihood of incumbent reelection or increase the number of racial minorities in legislatures.

While gerrymandering is a problem, I do not think that it is a key cause of distortions in the electoral system. Gerrymandering only affects election outcomes at the margins. Ideally, we should avoid it, but there are much bigger issues at stake.

Ideologues Have a Veto

When you put all of these factors together (non-competitive elections, very low primary turnout, ideological primary voters, centralized power in Congressional leadership, and gerrymandering), you have an extreme concentration of power. If you add on the enormous growth in the power of the federal government over the last 90 years, it is not difficult to understand why most American citizens are alienated from the federal government and politics, and have a negative view of both parties.

Note that none of this has anything to do with the U.S. Constitution. All of these trends have occurred without any important changes to that foundational document.

Goals for Electoral Reform

We must reform the terms of political competition in the United States. Replacing leaders with "better people" is not enough. The terms of political competition produce the incentives, which determine the behavior of our political leaders. Once we reform the terms of competition, our leaders and institutions will start behaving in very different ways.

I believe that any reform of our electoral system must start with the following principles:

1. Elected representatives must better reflect the ideological diversity of voters. Moderate voters, who make up a sizable share of the electorate, must be represented in Congress and state legislatures.

2. Elected representatives must also reflect the geographical diversity of voters as well. Americans would be very reluctant to give up "their" representative, and since much diversity in the nation is geographical, they should not have to do so.

3. The general election, where turnout is high and the electorate far more representative, must be the decisive election in determining which candidate wins.

4. We must remove the de facto duopoly that the Democratic and Republican primaries have over candidate selection.

My Proposal

This is one issue where supporters of Progress may have widely divergent views, but my preferred electoral reform would be to establish the following for all federal, state and local elections:

1. Establish an Independent primary.
2. Shift to ranked-choice voting.
3. Shift from single-member districts to multi-member districts for the U.S. House, Electoral College and state legislatures.
4. Select legislative leadership using ranked-choice voting by the entire membership.

An Independent Primary

To abolish the de facto nominating power of a small minority of partisan primary voters, I propose that we establish Independent primaries for federal, state and local elections. An Independent primary would function just like our current Democratic and Republican primaries, except it would be open to only Independent voters and candidates. This would empower the single largest bloc of voters in the American political system: Independents.

Existing Democratic, Republican, Green, and Libertarian party primaries would remain unchanged. Voters who are registered party members would still nominate their candidates in the partisan primaries before the general election. Ideally, the primaries would be closed primaries (i.e. only party members can vote in them), but that is not essential to the plan.

The big difference would be that the huge bloc of Independent voters would also be able to vote in their own primaries. Any candidate who is not running under a party label would be allowed to seek the Independent nomination. Any voter who is not registered as a voter in a specific party would be able to vote in the Independent primary.

The winner of the Independent primary would automatically be on the general election ballot. Currently, Independents and new third parties need to mount separate petition drives to get on the ballot. In some states, the number of required petition signatures is so high that they realistically cannot get on the ballot.

Independent candidates would also have all the rights and obligations of the Democratic and Republican nominees. This would affect fund-raising rules, campaign spending, advertising rules, and debate appearances. Hopefully, all of these changes would enable Independents to generate greater free media coverage.

An Independent primary would probably create a three-way race in most general elections. In some cases, the Independent nominee would be to the left of the Democratic party or to the right of the Republican party, but in most cases, Independent candidates would probably be someone from the ideological center. This would mean that Centrist Independents would finally have a candidate to support in the general election.

Ranked-Choice Voting

An Independent primary would make it easier for Independents to get on the general election ballot, but under the current electoral system, they would probably lose. Under our current plurality-voting system, voters are worried about wasting their ballot by voting for a candidate who cannot win.

Ranked-choice voting would end those fears. Ranked-choice voting is currently used in Ireland, the Australian Senate, and Malta.

In ranked-choice voting, voters do not just vote for their favorite candidate. Instead, voters rank the candidates. So let's say that I am a center-right voter. Under the current system, I would probably vote for a Republican candidate, and that would be the end of it. Under ranked-choice voting, I might rank the Independent as my favorite candidate, then the Republican as my second, then the Libertarian as my third and the Democrat as my fourth.

Under the ranked-choice voting system, if no candidate wins a majority of votes, the candidate with the least amount of votes is eliminated from contention and their votes are shifted to the voter's second favorite candidate. This continues until one candidate receives a majority of the vote. So I could vote for the Independent candidate or third party candidate and not worry about accidentally helping the Democrat win.

In the vast majority of the cases, small third-party candidates would be eliminated quickly. Vote counting in most districts would shift to a three-way race between Democrats, Republicans, and Independents.

All Democratic voters in Red districts would have a strong incentive to support a centrist Independent candidate as their second option. So would Republican voters in Blue districts. A de facto political alliance between Independents and the minority party would be a formidable force in the vast majority of electoral districts.

The exact outcome would vary greatly by election, but it is not beyond the realm of possibility that Independents would win up to one-third of the seats. For virtually all Presidential, Gubernatorial and Congressional elections, Independents would have a real chance of winning.

With three viable candidates, neither the Democrats nor the Republicans would be able to win a majority on the first round of counting. Many Democrats and Republicans would rather vote for Independents as their second-favorite candidate rather than have their hated opponents elected. This would make it quite possible for Independents to win a majority in later rounds of counting.

Moderate Democratic candidates and moderate Republican candidates would have a strong incentive to choose to run as Independents as doing so would give them a better chance of getting to the general election. Knowing that they would not be filtered out by more ideological primary voters will open up the general election playing field.

Ranked-choice voting in three-way races including viable Independent candidates would give major-party candidates a powerful incentive to move toward the political center and run more positive campaigns. Neither Democrats in liberal districts, nor Republicans in conservative districts could afford to ignore the threat of a viable centrist Independent candidate.

Ranked-choice voting is not some pie-in-the-sky idea. There is currently a great deal of momentum for it in the United States, though it does not receive much national media attention.

Ranked-choice voting has already been implemented via popular initiative in the states of Maine (in 2016), Alaska (in 2020), and Nevada (in 2022). Particularly in states where referenda or initiatives can change the electoral law, such a change is very achievable. If ranked-choice voting were implemented in the third of states where citizens can choose their electoral system, it would have a major effect on federal politics.

Even if only 5 or 10% of Congressional and state legislative elections were won by Independents, it would send a thunderclap through the entire American political system. Governing majorities would immediately be much harder to construct without support from Independents. Rather than being forced to caucus with either Democrats or Republicans, Independents would have the incentive to create their own caucus. Partisan leaders would be forced to negotiate with a bloc of elected Independent senators, and they would have little leverage over them.

Toning Down the Negativity

One of the best outcomes of ranked-choice voting is that candidates have a strong incentive to run positive campaigns. In our current system, candidates have a strong incentive to run highly negative campaigns that focus on making their opponents look bad. They do so for one reason: it works. Negative campaigning hurts both candidates, but it hurts the opponent even more. So candidates win elections by destroying their opponent.

Major-party candidates would want to be perceived as the second-best option for Independent voters. Very few candidates will be able to win a majority of the vote on the first count. Attacking a person's favorite candidate is a terrible way to win an electoral majority in ranked-choice voting, so candidates would probably be forced to change their campaign style.

Under ranked-choice voting, major-party candidates cannot win elections simply by demonizing the other side. Attempting to do so would only increase the chances that Independents would win.

Multi-member districts

Creating an Independent primary and ranked-choice voting would go a long way toward removing the de facto veto power of ideological activists in the primaries. It would not, however, overcome the lack of representation of Republicans in Blue States and Democrats in Red States. While each are a minority of voters in those states, they still make up a sizable portion of the electorate. Despite this, they have very little representation.

To remedy this problem, I believe that adding in one more reform would also be justified: convert U.S. House and State Legislative seats into multi-member districts. Multi-member districts are somewhat of a blend of America's current single-member district system and the proportional representation system that is common in Europe. Multi-member districts are currently used in Germany, New Zealand, Scotland, and Wales.

Multi-member districts have the advantage of representing ideological and geographical diversity, and eliminating gerrymandering. Even if Independents win absolutely no elections, giving conservative voters in California and liberal voters in Kansas representation would be a big step forward in federal representation. So would the elimination of gerrymandering.

Multi-member districts would have their biggest effect in states where one party has a huge partisan advantage (i.e. Red states and Blue states). Democrats in Red states currently have virtually no representation. The same goes for Republicans in Blue states. Under multi-member districts, the minority party would get something like 40% of the seats, a radical change from our current system.

Converting the U.S. House from single-member districts to multi-member districts in most states would be quite simple: just establish each state as one multi-member district. Since the vast majority of states have 10 or less House seats, this is a fairly easy conversion.

Let's use Colorado, a medium-sized state, as an example. Colorado currently has 7 seats in the U.S. House. Colorado would go from having 7 separate single-member districts to one 7-seat multi-member district. So if the Democrats get 41% of the vote, Republicans get 39% of the vote, and the Independents get 14% of the vote, the parties would get 3, 3, and 1 seat respectively.

While combining multi-member districts and ranked-choice voting is more complicated when it comes to counting votes, it is not necessarily much more difficult for voters. To make the voting process easier for voters, they should be allowed to rank either parties or individual candidates. By voting for parties, voters would effectively agree to the rankings established by the results of the primaries.

Voters who vote for individual candidates would probably have to be fairly well-informed about each candidate. It is not, however, difficult for even casual voters to understand what each of the political parties stands for.

Uninformed partisan voters would simply vote for either Democrats or Republicans as their first choice and then Independents as their second choice. Many uninformed voters who dislike both major parties could just vote for the Independent "party" as their first choice and then either the Democratic or Republican party as their second preference and then stop.

My proposal does leave something of a problem for very populous states such as California (with 53 House seats), Texas (with 36 seats) New York, and Florida (with 27 seats each). Rather than one very large multi-member district, each of these states should probably be divided up into multiple districts with fewer seats. This would break up the power of the dominant party (either Democrat or Republican), and enable representation of the minority party and Independents, while still preserving a close geographical link between voters and representatives.

Even better, entire metro areas with a population of over 2 million or so should comprise a single district. This would give them separate delegations to metro areas with enough of a population for 3 House seats. Geographically distinct rural regions would form their separate multi-member district. The number of seats in each district would be determined by population. If multi-member districts are required to consist of entire counties, this would undermine the opportunities for gerrymandering.

To use a particularly complicated example, let's consolidate California's current number of 52 House districts into 7 different multi-member districts. Four districts would represent the four largest metro areas in the state, while the other 3 districts would represent separate rural regions. (All the numbers below are estimates only and would change with each census).

Los Angeles metro area: one 17-seat district

SF Bay metro area: one 9-seat district

San Diego metro area: one 4-seat district

Sacramento metro area: one 3-seat district

Northern rural areas: one 5-seat district

Central rural areas: one 9-seat district

Eastern rural areas: one 5-seat district

The Electoral College, which indirectly elects the President, could also function with identical multi-member districts. Electoral College votes would no longer be passed to one candidate as a single huge bloc. Instead, states would be divided up into multi-member districts, each of which would distribute Electoral College votes in a more representative method. This maintains the Electoral College while diminishing its distortions of the popular vote.

A similar electoral system could also be implemented for state legislatures, except each federal district might be divided up further into smaller districts. Currently, the number of state legislative districts per state varies between 49 for the state of Nebraska and 253 for Pennsylvania. Consolidating the current districts into multi-member districts with approximately 3-9 members each, which roughly correspond to the proposal above seems quite workable.

Departisanizing Legislative Leadership

The final reform that I propose is replacing partisan legislative leadership positions at the federal and state level with non-partisan committees representative of the entire chamber. This may seem a bit "pie-in-the-sky", but we already have a model for how it might work: the Nebraska state legislature. The Nebraska state legislature is the only non-partisan legislature in the United States, and it has found a way to deliver results without party leaders.

To avoid getting bogged down into details in the main section of this book, I have moved the details of my proposal to Appendix A at the end of this book. In the current section, I will only go over the main principles of my proposal, which are:

1. Abolish all partisan leadership positions, including Majority Leader, Minority Leader, and Whips.

2. Elect Speakers via secret ballot and ranked-choice voting. This will make the Speaker representative of the entire legislature, not just the majority of the majority party.

3. Shift the power to set the legislative agenda to a non-partisan Executive Board elected by all members via secret ballot and ranked-choice voting.

4. Shift the power to set committed assignments to a non-partisan Committee of Committees elected by a similar means.

5. Members of those committees may only serve one two-year term every 10 years. Nor may they serve on any other committee. This will limit their ability to hoard power over time.

6. The vast majority of policy negotiations will be shifted back to the committees (as they were before 1970).

Our current leadership system gives power to the majority of the majority party, virtually all of whom are elected by low-turnout primaries and non-competitive general elections. Now, Independents and moderates within each party would be empowered. And because of my other proposed reforms, those two groups would be far bigger than they are currently.

The combination of Independents, potential third parties, Democrats from Red states, and Republicans from Blue states would form a significant bloc in Congress. With such a bloc in the center, less partisan centrists would have a real chance of getting elected to governing committees.

Because those non-partisan committees would control the legislative agenda and committee assignments, this change would ripple through the entire institution. Whereas our current system empowers ideologues from non-competitive Blue/Red states, the new system would empower those who are willing to create centrist majorities on each issue. Non-elected bureaucrats would have to shift their stances to maintain Congressional funding.

How Do We Get It Done?

The combination of all four of my suggested electoral reforms would create a powerful political realignment. Independent candidates would be empowered, party primaries within the dominant party would lose their veto power, minority parties within Red/Blue states would be represented, and legislative leaders would be far more representative of the American people. .

There is only one problem: under our current system, the people who have the power to change the system are the very people who benefit from the status quo. That is why Congress and state legislatures have no incentive to reform the system. Any real reform would probably end many of their political careers, so of course, they oppose it. They are part of the problem, not the solution.

Congress and state legislatures will probably never pass my proposed reform agenda because they are dominated by Red-state Republicans and Blue-state Democrats who are nominated by ideological activists. Nor is amending the Constitution possible, as both parties also control that process.

State-level Initiatives

The only way to reform the electoral system that bypasses both Congress and the state legislatures is state-level initiatives. Initiatives enable citizens to sign petitions to place the question directly on the ballot for popular vote. If the initiative wins a majority of the vote in one election, it becomes law in that state.

Initiative and referenda rules vary greatly by state, but a total of 14 states allow direct initiatives while another 7 states enable the state legislatures to put referenda on the ballot. In general, western states allow initiatives and/or referendum, while eastern states do not.

A total of 16 states enable direct initiatives to amend the state constitution, which typically defines the electoral system. California, Florida, Illinois, Michigan, and Ohio are the most populous states that allow this process. Together these 16 states make up a sizable portion of the American electorate.

A well-funded initiative drive to get all four of my proposed reforms onto the state ballot might realistically achieve success within a few election cycles. As mentioned before, Maine, Alaska, and Nevada have already passed initiatives to establish ranked-choice voting. The ranked-choice movement is gaining momentum in other states.

I believe that a well-funded initiative drive across many states could get a great deal of voter support. Because of the expense of modern politics, a nation-wide movement would probably cost millions or even tens of millions of dollars. But the partial success in Maine, Alaska and Nevada shows that committed voters can get by on shoe-string budgets.

Of course, both major parties would fight hard against implementing my suggested reforms and deliberately cause confusion about the motivations and likely outcomes of the reforms. Democrats will claim that that reform is a right-wing conspiracy to overthrow democracy and disenfranchise racial minorities. Republicans will claim that reform only benefits liberals and increases the growth of the Deep State. They will inevitably fight back, as fundamental reform would be a threat to their control over American politics.

However, I believe that the American people are so fed up with both parties and the toxic political culture that they have created that initiatives will succeed in at least one state. Success in any one state would cause momentum for these measures to make it onto the ballot in additional states. At some point, I believe, the dam will break and substantial progress will occur.

Let's start that process.

Reforming Legislatures

The only plank on my reform agenda that could not be implemented by state-level initiative is changing how Congressional leaders are elected. State legislative rules also very greatly by state, but most determine their own rules. For this reason, it will be very hard for voters to force through reform.

Reforming legislative bodies will have to come after reforms to the electoral process. That can only be achieved when Independents and moderates make up a sizable bloc in Congress, and they can use that influence to force through institutional reforms. In other words, electoral reform will enable legislative reform.

All it will take is for a handful of small states or one big state to start electing a substantial number of Independents and moderate partisans to Congress and state legislatures. Fortunately, because the partisan balance between Republicans and Democrats is so tight, this is probably all that would be needed.

A handful of Independents and moderates would be highly influential, because their support would be needed to pass major legislation. This bloc could withhold their vote until the party leaders agree to reform the legislative process. This, combined with a series of state-level initiatives, could generate real pressure for reform from below. At some point, centrists would grow into a critical mass that could force radical electoral change across the entire nation.

If a sizable number of states adopt my proposed electoral reforms via state-initiative, and then this is followed by legislative process reforms in Congress and those state legislatures, this will create a fundamentally different political system. I believe that the positive results will be so obvious that other states without an initiative process will be forced to copy the reforms.

Conclusion

Rather than promoting progress and upward mobility, our political system undermines both. The terms of political competition have been so corrupted that good policies are extremely difficult to implement and bad policies are even harder to repeal.

We must reform the terms of political competition by doing the following:

1. Establish an Independent primary.
2. Shift to ranked-choice voting.
3. Shift from single-member districts to multi-member districts for the U.S. House, Electoral College and state legislatures.
4. Select legislative leadership by the entire membership using ranked-choice voting.

These reforms will not only enable a Progress-based reform agenda to be implemented, but they will also undermine the power of the ideologues who are doing so much to undermine confidence in progress itself.

DECENTRALIZING POLITICAL POWER

The Third Key to Progress: Decentralized political, economic, religious and ideological power. Of particular importance are elites being forced into transparent, non-violent competition that undermines their ability to forcibly extract wealth from the masses. This also allows citizens to freely choose among institutions based upon what they have offer to each individual and society in general.

As I have argued throughout my *From Poverty to Progress* book series, progress has historically come from societies creating a food surplus and then transporting that surplus to the cities where innovations in new technologies, skills and organizations take place. City-dwellers then copy the innovations that work best. Sounds pretty simple. Unfortunately, it is not so easy. Whenever farmers create a food surplus that can potentially lead to the growth of dynamic trade-based cities, elites in those societies have other ideas.

Unfortunately, throughout most of human history, the bulk of the food surplus has been extracted by political, economic, or religious elites in the form of taxes and land rents. Rather than allowing specialists in cities to consume this food surplus, the elites spent the food surplus on conspicuous consumption, military conquest, signaling their social status, or celebrating their religious or ideological visions. These elites effectively stifled the growth of trade-based cities, which in turn stifled the possibility of progress.

Sometimes these elites extracted wealth from the peasantry individually, as in European feudalism, but, more often, elites established centralized extractive institutions to do so on a vast scale. Usually operating as government-sanctioned monopolies, these extractive institutions channeled the food surplus generated by farmers towards elites. Unfortunately, through most of human history, the more productive farmers have become, the more the extractive institutions funneled that wealth to elites.

And even worse, elites funneled this food surplus into building powerful military machines that competed against each other to expand the scope of extraction into neighboring areas. The Chinese, Roman, French, Ottoman, Persian, Spanish and Portuguese empires are just a few of the dominant empires that have chosen this path. Many other potential empires attempted to do the same, but they were outcompeted by their more famous competitor empires.

For this reason, the decentralization of political, economic, religious, and ideological power is essential for innovation and progress. Ideally, this decentralization comes from the creation of institutions that compete against each other without the use of violence. When institutions compete peacefully, they can no longer acquire all their resources by extracting them from farmers and urbanites.

Organizations that are forced to compete non-violently have the incentive to offer material benefits to the masses in order to acquire more resources. The people are then no longer beasts of burden to be exploited, but potential customers, employees, investors, and voters.

Organizations that compete non-violently have a strong incentive to embrace new technologies, skills, and processes that give them a competitive advantage against other institutions. At this point, instead of having the incentive to stifle progress, elites suddenly had the incentive to promote progress.

Modern societies have evolved many means by which to force elites to compete against each other non-violently. For instance, political parties, the rule of law, and elections force political and ideological elites to do this. So do markets, property rights, and corporations. Meanwhile, the separation of church and state and the concept of religious liberty forces religious elites to compete non-violently against each other for worshipers.

And the specialization of institutions in modern society means that an institution can compete in only one of those spheres. They must specialize in politics, economics, or religion. When elites compete non-violently, the rest of society has the opportunity to choose which sub-section of the elite most benefits society. And, given so many options, they can mix and match as they choose.

Today, we take all of that competition for granted, but for millennia, Agrarian societies (like authoritarian regimes today) strictly limited competition by imposing government-sponsored monopolies. These monopolies enabled political, economic and religious elites to extract wealth from the masses. More recently, ideological elites have played that role. Any new organizations that could create wealth that will benefit the masses are a distinct threat to elite power, as they could become power bases for rivals.

Forcing elites to compete non-violently against each other is critical, because it changes the way that people become wealthy. Rather than conquering new lands or squeezing taxes from the peasantry, modern elites become wealthy by creating wealth. They do so by creating innovative new technologies, skills and social organizations. The innovators gain vast wealth from those innovations, but the masses as a whole receive far more of the benefits.

Dangers of Centralization

Today, the United States and Europe run the risk of undoing a significant amount of progress that came from their earlier decentralization of political power. This centralization of power undermines the ability of state, local governments and non-political institutions to experiment with differing policies and copy what works. Lower levels of local experimentation are undermining progress and upward mobility.

In both North America and Europe, there has been a relentless centralization of political power over the last 60 years. While nowhere near as threatening to progress as earlier agrarian regimes or modern totalitarian regimes, this centralization drastically reduces the diversity of policy-making options that are necessary to foster innovation.

While it is tempting to force the supposed "best" solution onto a large number of people, it is usually far better to allow a great deal of experimentation at the local level. When local governments implement different policies, this gives everyone the ability to assess the outcomes of those policies.

If the policy works well on the local level, then other localities will probably copy it. If the policy fails or causes significant negative side-effects, then other localities will avoid copying it. All that is needed is an open mind, clear metrics, transparency and a willingness to copy the successful policies.

Elites within centralized political institutions have strong personal, financial and ideological interests that bias their decisions. Even when they arrive at the best solution, the situation can change substantially over time, making the solution less than ideal at a later date.

Rapid technological innovation virtually guarantees that most decisions will become obsolete within a generation. But once a policy is enacted, bureaucratic and political forces make it very difficult to modify or eliminate obsolete policies.

Centralization Accentuates Partisan Conflict

An additional result of this relentless centralization over the last century has been ever-increasing partisan conflict in federal politics. In the *Promoting Political Competition* chapter I discussed the effects of our electoral laws on this partisan conflict. Here, I will focus on the problem of over-centralization.

Relentless, never-ending trench warfare between liberal Democrats and conservative Republicans dominates the federal level. Each party tries to use the federal government to impose the values of a political minority on the entire country. Neither party is successful enough to feel like they have won, but both have been successful enough to enrage the other side. Whereas various sub-national groups within America were once largely allowed to go their own way, now strong federal power makes that impossible.

Both parties know that they are engaged in a permanent zero-sum struggle to impose their will on the entire nation. It has become so commonplace that most people assume that this is the way it has always been. But this is actually a relatively new phenomenon. The overall distribution of governmental power in America was very different in the past.

Our Decentralized Past

Our current over-centralization is a radical departure from the first 150 years of American history. Until 1930, virtually all government took place on the local and state level. Outside of the military and the post office, the federal government played very little day-to-day role in people's lives.

The American political system was based upon the concept of federalism. Most power resided with state and local governments, and it was expected that they would each experiment with different policies based upon local conditions. When a policy proved successful, it was quite likely that other neighboring districts and states would learn of the results and copy them. Gradually, what worked would spread from state to state and policies that were not perceived to work as well would not.

While we tend to think of America today as more diverse than ever, this is not true. Yes, America is more racially diverse, but we are far less diverse based upon ethnicity, religion and region. Just like a tourist moving through the European Union today, as one moves from state to state and even city-to-city, travelers were are struck by the enormous diversity of the United States.

While Americans today now think of Whites as one group, few people outside the Deep South used to think in those terms. Instead, they saw English, Scottish, Irish, Germans, Italians, Russians, Poles, Dutch, Portuguese, French, Hungarians, Greeks and many other ethnic groups. Each ethnic group was concentrated in certain neighborhoods and regions. With the exception of the English, none were evenly spread across the nation.

Even within each ethnic group, there were different religious denominations: Anglicans, Methodists, Baptists, Catholics, Mormons, Quakers and Jews. Finally, there were very large regional differences between Northerners, Southerners, Midwesterners and West Coasters. Even Southerners were split between the patrician Deep South and rowdy Upper South. Only the Deep South was a biracial society.

Most people thought that their group was best, but in general, people went their own way without thinking much of the other groups. The biggest exception to this rule, of course, was the outrageous suppression of Black rights through slavery and Jim Crow segregation.

What allowed all this to work (except for the Blacks) was a highly decentralized political system. Each town, city and state was run by a unique coalition of minority groups, none of which was powerful enough to oppress the other. Each party was a smaller coalition of minority groups who hoped to influence local power.

None had any expectation of controlling the federal government, except for the Northern WASPs (White Anglo-Saxon Protestants), who had power over the majority Republican party. And those WASPs rarely tried to intervene in what they deemed to be local and state affairs.

The system had its drawbacks: Blacks were terribly oppressed by the White majority in the Deep South. Some regions were economic backwaters with little chance of economic development. Fortunately, with the two big exceptions of the Civil War/Reconstruction and the Civil Rights movement, violent conflict was fairly contained.

These two exceptional events were based upon differing opinions of whether the majority of White Southerners could oppress Blacks, and whether Northern WASPs, who typically controlled the federal government had the right to intervene on behalf of Blacks. For most of American history, Northern WASPs preferred to look the other way, but during those two great conflicts, they saw it as their duty to liberate Blacks from oppression.

Within certain limits defined by constitutional rights, we need more decentralization. This could do much to tone down the ideological hostility that is wearing away at the fabric of American society.

If the Democrats want to enact a Single-Payer health insurance system, let them try it out in California or Vermont. If the Republicans want to radically cut taxes, spending and regulation, let them try it out in Utah or Kansas.

Then let the rest of America wait for the results to come in. States that like the results can implement similar policies. States that do not like the results can go in the opposite direction. In the long run, we will get to good results faster with 50 states experimenting rather than one federal government imposing its will.

Better yet, because American citizens can relocate to different cities and towns, people can effectively choose their own policies with their feet. Minorities who feel discriminated against in ways that are not reflected in the Constitution can move to cities or states where they feel less discriminated against.

Reducing the Scope of Federal Government

I believe that the only way to enable the kind of decentralized experimentation that leads to progress is to radically reduce the scope of the federal government in domestic affairs. While this may seem like a radical change today, it is really just restoring what worked in the past.

The U.S. Constitution was supposed to create a fairly clear division between the powers of the states and the powers of the federal government. Article I, Section 8 clearly enumerates the powers of

Congress. All other powers were then reserved to the state governments or the people themselves. State governments could delegate power to county and local governments at their discretion. This is effectively how the American government functioned until 1930.

Starting in the 1930s, and then accelerating since the 1960s, the federal government has gradually surpassed state governments in dozens of policy domains. The "necessary and proper" clause of the Constitution has been used to expand the power of the federal government far beyond its original intent. Through a combination of social legislation, aid to states, federal court rulings, mandates and regulations, the federal government now highly constrains the ability of state and local governments to experiment.

The Constitution of 1787 was specifically written to ensure the federal government had the power in external affairs. That dominance should continue, as there is no viable alternative.

However, in order to facilitate state-level policy experimentation, we should radically limit the power of the federal government in domestic affairs. In general, the powers of the federal government should be limited to external affairs or to policy domains that would be very difficult for state governments to administer.

More specifically the federal government should be more clearly enumerated and restricted to the following policy domains:
- Military
- Declaration of war
- Foreign policy
- Foreign intelligence
- Foreign trade and customs
- Immigration and naturalization
- Federal courts and prisons
- Security for federal installations and personnel
- Enforcement of free trade between the states
- Coinage/print money and service federal debt
- Pensions, benefits, and health care for retirees (Social Security and Medicare) and federal employees

- Management of federally-owned lands
- Levy taxes to pay for federal spending
- Federal aid to state or local governments with below-average per capita GDP or experiencing natural disasters. Such aid should not be contingent upon any change in state or local policies, except to insist that they measure results and transparently publish outcomes.

We should also specifically enumerate a few powers that should remain shared by both the federal and state governments:

- Protection from terrorism, violent political movements, and organized crime
- Science, research, and technological innovation.

My guess is that there are other lesser powers that it would make sense to leave on the federal level, but this list is a good starting point. The general principle should be that, if a policy domain is domestic in nature and state governments can realistically administer it, they should do so exclusively. This list still encompasses a vast swath of government power, so it will not eliminate the federal government.

All other powers should be transferred to the states, who can delegate those powers to local governments as they choose. Any federal laws, regulations and executive orders in those domains would be null and void unless confirmed by the majority of each state legislature. All federal departments and agencies in other areas, except in the domains listed above, would be transferred to the individual states. State legislatures would have the option of adopting federal policy as their own or creating their own policies.

If federal powers were restricted to these policy domains, this would be a vast shift of political power from the federal government to state governments. Policies in the domains of education, energy, commerce, labor, social welfare, housing, agriculture, drugs, art, urban development, transportation and the environment would all be shifted to the state governments.

Most of the proposed federal powers listed above are fairly self-explanatory and non-controversial. Military, foreign policy, foreign trade and immigration are natural federal powers, as they interact with nations and persons outside the United States. We also need the federal government to enforce interstate free trade, coin money, service the federal debt, run federal courts, prisons and lands. And, of course, the federal government would need to levy taxes to pay for all of those programs.

Exceptions

In addition to the obvious federal powers listed above, I think that it makes sense for the federal government to still be active in some domestic policy domains. It seems perfectly reasonable for the federal government to be able to give aid to states with below-average per capita GDP. This would help to even out the ability of poor states to fund desirable state programs. This was part of the original intention of federal aid to states, but the program has gone far beyond the original vision.

Before the 1960s, federal aid to the states was almost non-extent. States liked it that way, as it gave the federal government little leverage over them. Federal aid to the states grew rapidly in the 1960s and 1970s, particularly under the Nixon administration. The general concept of federal aid to the states is reasonable, but it has led to a huge number of federal mandates and expansion of federal power into policy domains that were previously restricted to the states. This undermined the ability of state governments to experiment with different policies.

Federal aid to states with above-average per capita GDP, however, is very difficult to rationalize. It is fundamentally unfair for citizens from poorer regions to subsidize citizens with far greater means to fund their own programs. The United States is already one of the richest societies that has ever existed. If a state that exceeds the average level of income cannot afford to pay for its own programs, they are doing something fundamentally wrong. Taxpayers should not subsidize the rich.

In addition, it seems reasonable for the federal government to make emergency payments to states that have recently experienced a natural disaster. The states can handle emergency preparedness, but a sudden disaster can easily sap their ability to pay for reconstruction costs.

I also believe that the federal government should have the power to fund science, research and technological innovation. Science and technology are fundamentally the same across all states, so having a concentration of effort at the federal level makes sense.

The main budgetary items that would remain with the federal government would be the military, Social Security and Medicare.

Social Security and Medicare should continue to be run by the federal government, mainly for administrative reasons. Having individual states fund their own pension programs would be very cumbersome. Beneficiaries contribute to the program as workers for decades, while they receive benefits in later decades. If, for example, a worker is employed and pays taxes in California, Idaho, Colorado and Washington during their productive years, and then retires to Arizona or Florida, it would be an accounting nightmare to agree on who should pay retirement benefits.

The states of California, Idaho, Colorado and Washington would all benefit from previous contributions without having to pay for subsequent benefits. Meanwhile, Florida and Arizona would get stuck paying the tab without having received any earlier contributions. Perhaps there might be a complicated transfer system for Social Security or a way of making the Social Security Administration answerable to a consortium of state governments, but maintaining it as a federal program seems more sensible.

Would this enumeration of federal power lead to radical changes in policy? In some cases, yes, but in other cases no. My guess is that more liberal states would copy federal programs and legislations and make them more progressive. It's likely that more conservative states would seriously cut back on current federal policies or perhaps even eliminate them. The result would be policy that more accurately reflects the diversity of political opinions across the American people.

Toning Down the Partisan Conflict

I believe that the transfer of power from the federal government to the many state governments would substantially lower the toxicity of partisan competition. The federal government would focus largely on external affairs, where there tends to be more bipartisan agreement.

While partisan conflict would hardly disappear, the stakes of federal elections would be radically lower. Federal politics would be of less importance, and would presumably receive less media coverage, except during time of war or foreign crisis. The main focus of domestic power would be on the state level.

State-level parties would no longer be defined by their national brand. Wyoming Democrats might start to support very different policies to California Democrats. California Republicans might shift towards the center in order to become competitive again.

Most importantly, state policies would better reflect their state's unique political culture. Liberal Democrats would be able to do their own thing within their own states. Republicans within the more liberal-leaning states would likely shift to the center to become more competitive. If they failed to do so, this would leave room for a centrist third party or Independents.

Conservative Republicans would be able to do their own thing within their own states. Democrats within those more conservative-leaning states would probably shift to the center to become more competitive. Because the locus of power would now be on the state level, the trend toward the nationalization of politics would be reversed.

It might even be possible for Republican states to learn from experimentation that took place in more liberal states, and for Democratic states to do the equivalent.

Massive Federal Debt

A major cause of federal expansion since the 1930s has been the ability of the federal government to run massive deficits each year and then finance them through bond issues. While, in certain circumstances, this is a reasonable strategy, it has become the standard operating procedure rather than an exceptional practice. Bond issues make perfect sense for investment in infrastructure and for funding wars, but as a means of funding ongoing spending, they are dubious at best.

The ability of the federal government to keep pumping money out to failed programs is what enables those failed programs to survive for decades. If the federal government were forced to balance its budget, then Congress would be much more willing to cut back or eliminate failed programs.

I do not believe that we can drastically limit the power of the federal government and impose balanced budget requirements via incremental reform. Republicans whine and complain about the federal government, but, once they get in power, they typically just shape the increase of growth to their partisan advantage. Republicans cut taxes, and do little else.

Since the 1980s, it has been a consensus within the Republican party, to constrain the growth of federal power, you should focus on cutting taxes. They have often claimed that cutting taxes would create a deficit, which would then force matching cuts in spending. In the late 1990s, this strategy appeared to be working, as the federal government achieved balanced budgets between 1998 and 2001.

Rather than continue balancing the budget, however, the GW Bush administrations cut taxes, launched two wars, increased spending, established new federal programs and expanded federal mandates on the states. In the early 2000s, cutting taxes shifted from a long-term goal to shrink the federal government to a short-term goal of repaying upper-income voters for their support. Cutting taxes became an end to itself.

Starting in 2002, federal deficits reemerged. This trend drastically accelerated during the Obama administration. Government spending as a percentage of total GDP soared from just over 30% in 2000 to almost 50% under the Biden administration. If the Biden administration has successfully passed the Green New Deal, total government spending will have soared well past 50% of the total economy.

This increase in federal spending without increasing taxes has created a massive increase in federal debt. In 2000, federal debt was 54% of the total size of the American economy. By 2022, it had grown to 123%. Or to put it another way, the federal debt exceeds $30 trillion, more than $85,000 for each man, woman and child. The total amount of federal debt is now *more than four times the level of just 20 years ago* (US Dept. of Treasury).

This is a stunning increase in centralized government and national debt. It is important to point out that this all occurred during 12 years of Republican presidents and Republican majorities in either the House or the Senate for all but 6 years.

Cutting taxes, the default Republican policy, does not work. More direct action is necessary. The federal government has become such a massive institution that cutting individual regulations, programs and mandates will take generations. The system has an inherent desire to grow, so merely limiting growth will be very difficult.

Balanced Budget Requirements

While the federal government has run up a massive debt, almost all state governments have constitutional or statutory rules that require a balanced budget every year. While the stringency of these requirements varies by state, their overall impact has been to create a radically different situation from the federal government.

Fiscal discipline has been enforced. The result is less spending, less debt, rapid spending adjustments during recession, and lower borrowing costs. Balanced budget rules forced elected officials to carefully consider the impacts of their spending decisions. Because they will have to cut one program or raise taxes to pay for another, they are far less likely to support untested spending programs. They are also more likely to cut spending on failed programs. Budgeting is fundamentally about making choices and, without balanced budget rules, politicians are unwilling to make those choices.

Opponents of balanced-budget amendments correctly point out that they would require massive spending cuts during recessions, exactly at the time when federal stimulus spending is required. We would not want strong increases in federal spending during times of strong economic growth followed by big cuts during recessions. A more consistent level of spending would be more desirable.

To overcome this problem, many states have budget stabilization funds, into which surplus funds can be contributed. These surpluses can then be applied to budget deficits during recessions. These funds are commonly known as "rainy day" funds.

The federal government should follow a similar policy. A few simple budgetary requirements should be followed:

- The President may only sign a budget if it is in balance or surplus.

- Congress is prohibited from carrying over a deficit into the following fiscal year.

- If Congress passes a budget in deficit, the President shall have the power to reduce or eliminate spending on any program until the budget is brought into balance.

- The federal government may establish a budget stabilization fund to apply excess revenue to make up for future deficits.

Ideally, these requirements should be appended to the U.S. Constitution. If this amendment is combined with the strict enumeration of federal powers that I mentioned earlier, it would be relatively easy for the federal government to balance its budget. Strict enumeration would significantly cut federal spending while keeping revenues intact. The federal government deficit would suddenly be converted into a surplus.

So How Do We Get There?

In order to decentralize political power in the United States, I have proposed a number of fairly radical reforms. While I do my best to work to keep my proposed reforms in this book within the confines of the current U.S. Constitution, the ones discussed in this chapter are so fundamental as to require a series of constitutional amendments.

As everyone who follows American politics knows, it is very difficult to amend the U.S. Constitution. In almost 250 years, the Constitution has been amended only 27 times, and ten of those amendments were passed immediately after writing the document. Another three of them were implemented immediately after the Civil War.

Convention of the States

There are two different means by which to amend the U.S. Constitution. Until now, the only successful method for proposing an amendment is by two-thirds majority vote in both the House and the Senate. A proposed amendment becomes part of the Constitution as soon as it is ratified by three-fourths of the states. Today this would mean ratification by 38 of the 50 states.

Many people believe that this is the only method to amend the constitution, but actually there is a second: a constitutional convention called for by two-thirds of the State legislatures. Currently, this would require approval from 34 of the 50 states. Such a convention cannot enact constitutional amendments. They would only have the power to propose amendments.

A proposed amendment would still need to be ratified by three-fourths of the state legislatures. This clause was specifically added to the Constitution to ensure that the states had a means of checking the growth of federal power. It is time that we used that power.

Since 2013 there has been a movement within state legislatures to call a Convention of States. The proposed convention would only be authorized to discuss amendments that "limit the power and jurisdiction of the federal government, impose fiscal restraints, and place term limits on federal officials. (COS action)."

The first two proposals to "limit the power and jurisdiction of the federal government" and "impose fiscal restraints" are well within the scope of many of my proposals. Personally, I do not have a strong opinion on term limits. It might be a good thing, but my guess is that it will not make much of a difference.

As of 2022, 29 of the 34 state legislatures have approved varying forms of resolutions to call a Convention of States. Most focus exclusively on a federal balanced budget amendment. Nineteen have passed a specific application that calls for limiting federal powers. Six other states' applications have passed in one chamber but not the other. Fourteen other states have pending legislation (COS action).

Progressives Should Embrace Decentralization

Currently, progressive Democrats perceive decentralization of power from the federal government to the states to be a conservative Republican proposal and are strongly against it. I think that this is a big mistake.

Progressives should embrace decentralization as a great opportunity. Decentralization would allow California, New York, Washington, Hawaii and Vermont to construct social programs and regulations that are far more progressive than anything currently in existence in the federal government.

Decentralization of power would prevent conservative Republican presidents and Congress from cutting social programs, environmental regulations, abortion rights and many other policies that are near and dear to the hearts of progressives. After the Obama and Biden administrations, it should be painfully obvious to progressives that they will never be able to implement their maximalist agenda on the federal level.

Progressives should shift their focus from winning a short-term 51% majority on the federal level to empowering their supermajorities in the most liberal states. As of 2022, Democrats control at least 60% of the seats in state legislatures in 12 states: California, Connecticut, Delaware, Hawaii, Illinois, Maryland, Massachusetts, New Jersey, New Mexico, New York, Rhode Island, and Vermont (National Conference of State Legislatures).

All of these states are wealthier than the rest of the United States, so they clearly have the funding capacity to implement sweeping progressive changes. Why not empower state legislatures and executives in those states to implement a truly progressive agenda? Why ignore your strongholds in progressive states to focus on fighting an unwinnable battle on the federal level? Any progressive achievement on the federal level can easily be undone by Republicans at the next election, whereas that seems very unlikely in the 12 states listed above.

And, if progressives are correct and their policies work well, then this will build support for progressive reforms within more centrist states, such as Virginia, Maine, Minnesota, Pennsylvania, Michigan, Arizona, Nevada, Oregon, Colorado, and New Hampshire. Support might even grow in more conservative states. If progressive policies work well, then decentralization of power from the federal government to the state governments would work to the advantage of progressives.

Enable Metro Areas to Compete

While 50 states experimenting independently and copying whatever works from those experiments would be a vast improvement, perhaps we can do better.

The Commercial societies from European history, such as Venice, Florence, Bruges, Antwerp and Amsterdam, give strong evidence that individual city/states competing against each other and copying what works can lead to greater progress. As I claimed in my first book, these Commercial societies essentially invented progress. We need to find a way to copy what worked from them within the confines of modern nation states.

There is currently one small-scale political movement that has proposed making those Commercial city/states their model for political reform: the Charter City movement. The Charter City movement seeks to found new cities who are "granted special jurisdiction to create a new governance system and enact policy reforms."

As I see it, the Charter City movement essentially wants to implement libertarian principles on the local level. While the Charter City movement is trying to establish city/states in developing nations (without much success so far), no one has tried to do this within the United States. It seems like a utopian and unconstitutional idea, but it is not.

Even if the Convention of States that I mentioned above never comes to pass, state constitutions allow cities to secede from the state to form their own states. So far only Maine (in 1820) and West Virginia (in 1863) have done so. Unfortunately, no one has thought through the great benefits of secession at scale.

States are not allowed to secede from the Union, as Abraham Lincoln made clear in 1861. The Civil War was the result of the last attempt to do so. Fortunately, the Union was preserved and the slaves were freed. I hope that the United States never has to go through anything like that again. I agree with Abraham Lincoln that state-level secession from the Union is a bad idea.

I also do not think that it is a good idea for individual cities or counties to secede from a state. This level of government is too small in geographical scope to work in practice, and most city and county borders are meaningless when it comes to everyday economic interactions.

A Republic of City/States

I believe that metropolitan governments are the best level of government for solving problems in a decentralized manner. Metropolitan governments are not the same as city governments. Metro areas include the downtown, all the surrounding suburbs, and all nearby satellite cities and their suburbs. Metro areas do not include the sparsely populated rural areas that are technically within city or county borders. So metro areas are based upon population density and economic interactions, not county or municipal borders.

Men in smoked-filled rooms created our current state, city, and county borders sometime in the past. Metro areas evolved organically due to the economic forces that economists call "agglomeration" effects.

The U.S. Census Bureau has created a geographical concept called Metropolitan Statistical Areas (MSAs) to capture their agglomeration. By analyzing commuter patterns, MSAs lump together the geographical areas that interact with each other daily.

MSAs are de facto metro areas. Metro areas include a very high level of interaction between many different people in one small geographical area. This is exactly what you need for progress to work.

To give one example, the San Francisco Bay area is one metro area. It consists of the city of San Francisco, Oakland, San Jose, and all the nearby suburbs. Nearby Sacramento is a different metro area. So are the Los Angeles and San Diego metro areas. Altogether, the vast majority of Americans live in a metro area, and most live in one with a population of over two million.

Metropolitan-level governments are common in Europe and the rest of the world. Unfortunately, they are almost non-existent in the United States. Given that the metro area is the only level of government that has evolved rather than being established centuries ago, this is a major oversight.

While creating yet another level of government in the United States would probably fail and could well do more damage than good, perhaps we can upgrade entire metro areas into fully-fledged states. The United States has a robust tradition of federalism with a relatively clear division of responsibility between local, state, and federal governments. We should leverage this federalist tradition to create a workable decentralization of power that radically increases decentralized policy experimentation.

Not surprisingly, the metropolitan level is roughly analogous to the old Commercial city/states of European history. This level of government is very common in Europe, but, because Europe has much more centralized governance, those metro areas do not have much leeway for independent experimentation.

State governments in the United States have much more leeway for policy experimentation, and that leeway is enshrined in the Constitution. Unfortunately, the United States is almost completely lacking in metropolitan-level governments.

Create New States

I believe that I have figured out a way to effectively recreate the old European city/states within the current American federal system. Rather than trying to create a new level of metropolitan government, *we should expand the number of states.* The United States has had 50 states for so long that we forget that this has not always been the case.

One of the most important achievements of the Founding Fathers was to ensure that new western territories did not become colonies of the original 13 states. Instead, as the population migrated westward, territories were gradually transformed into self-governing states. As pioneers gradually migrated westward, the United States grew from 13 states to the current 50.

I propose that we "crank up the volume" of American federalism by creating 36 new states. If all 36 metro areas in the U.S. with a population of over 2 million seceded to form their own states, they would each have their own governor, their own state legislature, their own tax system, their own court system, and a great deal of constitutional leeway to experiment with different policies. These new states could maintain the same city governments that were already in existence if they chose to do so.

Together, these 36 metro areas comprise a total population of 161 million in 2020, or 49% of the United States. The largest metro areas that could receive statehood are New York City, Los Angeles, Chicago, Dallas, and Houston. The smallest metro areas would include Las Vegas, Cincinnati, Kansas City, Indianapolis and Cleveland.

Under the U.S. Constitution Article IV Section 4, state-level secession within the Union is permitted by "the Consent of the Legislatures of the States concerned as well as of the Congress." The wording is a little vague, and to the best of my knowledge the U.S. Supreme Court has not offered an official interpretation of this clause, but the Constitution clearly allows for the creation of new states.

What is not clear is whether states can initiate the process without final Congressional approval. Remember that the U.S. Constitution was written to define the powers of the federal government only. The U.S. Constitution was never intended to define the powers of state governments.

Presumably, there would need to be some sort of proof that the affected metro areas want such a change, such as a referendum. So this would be either a two-step or a three-step process:

1. Referenda or legislative action within the counties or cities affected.

2. A majority vote of all affected State Legislatures (because some metro areas cross state boundaries).

3. (Perhaps also) Majority vote by both the U.S. House and Senate.

If Congressional legislation is required, it could presumably be done in one simple majority vote granting all metro areas with a population over 2 million the right to form a new state. New states might be created as each census reveals more metro areas with other 2 million people. Few pieces of legislation would do more to lower the levels of partisan conflict within state legislatures than a clean separation of liberal metro areas from the conservative remainder of the states.

The push for creating new states could come from voters in metro regions who want their metro to secede from the state. Or the push could come from rural voters outside the metro area who want to kick them out of the state. Currently, the partisan divide is so strong that I could see either movement gaining traction fairly quickly once the idea becomes part of the political discourse.

Under my proposal, the 50 states that are currently in existence would remain. They would, however, be restricted to rural areas and cities with populations under 2 million people. To use Illinois as an example, the entire Chicago metro area would secede from the state of Illinois to form its own state. The state of Illinois would remain, but with fewer people.

Some of these states might decide to start with a clean slate that did not automatically duplicate all existing legislation and regulation from their previous state. This would allow them to take a look at massively reducing policies that no longer make any sense. Because they would have to hire new metro-level bureaucrats, there would be far less resistance to fundamental reform. This is exactly what the Charter City movement is trying to do abroad, but has so far failed to achieve.

Without the more liberal Chicago voters, the state of Illinois could implement sweeping changes that they otherwise would not be able to pass. The fledgling state of Chicago might be able to do the same but in the opposite direction. The new state of Chicago might resemble the new state of Seattle more than the updated version of Illinois.

Redrawing state borders would lead many governments to have a massive rethink of current policies, regulations, programs, and processes. Some might be more favorable to liberals, while others might be more favorable to conservatives. Some would prefer to pursue pragmatic centrist policies. If federal regulations and mandates were simultaneously reduced to allow states more freedom, this would create even more opportunities for local experimentation.

Given this redefinition of the concept of states, liberal voters who previously thought of states' rights as an excuse to oppress Blacks might see things in a very different way. After four years of living under Trump with the possibility of four more in the future, Los Angeles and New York City voters might become hard-core advocates of state rights.

Opinion polls consistently show far more confidence in local and state government than in the federal government. While trust in the federal government is at or near all-time lows (24%), state (65%) and particularly local government (74%) gain net positive support from voters (Deloitte, Gallup).

I believe that having 86 states, all with much smaller populations, would give people a much greater connection with their government. Each state would be more homogeneous, but the ability to go its own way would empower greater diversity between states.

The great diversity of America could be represented on the state level rather than trying to force an epic zero-sum conflict on the federal level. It would also give us far more policy variations to experiment with.

Given that the United States has worked out the powers of the state and federal government, I do not see any long-term problems with creating more states. The biggest complication would be in the U.S. Senate, which would suddenly grow from 100 Senators to 172. Both parties would be very nervous about accidentally empowering the other party with more states. Each would weigh the partisan consequences carefully.

It would take some sophisticated mathematical computations to see which party would benefit from 72 new Senators. I admit the possibilities of a partisan shift, but we should not assume that the change will be big until we have better data. Particularly when the creation of new states is combined with the slimmer federal government that I proposed earlier, the consequences of new Senators would be much less extreme.

I believe that greater decentralization and the creation of more states will greatly power down the intensity of conflict between the two parties. With many more states that are all more homogeneous, we could let them experiment with different policies without huge partisan conflict on the federal level.

With lower federal taxes and spending, the federal government would become less important, except in natural security issues. This would dampen down the consequences of losing federal elections.

Liberals might shift to implementing vastly increased welfare states in the biggest metro areas without the encumbrance of Republicans.

Republicans might not feel like liberals were trying to impose their will on them and be less worried about experimentation in liberal states.

Republicans might shift to cutting taxes, spending, and regulations in their states. Liberals would be less worried about the negative effects on poor people, because poor people could move to states with expansive benefits. Fewer people would be forced to accept policies that fundamentally conflict with their beliefs.

The very ideological elected officials of cities would be forced to modify their stances somewhat, because they would now have to appeal to far more moderate suburbanites. This would probably not have a big effect in the very large metro areas on the Pacific Coast and Northeast, but it would in the rest of the nation.

My proposal would also help to solve the problem of gerrymandering. Because states would be much smaller in both population and land area, there would be fewer opportunities for gaming the system. This would not eliminate the problem, but it would probably reduce it simply because voters within states would become more homogenous.

In addition to the federal government giving states greater autonomy by eliminating regulations and mandates, city governments within metro areas should transfer many of their powers up to the new states. Currently, most metro areas are a labyrinth of mayors, councils, county governments, school boards, utility districts, water districts, and other authorities and special districts. Because each of them is so small and many are specific to a small policy domain, voter turnout is very low. They also receive very little media attention.

The combination of low turnout, low media coverage and focus on one small policy domain, makes these local entities ripe for capture by special interests. It also means that it is hard to implement change across an entire metro area. By handing over some or all of these powers to much smaller state governments, we could make the new states more efficient and representative. City, municipal, and country governments within rural states would remain the same.

My proposal would effectively meld local and state governments together within metro areas and remove federal restrictions on autonomy and experimentation. More power to more states would make the government more representative, more effective, and more willing to experiment. This type of decentralization is exactly the kind of condition that makes progress possible.

The EU Has Gone Too Far

So far, I have mainly focused on the United States, but I would like to briefly discuss Europe.

The European Union has moved far beyond its original vision of a free trade zone with democratic governance and peaceful conflict resolution. The Union is increasingly trying to eliminate diversity between European nations in the name of "harmonization." Europeans seem to have forgotten that it was the fragmentation and diversity of political institutions that originally made Europe the most dynamic economy in the world.

I lived in Europe during the 1980s when this process was getting started. I was a big fan of European integration, but gradually over time, I have come to realize that the process has moved much too far. When European judges and bureaucrats nullify perfectly good legislation or regulations just because it is different from EU standards, this undermines the very foundation of what made Europe great in the first place.

The failed attempt to ratify a treaty establishing a Constitution for Europe in 2005-06 should have been a wake-up call. Referenda in France and Netherlands led to defeat. Rather than embarrass themselves with further evidence of popular opposition, further referenda were canceled in the Czech Republic, Denmark, Ireland, Poland, Sweden, and the UK. After a "period of reflection," a slightly modified Treaty of Lisbon was implemented anyway.

The subsequent withdrawal of the United Kingdom from the European Union, the economic stagnation over the last 15 years, and the rise of anti-EU parties on both the Right and the Left show that the failure to ratify was not an isolated incident. The fate of the European Union is uncertain, and the EU has no one to blame but itself.

Bureaucrats and judges in Brussels are relentlessly taking away power from democratically-elected national assemblies. Any objection to this trend is dismissed as mindless "populism." But one does not have to be a "populist" to be concerned by this centralizing trend.

It should not be a surprise that Europe has been experiencing some of the slowest economic growth in the world for quite some time. As of today, the European economy has essentially been stuck in a stagnant economy since the recession of 2008. Per capita GDP has not budged for 15 years... and counting. At the time of writing, the economic situation only appears to be getting worse.

Enabling national and local governments to experiment with different policies will lead to greater innovation. Those innovations can make a big difference in reinvigorating European economic growth.

The European Union should not give up on its original goal of free trade, peaceful conflict resolution, and democratic governance, but judges and bureaucrats in Brussels need to give nations and regions greater license to go their own way. Diversity within the European Union is not a threat to the future of the Union, it will only strengthen it.

Allowing nations to go back to using their national currencies, while still keeping the Euro for international business and tourism would be a big step toward loosening the reins. Each of these national currencies would freely float relative to both the other national currencies and the Euro. This would allow each nation to pursue its own monetary policy without negatively affecting other nations.

To make this workable, businesses throughout Europe might be required to accept both the local currency and the Euro. Customers would be allowed to pay for an item using either currency. Given that the vast majority of transactions are now conducted digitally, this does not seem unworkable.

Allowing nations to protect their own borders against immigrants within Europe and those coming from outside Europe could greatly tone down the tense politics regarding immigration and multiculturalism. European nations who want to accept immigrants or migrants should be allowed to do so. European nations who want far fewer immigrants or migrants should also be allowed to act on that wish. They should also be allowed to choose which immigrants or migrants to accept.

Each European nation should also be allowed to determine its own agricultural and energy policies. Currently, the European Union is trying to force Green energy and agricultural policies on its member nations. Some nations like that, while others do not. Each should be able to choose for themselves.

Decentralizing the EU, particularly in the domains of finance, immigration, energy, and agriculture might be a way to save the Union. A decentralized EU is far better than an overly-centralized EU or no EU. If Brussels continues along its current path, it will get the least desirable of all outcomes.

The problems within the European Union go beyond policy. Brussels and many other institutions in Europe seem intent on abolishing national identity and replacing them with a common European identity. Changing identity is not in itself a problem, but when it is accomplished by centralized institutions without much public influence, it is very troubling.

These elites have convinced themselves that nationalism is dangerous and out-moded in the modern world. They equate nationalism with war, authoritarianism, emotionalism, and conflict. However, war, authoritarianism, emotionalism, and conflict existed long before nationalism and will continue to exist even if nationalism is eliminated.

There is nothing inherently wrong with national identity. It seems to be a core need of the vast majority of people to identify with a group that transcends their immediate family. Perceiving oneself as a citizen of the world or a continent is fine for some intellectuals, but it is too high a level for most people.

The only real alternatives to national identity are the identities of the clan, tribe, race, ethnicity, religion, or empire. The nation state has proven itself as the most effective means of preserving cultural diversity while maintaining effective institutions in a specific geographical area.

There is absolutely nothing wrong with Danes, Poles, Italians, Greeks, and, yes, even Germans being proud of their national traditions and accomplishments. Nor is there anything wrong with each of them wanting to preserve those traditions by establishing separate institutions governed solely by elected national, regional, and local legislatures.

If Brussels is not careful, all the wonderful national diversity throughout the continent will be eliminated for the sake of harmonization. Rather than leading to a higher form of identity, this harmonization will probably lead to people without a true common sense of identity. After all, if every European nation follows the same diversity policies, there will be much less diversity between European nations in the long run.

Above all, European judges and bureaucrats must allow national and local experimentation. Perhaps every European standard is better than all the previous local standards, so it should be imposed. But what about 20 years from now? How do you know what works if no variation is allowed? Variation enables evolutionary processes to find a way and to develop.

Europe, the homeland of Commercial societies, needs to rediscover the local experimentation that once made it the most dynamic continent in the world. The alternative may be Brexit on a much greater scale.

Conclusion

Both the United States and the European Union should embrace decentralization and local experimentation. The enormous growth of centralized government in both territories has been a major issue undermining long-term economic growth. By enabling metropolitan areas to experiment with different policies while the central government protects basic rights, we can identify policies that work. Then those policies that work can be copied by other metropolitan governments. In this way, decentralized experimentation can help to promote progress.

PROMOTING PROGRESS

IDENTIFYING POLICIES THAT WORK

How Progress Works:

People copying successful technologies, skills, and organizations and then modifying them to solve different problems. This enables innovations that work to spread into new companies, new sectors of the economy, and new geographical regions. This step is critical to ensure that progress is widely shared.

The concept of innovation has been all the rage in 21st Century America. No matter where one looks – books, media, or corporate board rooms – there is a focus on this concept. And for good reason. Innovation is critical to progress. I would like to make the claim, however, that copying is at least as important as innovating.

Copying others is a unique human behavior that enables progress to work. Humans can see a technology or skill being used by another person, identify its purpose, assess its usefulness compared to their own toolkit, and then decide whether to copy it. While other animals may have this skill (for example, young birds and mammals learn from their mother), the human species has taken this to a new level.

There are real benefits to being the copier rather than the innovator. The innovator has to go through all the hard work of designing a new piece of technology, testing it, and iterating on the results. The innovator also has to go through the hard work of learning all the necessary new skills related to that technology. They have also invested the time to learn how to adapt their social organizations so they are best placed to use those technologies. The copier can just wait, watch the results, and copy only when it looks like the original innovators have come up with a superior solution.

No matter what domain you seek to enter, there is one Golden Rule of Success: Copy the Successful. It does not matter whether you want to be an athlete, artist, business leader, political leader, doctor, farmer, or welder. The simplest way to get better at something is to copy those who are most successful in the field. By copying the best, you are effectively learning from all the trial-and-error attempts made by those who came before you.

Unfortunately, copying is not so easy. Particularly when we focus on government policy, it can be difficult to identify which policy actually works. When one copies an individual or a specific technology, or skill, it is much easier to identify it. The actual impact of government policy, however, is spread throughout society, so it is very hard to differentiate policies that fail from policies that work.

Progress Is More Than Economic Growth

So far I have argued that supporters of progress should roll back policies that undermine long-term economic growth. In a later book in this series, I will argue for a set of policies to create a prosperous working class and a clear pathway so that youths from a low-income background can enter that class. Together, these policies will lay a solid foundation for widely-shared economic growth.

However, not all domains of the human experience are directly related to economic growth. In many of those domains, private industry has no real profit incentive to solve the problem, so market-oriented solutions are difficult to establish.

For this reason, governments have stepped in to establish programs related to education, retirement, health care, poverty, disability, unemployment, housing, homelessness, and other social policies. Altogether these policies encompass a large percentage of the nation's total economic activity.

Making these social policies more effective is one of the most important things that governments can do to promote material progress. Unfortunately, the American government has not been very successful at doing so on either on the federal or the state level.

Currently, our political system boils down to Democrats trying to increase spending on social programs and regulations as much as possible, while the Republicans are trying to stop that expansion. In that perpetual partisan conflict, no one stops to think about what really matters: whether a program actually produces the desired results.

I believe that the American people want the government to show better results. A government that spends far less money but produces far greater results would do much to heal the bitter partisan divide and restore confidence in our institutions. A slimmer more effective government that helps the less fortunate more than it does today would be popular with the vast majority of voters.

Rather than wasting billions or even trillions on programs that do not work, we could shift funding to those that do. We could have a smaller government (which the Right wants) along with a government that helps those most in need (which the Left wants).

Why Government Fails So Often

Despite the American government spending almost 50% of GDP, it is difficult to point to many real policy successes over the last 50 years. Think about it; what would you consider to be a great accomplishment of government over the last 50 years to be? And remember, I am talking about *results*, not legislation or spending.

The fundamental problem is two-fold:

1.   Our political system has not identified policies that actually work.

2.   People involved in politics do not care.

The problem is not bad people. The problem is a bad implementation and evaluation process.

At its core, democratic governance involves the following process:

1. Citizens raise problems that they think the government should solve.

2. Policy experts propose solutions to those problems.

3. During elections, candidates decide which issues they want to prioritize and their proposed solutions to those high-priority problems.

4. Voters choose their favorite candidate.

5. Elected officials attempt to form majorities to pass legislation on the few problems deemed the highest priority.

6. Bureaucrats implement those solutions.

7. Everyone cheers and then goes home!

Our political system is pretty good at bringing problems into the political arena and then prioritizing them according to popular opinion. Our political system is also pretty good at throwing up a wide variety of plausible solutions. That is a start, but it does not complete the process.

Our political system is unfortunately very poor at implementing solutions that actually work and then iterating based on results. The American people know it and are gradually losing confidence in our governing institutions.

Elected officials, campaign donors, activists, and their allied media outlets do not care that the policies they so avidly promote are very unlikely to produce results for the people. Most of them are so sure that they know what works, that they assume their opponents are idiots, corrupt or stupid.

Most people in politics believe that all that they need to do to solve problems is to show courage and fortitude in the political struggle. When that struggle finally leads to the desired legislation, they cheer and then just move on to the next issue.

Hold on. Identifying problems, and their possible solutions, and implementing them is the easy part. The really hard part is figuring out what works. Many activists claim to care about people, when what they actually care about are their ideas.

Imagine if entrepreneurs, who play such an important role in promoting progress, had a similar mentality. They start out with a great idea of how to solve a problem that other people want to be solved. Then they form a company. And then... they cheer, pat themselves on the back, and go home?

Sorry, that is not how it works.

Experienced entrepreneurs know that the hard part has not even started. They still have years, or more likely decades of hard work to define a business model, experiment with new technologies, raise capital, hire workers, identify customers, and market to those customers. And even after all of that work, the vast majority of companies fail to make a long-term profit.

The same goes for engineering, another profession that plays an important role in promoting progress. When senior executives or the marketing team come up with a "great idea" for a product, experienced engineers know that this is just the beginning of a long arduous process that may or may not succeed.

Unfortunately, great ideas rarely lead to success. Everyone with any experience in business, engineering, or technology knows that there is a huge gulf between a great idea and a profitable product. In politics, great ideas get implemented, but then no one looks at the results. In business, it is all about results, and "great" ideas are a dime a dozen.

Some portray business as cold-hearted because all business leaders do is focus on the bottom line. But not caring about results is the height of self-indulgence. If you do not care about results, you do not care about people. It is results that affect people's lives, not good intentions.

Some less idealistic elected officials and campaign donors do not care about results for different reasons. While they claim to care about the people, they mainly care about building coalitions. They do not care about the ideas themselves as long as they can construct a majority coalition to pass legislation.

In some ways, this is a very pragmatic attitude, but it can often degenerate into power politics for its own sake. In practice, this attitude becomes all about using the power of the government to tax, and distribute money and jobs to one's supporters in return for their votes. This is very similar to the viewpoint of the old corrupt urban machines that used to dominate the politics of American cities.

What most people do not realize is that government bureaucrats have a huge amount of latitude as to how to implement legislation. Despite often being hundreds of pages long, Congressional legislation is often vague about many important points. And Congress often deliberately leaves important points vague as they do not want to get too bogged down in the details.

Congress focuses mainly on the intent of the legislation and who receives the money and jobs. Most Congresspersons are not interested in the details of implementation or the evaluation of policies because they are more interested in pushing through the next round of legislation.

No one in our political system has the incentive to focus on results, even though results are what people actually care about. Most regular people do not want to be involved in politics. In fact, they hate politics. They just want to live their lives and have government solve those problems that they cannot solve through their own efforts.

Both the idealists and the machine politicians are wrong. It is results that matter because it is results that affect people's lives. Rather than focus on intentions and who receives the money and jobs, we would be much better served as a nation if our political system focused more on results.

Experts Do Not Know

Some people claim that we can solve the problem by deferring to experts. They claim that our political process is bad at solving problems because politicians do not listen to experts. Policy issues are very complex, and it takes deep expertise in one domain to truly understand what works.

My formal academic training is in the field of Public Policy. I received a Ph.D. in Political Science and Public Policy from Brown University. I taught many university-level policy courses when I was a professor. I think that it is correct to say that I am an expert in a number of policy domains, including many that are in this book. I have a deep respect for the importance of policy knowledge.

However, I am here to tell you that experts are just as fallible as non-experts. The fundamental problem is that modern societies are extremely complex, policy impacts span across many different domains, and no one person is an expert on all of those domains. More to the point, experts often base their opinions on the same ideological assumptions that political activists do.

Another fundamental problem is that, on issues that are relevant to public policy, experts often disagree. This should not be a surprise. Where experts are in total agreement, this is generally on issues that are not problems that government wants to solve. Experts agree that the Earth is a sphere, but this is not particularly relevant to any policy issue.

Unfortunately, the view that we should defer to experts often degenerates into something like a Cult of the Expert. What this actually entails is deferring to a sub-group of experts who have the same ideological assumptions as the people who are promoting the Cult of the Expert. So behind the Cult of the Expert actually lurks the Cult of the Ideology.

Even though experts are just as ideologically biased as the rest of us, this does not mean that they do not have a role to play. Experts are excellent at presenting policies that might work. If we listen to a wide variety of experts with differing ideological biases, we greatly increase the chances that one of them will work.

But how do we sort through all the conflicting policy proposals that experts make so that we can identify the one that actually works?

Experimentation

We need to figure out better ways of actually implementing solutions to the problems that people care about. At its most basic, we need to develop a methodology for implementing the best possible solution, given our resources in a highly complex society. Modern societies are so complex that no one truly understands the results of many of our policies, the incentive those policies create, and the second-order behaviors of people as a result of those incentives.

This is a tough nut to crack that gets to the heart of trying to use policies to get desired results in extraordinarily complex societies. Fortunately, we can copy a methodology that is quite common in other domains.

Medical researchers also face very high levels of complexity within biological systems that they do not fully understand. They have developed methodologies to partially overcome that problem.

Congress funds medical research but does not tell researchers what works. Congress gives medical researchers funding to solve a problem, usually involving curing a specific disease or ailment. Congress also gives medical researchers the latitude to conduct research, develop options, and experiment with each of those options while forcing each to use a rigorous methodology.

Imagine if we did that for every issue!

Randomized Controlled Trials

As Jim Manzi pointed out in his book *Uncontrolled*, a time-tested methodology for determining the most effective policies is Randomized Controlled Trials (RCTs). Widely used in the medical field and rapidly catching on in business, RCTs are an experimental form of impact evaluation in which potential recipients are randomly sorted into two groups: an experimental group, which receives the treatment, and a control group, which does not.

In this book series, I have applied the concept of evolution to a number of areas. I believe that the concept of evolution is extremely useful for understanding complex interactions.

One can think of RCTs as a controlled experiment in evolution. If the government systematically performed RCTs using many different policy options, we would create the variation necessary to fuel evolution. By using clear metrics of the results, we would be measuring outcomes in the same way that evolution "measures" results by the probability that a variation leads to survival and reproduction.

For example, let's use the testing of a Covid vaccine as an example. Health researchers might post a call for volunteers to participate in a study. They might receive a small financial reward and a warning of potential risks. All those who volunteer are sorted into two groups: one that receives a Covid vaccine, and another that receives an injection of a placebo. After a period of time, the researchers look at the difference in the number of participants who actually got Covid. If the difference is statistically significant, and if there were no adverse effects, then the vaccine is deemed effective.

If done rigorously and with a large enough sample size, RCTs are the gold standard in identifying which public policies work. Unfortunately, they are rarely used in the field of public policy.

We have run enough RCTs to know that *most government programs fail to achieve positive results*. Unfortunately, we have not run enough RCTs to identify which policies *actually do work*.

Widespread use of RCTs that force the government to focus on results would do much to rebuild the confidence of the American people in their government. Citizens intuitively understand that both sides in the partisan wars just want to win, ram through their policies, and ignore results.

Negative public attitudes towards our institutions are not solely based on populism or irrational distrust of experts. The people intuitively understand what most policy experts know but rarely talk about.

The Iron Law

The dirty little secret of policy evaluation is that the vast majority of government programs that are subjected to rigorous evaluation, including RCTs, show no net positive results. And once one adds in the funding spent on the program, then the net impact is invariably negative. This outcome has been so consistent that policy experts now expect those results.

These results are so consistent that Peter Rossi, an intrepid evaluator of social programs, coined the term the "Iron Law" of policy evaluation. The Iron Law states that "the expected value of any net impact assessment of any large-scale social program is zero." In other words, the program does not show positive results (Rossi).

Rossi followed up this Iron Law with the even more depressing "Stainless Steel Law." The Stainless Steel law states: "The better designed the impact assessment of a social program, the more likely is the resulting estimate of net impact to be zero." In other words, the more rigorous the test, the worse the results.

And Rossi was not some right-winger who hates social spending. He was a left-of-center policy analyst who wanted social policies to work better!

It is astounding to me that the Iron Law is not more widely known. It gets to the very core of the ability of our government to solve problems. Why don't more people know about the Iron Law of policy evaluation!?!

Moreover, to the best of my knowledge, no public policy expert has refuted the Iron Law. Instead, they just ignore it and move on. But ignoring the results of policies is getting increasingly difficult to do. If anything, as we gradually increase the usage of RCTs and post the results to the internet, more and more evidence for the Iron Law keeps piling up.

Within the policy evaluation field and to a lesser extent among the few political leaders and policy wonks who care about results, the Iron Law is like the body buried in the basement that everyone in the family knows about but does not talk about. And they pretend not to notice that Weird Uncle Joe supposedly went for a walk one day and never came back!

On the rare occasions that the subject of the Iron Law came up in my graduate-level classes, the professor sheepishly mentioned it, and my fellow students got nervous and confused looks on their faces. Then there was an awkward pause, and a brief conversation, before the topic turned to "more important matters."

Looking back, I am a bit embarrassed and ashamed that I was not willing to confront the significance of these findings. Quite frankly, I was unwilling to question my fundamental assumptions on the effectiveness of government policy at the time. It took me decades for the significance of the Iron Law to sink in.

Virtually everyone involved in politics or policy behaves on an implicit assumption that government programs typically achieve their goals. And those few who do know about the Iron Law, rarely speak up out of fear of starting an uncomfortable conversation with their superiors.

Both the idealists and the machine politicians who dominate politics hate RCTs and the Iron Law because they perceive them as undermining their entire view of the world. So they do not talk about either. To the extent that idealists and machine politicians think about results, they tend to suspect that their favorite policies will show bad results and be eliminated.

But that is exactly why we need RCTs at scale. And in the end, if the long-term decline of American confidence in our governing institutions is not reversed, any political victories scored by idealist and machine politicians will be very short-lived. In the long run, they need the public to be confident in the effectiveness of the government.

Most Good Ideas Fail

If we broaden the perspective, perhaps we should not be so surprised about the Iron Law. The reality is that the vast majority of new ideas fail to show results in the real world. Our world is very complex, and no one human or group of humans fully understands it.

No matter how "great" an idea is, it must also be better than all the other previous "great ideas" of the past that were tried and turned out to actually work. When one thinks of the millions of "great ideas" that billions of our ancestors experimented with, it should not be surprising that the vast majority of new ideas fail. Results are a very high standard that few ideas can meet.

Businesses, scientists, and medical researchers understand that most "good" ideas fail, so they have built methodologies to test them before scaling them up. If the government did the same, we could solve more problems than we can today.

Now I do not mean to claim that massively scaling up RCTs will solve all problems. Many problems simply cannot be solved. Many policy domains have characteristics that make controlled trials with large sample sizes difficult if not impossible. Other domains, such as civil rights and civil liberties, should not involve withholding benefits from some people. There are also ethical issues that are most commonly seen in medical experiments.

But any policy domain where one has a large number of relatively similar units, and it is possible to selectively extend money or services to some of them and withhold them from others is perfect for RCTs. The vast majority of social policies fall into this category. Education, health care, law enforcement, housing, environment, and many other policy domains are perfect for using RCTs at scale.

A Better Process

I believe that we should implement a better policy-making process that is more likely to yield positive results. The new process would look something like this:

1. When Congress passes legislation, instead of implementing a program, they clearly define the problem, determine how much money will be spent identifying the best solution to the problem, establish metrics of success, and identify possible solutions that need to be tested. No actual programs would be implemented at this time.

2. A newly-created Bureau of Policy Assessment designs a series of RCTs that will test each of the proposed solutions.

3. The methodology is posted on the internet as open for comment.

4. The methodology is vetted by a newly-created Congressional Committee on Policy Assessment and independent experts on RCTs.

5. Once approved, the executive bureaucracy runs the series of RCTs. For example, the U.S. Department of Housing and Human Services would run RCTs on policies related to housing.

6. The numeric results of the study are posted to the internet, and they are analyzed by the Bureau of Policy Assessment, the Congressional Committee on Policy Assessment, and independent experts.

7. For any programs that achieve positive initial results, steps #2-#6 are repeated with different groups of a larger sample size to verify the results and hone in on which specific characteristics of the solution that work best.

8. Based on the results, Congress could pass additional legislation that slowly scales up a new program and increases the number and size of the RCTs.

9. All beneficiaries of the new program are required to participate in RCTs so that the program can keep improving.

The above process is obviously a radical departure from current practice. Rather than Congress or state legislatures implementing a program, they should instead decide on which problem to solve and how much funding should be devoted to finding a solution. Federal or state bureaucrats would then be required to run hundreds of small-scale RCTs trying to identify the policy that most cost-effectively solves the problem.

Ideally, every reasonable policy option that does not conflict with fundamental constitutional rights or is prohibitively expensive should be tested. The policy that produces the best results relative to the cost should go on to further rounds of RCTs with larger sample sizes and different populations.

Some will probably complain that his new process is slow and cumbersome. They might claim that they will make it difficult for the government to react to sudden emergencies.

I would argue, however, that domestic issues rarely suddenly emerge. Think of homelessness, drug addiction, poverty, health care, education, etc. They are problems that have existed for generations, if not all of human history. Though political activists define every issue as a crisis, policy problems almost always have a long history.

I would also argue that it is far better to wait a few months or even years to implement a policy that actually works rather than rushing through a policy that is highly likely to fail. Our track record of implementing programs that show positive, long-term results is quite poor. Virtually every problem that we have today would be in a better place if the government had gone through this process five years ago.

It is important to remember that shutting down a program that does not work frees up additional funding resources for programs that do work. So a program that is determined to be a failure early in the implementation process should be viewed as a positive achievement. The alternative is wasting money for decades, while programs that actually do work are being starved for funding.

If a policy is a true emergency, then Congress can establish large amounts of money for a large number of rapid RCTs. Covid, for example, was such a sudden, unanticipated emergency in 2020. If all viable interventions had been tested using RCTs in 2020, we would know far more about what works today.

It is also possible to blend quick action with long-term RCTs. For example, we could have had a lockdown for the elderly and nursing homes, which were obviously the most vulnerable sectors, while subjecting vaccines, mask mandates, school closings, and business closings to RCTs. Fortunately, we did do RCTs for vaccines, but not for the other policies.

Of course, it is impossible in practice to test all possible ideas. Foreign policy, for example, is not very conducive to RCTs. Nor are policies with long delays between funding and receiving benefits, such as Social Security. It is also much more difficult to run RCTs on policies that have already been implemented, particularly if they are defined as an entitlement.

But we should experiment with a few of the policies that seem most likely to have positive results while carving out a domain for continual experimentation even after programs have been scaled up. After all, the best policy in 2020 may not be the best policy in 2030.

Most importantly, Congress and state legislatures should not authorize large-scale funding for a new program until it has passed many levels of rigorous RCTs. This would be a radical departure from current practice. Many elected officials would hate this because it undercuts their ability to force through a program regardless of results.

Doing so would effectively limit the power of elected officials and bureaucrats to decide *how* the government solves problems. In this sense, it would decentralize power. I know that this is not using the word "decentralization" in its usual sense, but my proposed process does undermine the power of political elites to determine *how* the government solves problems. They could only fully fund a new policy if it has already been rigorously tested and thereby proven to show net positive results.

Of course, Congress would still have the power to choose which problems need solving and the budget devoted to finding those solutions. Rather than just implementing a solution as they do today, bureaucrats should be required to conduct large numbers of small controlled experiments to see which policy option best solves the problem.

Rigorous RCTs

Not all RCTs are equally good. In order to properly run RCTs, they need to fulfill a number of rigorous requirements, including:

• The methodology used in the study must be fully vetted and approved by independent experts *before* the study commences.

• A large sample size must be used to ensure statistically valid results.

• Random sorting of participants into either the test group or the control group must be done *after* they decide to participate to eliminate selection bias.

• Double-blind experiments must be used where even those

conducting the experiment do not know which group each participant has been sorted into.

- To save cost widely available data should be used (getting the data is typically the biggest cost of running an RCT).

- A wide variety of interventions should be assessed. This may be within the same trial or in separate trials.

- Transparency of results by posting on the internet in understandable language.

- Short duration of tests, if possible, to enable rapid iteration.

- Initial trials should be followed up by long-term assessments to see if the impact lingers.

- There should be multiple rounds of RCTs in different geographical locations and with different demographic groups. This helps to verify the initial results and identify sub-populations with differing results.

The federal government and state governments should establish a Bureau of Policy Evaluation whose sole purpose is to run evaluation studies on specific policy problems. Congress should also establish its own Congressional Office of Policy Evaluation as a potential check. Those who staff these new organizations must learn how to effectively run RCTs from medical researchers and business analysts. They should also work closely with academic experts in policy evaluation.

These new institutions should establish best practices for running RCTs and posting those practices on the internet for all to see and comment on. These departments should also be insulated from partisan politics, interest groups, and the bureaucratic agencies that will actually implement the best policy in the future as much as possible.

An Example

Let me give a few examples of how this might work. Let's focus on teaching methods first. Education is the perfect domain for widespread RCTs. With roughly 100,000 schools and even more classrooms, the sample sizes could be in the millions. And there is no reason to wait for annual standardized tests. The testing could be delivered weekly, daily, or even hourly while the students learn.

Rather than teachers and administrators arguing over which teaching methods work, try them all at scale. Teachers in one class can each use one teaching methodology, while other teachers use different methodologies. To a certain extent, this is already done, but what if all students' test scores are matched to the teaching methodology? What if the content is delivered via computer along with assessments?

All subjects could be divided up into small ten-minute online modules with quick assessments to see if the student grasped the concepts. If the student fails to grasp the concepts, then a student could repeat the same content using another teaching methodology, to see if a different teaching method works better. Oh, by the way, this is good teaching practice anyway, so it would not interfere with student learning.

And this does not undermine our ability to have standards. All institutions are caught between trying to enforce certain minimum standards for all while still maintaining enough variation to allow the standards to improve.

RCTs are a perfect mechanism for doing this. With huge sample sizes, it would be simple for the vast majority of students to receive what is currently considered to be the most effective teaching methodology, while 20% get what other experts think might be a better method. Thus 80% of students would effectively be the control group, while the other 20% could be many different experimental groups.

That 20% might be randomly divided into ten different teaching methodologies. With digital technology, we could easily get meaningful results in just a few weeks. If one methodology outperformed the current standard, then it could become the new standard for the next group of students.

Constantly Improving Standards

Contrary to what most people in government think, uniformity is not a good thing; it is often a bad thing. Rather than thinking of a standard as what every person needs to receive, we should see it as what most people receive because it is currently the most impactful intervention.

We do not just want standards; we want *constantly improving standards*. And we want those standards to be based upon results, not politics, interest groups, or personal preference. RCTs at scale would enable the vast majority of students to get the best possible results, while still constantly trying to improve that standard.

If you add on all the benefits of federalism that I discussed earlier, I can foresee local and state governments conducting a vast number of RCTs. Federal aid to poorer state governments could be tied to states running RCTs. The federal government would give them the financial incentive by paying for these trials and the expertise for how to do so. If all levels of government are running thousands of different RCTs in dozens of different policy domains, imagine the learning that would take place.

The Politics of RCTs

A critical part of my proposal is that elected officials and bureaucrats would have to show enormous restraint. They must be required to follow the RCT methodology in a highly transparent and systematic manner.

The results and methodology would need to be accessible to all citizens via the internet, to ensure that no one cheats the system. And the results would need to be presented in a way that non-experts can easily read and interpret their results.

Most importantly, elected officials would have to have the discipline to eliminate funding for programs that show poor results, even if those programs are popular with voters, donors, the media, or interest groups. It would be very difficult for most current elected officials to show this restraint and the ones who do not may benefit more politically than those who do.

But seen from a different perspective, elected officials may learn to enjoy the benefits of my proposal in the long run. Not having to decide all the details of a solution takes a tremendous burden off their shoulders. Legislation could be radically simplified by merely determining:

- The problem to be solved.
- Possible solutions that might work.
- Metrics of success.
- The amount of funding devoted to experimentation
- The amount of funding for the most successful policy.

As far as I am concerned, this is just good management practice. Leaders generally get far better results if they target a problem to be solved rather than a solution to be implemented. Then give the experts the funding and the latitude to experiment. Only after a proposed solution has been proven at scale should funding be ramped up.

My proposal also has a tremendous benefit for elected officials and bureaucrats when it comes to blame-shifting. If they get complaints from an interest group that does not like the current policy, the elected official can say, "Sorry, but our RCTs determined that this was the most effective means to solve the problem that you earlier told me needed solving." And the bureaucrat can say, "Sorry, we tried that idea, and here are the bad results. Feel free to read the report on the internet."

My proposal virtually eliminates the most blatant type of favoritism of writing key clauses for interest groups that funded their campaign. High-level legislation generates far more public attention and media coverage than the details of the exact wording in bills and implementation.

My proposal has the advantage of radically reducing the amount of policy knowledge needed by legislators. Quite frankly, most legislators do not have much policy knowledge in any given policy domain. This is not a dig, just a statement of fact. And with so many different policy domains, how could they possibly have deep policy expertise in each?

Legislators typically reduce their needed knowledge in a specific area by relying on staff or on highly experienced legislators who have deep policy knowledge in that one specific domain. This gives those experts much more influence over the details of legislation than others. This is despite the fact that the experts received no more votes than less knowledgeable elected officials. My proposal would help to level the playing field by radically lowering the complexity of the legislation.

RCTs take much of the politics out of politics. Politics can never, and should never be taken out of the process for determining which problem to solve and how much funding to devote to it, but it can be taken out of much of the rest of the policy implementation and evaluation process.

We have already run a fair amount of RCTs on the federal, state, and local levels. The problem is that elected officials ignore the results if they do not like the outcome. RCTs are not popular because they overwhelmingly show that government programs typically do not work. This seriously undermines the morale of government bureaucrats, who want to produce results, even if they do not believe that RCTs are an effective tool for doing so.

Elected officials think that they have got away with it. They think that voters do not realize that RCTs show that government programs are overwhelmingly ineffective.

Obviously, voters are not reading those evaluation reports, but they do know that their government is not producing results. They grow increasingly weary of the inability of the government to solve problems, because they see it in their daily lives.

No one is fooled; they just don't see a solution other than "throw the bums out." Regardless of your ideology, voting for the other party does not solve the problem. It only makes our political system seem more dysfunctional as wave after wave of political tides shows no results.

Changing the process can only come through many years, perhaps decades, of voter education. *We need to shift the focus from intentions and redistribution to results.* And we need to make clear that the problem is not bad people, but a bad process.

Both Parties Should Support RCTs

The widespread use of RCTs is currently not supported by either political party. But I think both sides have powerful reasons for supporting them. Democrats want to use the government to solve problems. So they should have a strong desire to implement policies that work.

Under the current system, Democrats have dramatically increased social spending over the last 50 years. They are proud of that accomplishment, but they wonder why the American people have grown skeptical of their efforts. The lack of proven results undermines the Democrats' ability to win elections, even if they support solving problems that people care about.

Voters care about results. The more money the government spends without producing results, the greater the difficulty Democrats have in winning elections. If the Democrats focused like a laser beam on results and proposed ramping up RCTs and eliminating social programs that do not work, they would gain far more credibility with voters that they could use to increase spending on social programs that actually do produce results.

Far too many Democrats think that, once legislation is passed, the fight is over. But voters care about results, not legislation. They cannot identify the exact results of each policy, but they see the trend of massive spending and few results. Democrats must look in the mirror and recognize that good intentions which produce bad results undermine their cause in the long run. Democrats should strongly support RCTs and shifting funding based on results.

Republicans, who generally want to keep government spending lower, should also support RCTs. The best way to determine which programs to cut is to run RCTs (although this can admittedly be difficult after a policy has been fully implemented).

Republicans also have a great incentive to run RCTs before a policy has been implemented, when it is most appropriate to do so. For any given problem, it is always very possible that none of the proposed options work. RCTs are the best means for controlling government spending and cutting those that do not work.

Republicans should say: "Fine, you Democrats want this new social program? We will oppose it, but we will support funding for many small-scale RCTs to test whether those programs are as great as you say. We would also agree to authorize that program on the condition that the RCTs match best practices and that the results are published transparently on the internet in understandable language. We will also agree to increase funding for successful programs on the condition that we cut funding for other existing social programs that fail RCTs."

This will be very hard for Democrats to argue against. After all, they claim that their solutions work, so how can they oppose gathering more evidence to prove their case? Of course, it will delay implementation, but delayed programs that actually work are much better than no legislation at all or programs that do not work. Many moderate Democrats would agree to this compromise.

And Democrats can use the same logic on law enforcement issues. Democrats should say: "Fine, you Republicans want this new law enforcement program? We will oppose it, but..."

Cost-Benefit Analyses

Randomized controlled trials are not effective in all policy domains. For example, regulations that apply to the entire nation cannot be sorted into a control group and an experimental group. In such cases, Cost-Benefit analyses are the preferred method of policy evaluation (Caplan).

Cost-Benefit analyses put a dollar value on all known costs and benefits for each policy. All the costs and benefits are added up and then the policy is declared either net-positive or net-negative for society.

To be useful, Cost-Benefit analyses must measure:
- Intended outcomes
- Unintended outcomes
- Direct costs

- Indirect costs (usually because the policy changes people's incentives).

As with RCTs, CBAs are rarely done by the federal or state governments. Between 2003 and 2013, the federal government implemented over 37,000 regulations. CBAs were performed on only 115 of them (Caplan).

My proposed Bureau of Policy Assessment should perform CBAs on all federal rules, regulations, and executive orders before they are implemented. The bureau should also analyze all existing rules, regulations, and executive orders. They should assist state governments in analyzing the impact of their regulations. Above all, the results of CBAs should be published on a publically-accessible internet site along with easily-understandable conclusions.

While Cost-Benefit analyses can be very effective tools, I do not believe that they are as useful as RCTs overall. While a well-designed RCT is almost impervious to bias, this is not so for CBAs. It is always easy for analysts to make unrealistic assumptions that dramatically affect the results. Those assumptions are typically hidden back in a very difficult-to-read appendix.

Worse, analysts can bias the conclusions in a way that seems very neutral. It is very easy for an analyst who supports a policy to add another "benefit" to the list and conveniently ignore a plausible cost (or vice versa). So two analysts with differing political views could come to very different conclusions despite both using the CBA method.

Even with all the above limitations, however, CBAs can be effective tools in assessing the impact of federal laws. Particularly in domains that are not conducive to RCTs, CBAs should be routinely done for each regulation.

Conclusion

Our government desperately needs to win back public trust by producing positive results. The best means for doing this is the widespread adoption of RCTs early in the policy-making progress. Doing so will ensure that we can achieve progress in many areas of social policy where private industry does not have the incentive to invest. Most importantly, it will ensure that the benefits of economic growth are widely shared by the American people.

PART TWO: WHAT WEALTHY NATIONS CAN DO

P art Two of this book presents a Progress-based reform agenda for what wealthy nations can do to promote long-term economic growth. To narrow the focus to policies that are most likely to work, this agenda focuses on the Five Keys to Progress and How Progress Works:

The Five Keys to Progress

1. A highly efficient food production and distribution system.
2. Trade-based cities packed with a large number of free citizens possessing a wide variety of skills.
3. Decentralized political, economic, religious, and ideological power.
4. At least one high-value-added industry that exports to the rest of the world.
5. Widespread use of fossil fuels.

How Progress Works

Once a society achieves the Five Keys, progress comes from the interaction among the following:

1. Technological innovation.

2. People learning new skills to support those technologies.

3. People cooperating *within* organizations.

4. Competition *between* organizations for scarce resources.

5. People copying successful technologies, skills and organizations and then modifying them to solve different problems.

6. Vast amounts of useful energy being injected into the system.

ENERGY ABUNDANCE

The Fifth Key to Progress: Widespread use of fossil fuels.
The incredible energy density of fossil fuels injects vast amounts of useful energy into society, enabling it to solve a wide variety of problems. Without this energy, life would return to the daily struggle for survival that dominated most of human history.

B y far the biggest current threat to maintaining progress in wealthy nations are Green energy policies that seek to phase out fossil fuels, nuclear power, and hydroelectric power in favor of renewable energy. These policies have been staggeringly expensive. The world has spent *over $5 trillion* in global climate finance since 2011, the vast majority of which has gone to Green energy projects, such as wind and solar.

This makes Green energy policies the single largest peace-time government project in world history. And with global climate finance increasing towards *$1 trillion per year*, these policies are going to get more and more expensive (Global Climate Initiative).

What is worse, these Green energy policies have not been very effective at accomplishing their own stated goals. Global fossil fuel consumption continues to climb, and Green energy policies have produced very negative side-effects on the world economy. I will go into more detail about why Green energy policies cannot work in the *Cutting Global Carbon Emissions* chapter, but for now, I will say that Green energy policies have:

1. Failed to reduce global carbon emissions and will likely probably never be able to do so.

2. Had virtually no effect on current or future temperatures.

3.   Undermined economic growth in wealthy nations, particularly Europe.

4.   Undermined the standard of living of the working class and poor in wealthy nations.

5.   Undermined the ability of developing nations to experience economic growth.

6.   Undermined the national security of Europe (and they will do the same to the United States in the near future).

7.   Empowered Russia and China, two increasingly totalitarian powers.

8.   Kept more viable energy policies off the public agenda.

Given all the enormous contributions that fossil fuels have made to progress over the last 200 years, these Green energy policies are reckless, to say the least.

A Progress-based Energy Policy

To maintain progress, we need an energy system that is abundant, affordable, and secure. While other energy sources can supplement their use, only the widespread use of fossil fuels enables such an energy system. Solar, wind, nuclear and hydroelectric can each play a role, but only fossil fuels can do the heavy lifting.

Rather than dangerous Green policies that sacrifice human progress in the name of the environment, the West desperately needs a new energy policy that maintains progress while mitigating the negative consequences on the natural environment. If climate activists can overcome their prejudice against natural gas, nuclear and hydroelectric power, there is a Progress-based energy policy that would boost human progress as well as mitigating the negative consequences to the natural environment. That energy policy can make energy abundant, affordable, and secure while also lowering global carbon emissions and pollution.

A Progress-based energy policy should focus on completing the as-yet-unfinished Third Energy Transition (which I describe later). It should consist of the following steps.

1.   Construct an abundant, affordable and secure electrical grid based on natural gas, nuclear power and hydroelectric power. The exact blend will differ based on geography and local cost structure. In the United States, this will overwhelmingly mean natural gas, due to its huge cost advantage.

2.   Phase out coal power, by far the worst offender in carbon emissions, pollution and degrading health. Impose a coal tax on all goods mined, processed, transported and manufactured using coal or electricity generated from coal. This will give the entire world a strong economic incentive to move off coal.

3.   Roll back government restrictions on the exploration, drilling and distribution of natural gas on public and private land.

4.   Phase out all subsidies and mandates for renewable power. The focus should be on abundant, affordable, and secure energy sources. Renewable energy sources can act as a supplement where geography and economics allow, but natural gas, nuclear and hydroelectric power will do the heavy lifting.

5.   Leverage the technical skills of the American shale gas industry to spread the Shale Revolution throughout the world. This will make natural gas so affordable that the global energy sector wants to shift from coal to natural gas.

6.   Gradually shift the transportation sector from petroleum to electricity, starting with transport within wealthy metro regions and then expanding to longer-range transportation.

7.   Assist Asia and developing nations with the capital and technical skills required to gradually transition from coal and wood-burning to an electrical grid and industrial sector based upon a blend of natural gas, nuclear power, and hydroelectric power. Affordable and abundant natural gas is key to this transition.

8.   Create innovation prizes for new energy sources that have all the advantages of fossil fuels and nuclear power, but without pollution, radiation or carbon emissions.

This Progress-based energy policy will be more effective at lowering carbon emissions, pollution and health risks than the Green energy policy, and it will do so at a much lower cost. More importantly, this Progress-based energy policy will build an abundant, affordable and secure energy system that can power long-term economic growth.

This is not a hypothetical policy. Many nations have successfully transitioned their electrical grid away from coal to a blend of natural gas, nuclear and hydroelectric. Unfortunately, while the media and political activists focus on Green policies in Europe, they have missed far more successful energy transitions based upon natural gas, nuclear and hydroelectric.

Because energy is so critical to progress, the topic does not comfortably fit into a single chapter. For this reason, I will discuss my Progress-based energy policy in four separate chapters. In this chapter, I will explain energy policies to promote abundant, affordable, and secure energy in the short term in wealthy nations. Such an energy system is a cornerstone of promoting long-term economic growth.

In the *Technological Innovation* chapter, I will explain my proposal to establish innovation prizes to incentivize research on radical breakthrough energy technologies. If successful, this would probably be the greatest technological innovation of the 21st Century and do far more to lower global carbon emissions than current Green policies.

In the *Energy for Developing Nations* chapter, I will extend my Progress-based energy policy to include the needs of developing nations. To promote progress, all developing nations must build an abundant, affordable, and secure energy system.

In the *Cutting Global Carbon Emissions* chapter, I will explain how we can lower global carbon emissions while enabling developing nations to build their own abundant, affordable, and secure energy systems. While Green energy policies have failed abysmally at reducing global carbon emissions because they ignore the biggest contributors (Asian coal), my policy focuses on the most cost-effective means to reduce global carbon emissions while still maintaining progress.

Why Fossil Fuels Are Essential For Now

Fossil fuels are foundational to many of the technologies that make modern life possible. The railroad, marine diesel engines, steam turbines, automobiles, trucks, airplanes, electric motors, container ships, and the electrical grid are just a few of the thousands of industrial technologies that we take for granted today.

These fossil fuel-based technologies led to a standard of living for a typical person far beyond anything the richest men of the pre-Industrial era could imagine. Before the use of fossil fuels, economic growth and technological innovation mainly benefitted a very small portion of the world's population. Today, to a large extent because of fossil fuels, economic growth and technological innovation benefit the vast majority of the world's population.

Fossil fuels are critical to progress and economic growth because of their incredible energy density and the fact that they are affordable, easily stored and transported, reliable, controllable, and easy to scale to fit needs. And because of these characteristics, their geographical limitations are radically less than virtually all other energy sources.

All of these advantages explain why fossil fuels offered huge advantages over pre-Industrial energy sources such as human power, animal power, wind power and water power. Human power and animal power require food, which was the critical constraint on traditional societies. Humans and animals need food to survive and reproduce, and they need far greater amounts of food to increase production beyond subsistence levels.

Before the Industrial Revolution, societies were caught in a "Catch-22" situation. You needed more energy and food to create progress, but the people and animals required to produce that energy required more energy to do so. This is why there was such a long delay between the invention of agriculture and the Industrial Revolution. Gradually, a few societies overcame those limits by increasing per capita food production and distributing the gains to productive cities.

In addition to being one of the Five Keys to Progress, fossil fuels are also critical for two of the other keys: highly productive agriculture and export industries. Fossil-fuel-powered tractors, synthetic fertilizers, and petroleum byproducts played a critical role in radically expanding agricultural productivity.

And while some export industries do not require high amounts of fossil fuel usage beyond electricity, these industries are dominated by rich nations. The kind of high-value-added sectors that enable developing nations to export fall largely in the manufacturing sector. Manufacturing is critically dependent upon affordable, controllable, and secure energy at a level that only fossil fuels can provide.

Fossil Fuels Undergird the Balance of Power

Fossil fuels are not only a cornerstone of economic growth. They also play a key role in the global balance of power. World War II was the first war fought with widespread usage of industrial transportation devices. Tanks, trucks, jeeps, fighters, bombers, transport aircraft, aircraft carriers, cargo ships, submarines, and naval vessels all required vast amounts of petroleum.

It is not a coincidence that the Allies won the war, as they had far superior energy resources. While the United States had vast oil fields in Texas, the Soviet Union had vast oil fields near Baku, and the British Empire had access to vast oil fields in Persia, Germany, Italy, and Japan had none. This gave the Allies, particularly the United States, a huge advantage in mechanized warfare.

The grand strategy of the Axis powers was also to a large extent based on conquering and holding oil fields. The main reason why the Japanese attacked Pearl Harbor was that the United States had cut off oil shipments and Japan's only viable substitute source was modern-day Indonesia. Gaining access to these energy resources required the elimination of American bases in the Philippines.

Most historians of World War II regard the Battle of Stalingrad on the Eastern front as one of the decisive turning points of the war. The main reason why German forces were in Stalingrad in the first place was to guard the flanks of other German forces trying to conquer the oil fields of Baku. If they had succeeded and the Germans had been able to transport that oil to the front, all of their armored and aviation units would have been much more powerful.

Hydroelectric dams also played a pivotal role in powering American manufacturing during World War II. Dams built during the New Deal came online just as the war was getting started. Thanks to their enormous electrical output, American factories could rely on electric-powered hand tools. Throughout the war, American electricity output dwarfed all other nations combined. This energy enabled America's economic power to be translated into military power.

Energy sources were also critical to the Cold War. Without access to oil in the Middle East, Europe and Japan would never have been able to rebuild their economies after World War II. A de facto security guarantee for all oil transit out of the Persian Gulf was essential for the American grand strategy of containing the Soviet Union.

Petroleum also played a key role in maintaining Soviet power. Just as Putin does today, the Soviets translated energy power into military power. While the Soviet Union was able to industrialize and build a powerful military and space program, Communist economic principles proved unworkable. Between 1970 and 1986 the Soviet economy was at a virtual standstill. Only energy exports to Western nations enabled the Soviets to generate enough foreign currency to buy critical Western technologies that kept the system going.

The sudden drop in oil prices in 1986 removed the Soviets' only profitable export industry, so the entire Soviet economy collapsed. Then the entire Communist regime collapsed in 1991. This was one of the key events that enabled the dramatic increase in world progress over the last 30 years.

What About Other Energy Sources?

I do not claim that fossil fuels were the only energy source used by Industrial societies to power their progress in the past. Nuclear power and hydroelectric dams have provided a significant amount of electricity in the 20th Century, and they still do today. Unfortunately, their benefits are restricted to the production of electricity. This makes their application to industrial, commercial, and transportation sectors far more limited than fossil fuels.

In most circumstances, nuclear and hydroelectric are more expensive than fossil fuels and they take longer and are more expensive to construct. During construction, they also require substantial amounts of fossil fuels to power construction and transportation equipment, as well as the production of steel and other materials. Hydroelectric dams also require very specific geographic characteristics that most nations do not have in abundance.

Most importantly, neither energy source was important for any nation during or before their transition from poverty to progress. They only became important after they transitioned to progress. Thus widespread usage of fossil fuels is a Key to Progress, while nuclear power and hydroelectric dams are the results of progress. They are a useful supplement to fossil fuels, but they cannot entirely be substituted for them, particularly in the realm of transportation and industry.

Nor do I claim that we will never invent another energy source that has all the advantages of fossil fuels and none of their disadvantages. I believe that, as long as progress is maintained for the next century, it is very likely, perhaps inevitable, that we will do so. Later in this book, I will suggest policies that can help make it happen sooner.

Nor do I believe that solar, wind, and other non-hydro renewable energy sources cannot play a role in Industrial societies. Their use is rapidly increasing and their cost is rapidly declining. That is a good thing, and it is a result of the vast, decentralizing problem-solving network that is a modern society.

My claim is that solar and wind have made very little progress in *replacing* fossil fuels, nuclear or hydroelectric power, nor can they do so within the next one to three decades. Most likely solar, wind and other Green energy sources will never fully be able to replace those energy sources.

It is not a coincidence that the percentage of energy consumption made up of fossil fuels has hovered just above 80% for the last few decades. This is despite trillions of dollars of investments in renewable energy and constantly increasing global energy usage. Solar and wind are growing rapidly, but they are not replacing the use of fossil fuels to any significant extent. They are merely adding energy *in addition to* the current usage of fossil fuels. I believe that trend will continue for the next few decades.

Today virtually every mention of fossil fuels highlights the negative consequences of their use, particularly pollution and climate change. But it is important to realize that fossil fuels, despite their drawbacks, are a key foundation of progress. Quite simply, the modern world that we take for granted would not have been possible without fossil fuels.

Fossil fuels power innovation. Fossil fuels power economic growth. Fossil fuels power our education system, our transportation system, our communication system, our food production system, our health care system, and our military. Fossil fuels are key to generating all the wealth that pays for every government program we have. Before we try to eliminate fossil fuels, we need to make sure that we do not also eliminate all the benefits that have come from their use.

Quite simply, the prosperous world that we live in today would not have been possible without the widespread usage of fossil fuels. The Industrial Revolution in Britain might have been fueled by imported wood and charcoal, but it surely could not have spread to the rest of the world and lasted for centuries without fossil fuels. Without industrial technologies powered by fossil fuels, most nations would still be living at the same standard of living as they did in 1500: i.e. desperate poverty for virtually everyone but a few elites and a few lonely commercial cities.

Today the continued use of fossil fuels is under threat, particularly from those who are concerned about future climate change. Predicting the future is always hazardous, but I am extremely skeptical whether renewable energy can replace fossil fuels without drastically lowering humanity's standard of living and undermining progress.

We need a system that generates the abundant, affordable, and secure energy that is the backbone of progress.

Energy Transitions

While Green activists are typically highly critical of capitalism, our economic system started decarbonizing long before anyone had ever even heard of climate change. Modern industrial societies have gone through several energy transitions, each leading to less carbon-intensive energy sources.

Before the Industrial Revolution, burning wood was the primary source of energy. Today it is still used in many developing countries, especially in Sub-Saharan Africa.

Wood is a major source of air pollution and indoor pollution. Burning wood indoors, a primary means of keeping warm in many developing nations, is far more damaging to the lungs than the worst fossil fuel plants. The World Health Organization calls indoor air pollution "the world's large single environmental health risk (WHO).

Per unit of energy, burning wood releases more carbon than petroleum, natural gas, or even coal (Climate Registry). Wood also generates more air pollution. This is simple chemistry. Wood has a 10:1 C:H ratio, meaning that it consists of 10 carbon atoms per burnable hydrogen atom. It is burning the hydrogen that actually produces energy, while carbon is just an accidental byproduct of doing so. So, the lower the C:H ratio, the better it is for the environment.

Burning wood also leads to deforestation. We often think of deforestation as a side effect of industrialization, but it is actually a side effect of not industrializing. Because medieval farmers lacked the technology to burn fossil fuels, they clear-cut forests to burn wood to keep their houses warm. They also used wood as a material for constructing housing, fencing, wagons, tools and a host of other vital goods. Clearing forests was also essential for increasing farm acreage, which was necessary at the time because agricultural practices were highly unproductive.

The First Energy Transition

The First Energy Transition in human history was the transition from burning wood to burning coal. This transition began in the 16th Century in home heating in London. Coal consumption then gradually spread into industrial applications in the following centuries. It took off with the railway boom of the 1830s and kept increasing well into the 20th Century.

A key reason why the Industrial Revolution was such a key transformation in human history was the widespread use of coal. Coal was the first fossil fuel to be used widely. Without it, industrial growth could not have been sustained in Britain nor could it spread throughout the world. The transition from wood to coal was the first energy transition that involved a change from a diffuse, carbon-intensive energy source to a denser, less carbon-intensive energy source.

While wood has a 10:1 C:H ratio, coal has a C:H ratio of 2:1. So the First Energy Transition involved a shift to denser and less carbon-intensive energy sources (Smil).

Societies made this energy transition, not because they were concerned about climate change (they have never even heard of the concept). They made the transition because coal was a more useful form of energy, largely because it was denser in energy per unit of mass.

It was only with the Industrial Revolution that humans developed fossil fuels, concrete, steel and glass as substitutes for wood. Fossil fuels reduced the need to burn wood. Fossil fuels also reduced the farm acreage needed to grow horse feed. Tractors, synthetic fertilizer and other agricultural technologies reduced the need for more farm acreage. Concrete, steel and glass replaced wood in building, vehicles, and tool construction. All of these technology substitutions were good for the natural environment.

Notice that wood-burning did not go away during the First Energy Transition from wood to coal. Burning wood is still done today, though at a much smaller scale. Energy transitions typically add a new energy source, while diminishing but not eliminating, an old energy source.

The Second Energy Transition

The Second Energy Transition in the late 19th and first two-thirds of the 20th Century was from coal to petroleum. Just as coal was denser and less carbon-intensive than wood, so is petroleum denser and less carbon-intensive than coal. Oil has a 1:2 C:H ratio. Because petroleum is so useful in transportation, it has almost completely replaced coal in that sector. In industry and the electrical sector, though, coal is still widely used.

The Third Energy Transition

The Third Energy Transition in the 20th Century added natural gas, hydro-electric dams, and nuclear power. So far, natural gas has been the dominant energy source of this transition, for reasons that we will explore later. The Third Energy Transition is still ongoing, and far from complete. So far, this energy transition has done relatively little to reduce coal and petroleum use, but it has the real potential to do so in the future.

Natural gas has a C:H ratio of 1:4, so it releases far less carbon dioxide per unit of energy during combustion. Because it is a gas, it is far less dense by volume. Hydroelectric dams and nuclear power emit no carbon dioxide, except during the construction process.

Notice that, even without any knowledge of climate change, government regulations, or international treaties, our economic system has gradually adopted less carbon-intensive energy sources. Whether measured per capita or per unit of economic growth, global carbon intensity has been cut in half since 1920. In the United States, the decline has been over 80% (Our World In Data).

Opposition to the Third Energy Transition

The Third Energy Transition is the only energy transition that has faced substantial political opposition. While governments took little action to oppose the First and Second energy transitions, many have been quite hostile to the Third.

Due primarily to Green political activism, governments around the world have deliberately constrained the growth of natural gas, nuclear and hydroelectric power. In many cases, they have even tried to dismantle energy infrastructure after it has been constructed.

Later in this book, I will go into more detail on the subject, but slowing the Third Energy Transition down undermines economic growth, lowers the standard of living of the poor and working class, traps developing nations in poverty and undermines efforts to lower global carbon emissions. It is of the utmost importance that we roll back these misguided Green energy policies.

Fundamentally, climate activists are arguing for a Fourth Energy Transition to solar, wind, biomass, and other renewable energy sources. I will argue for completing the Third Energy Transition by focusing on natural gas, hydroelectric dams, and nuclear power. As we will see, the latter option is far more conducive to maintaining human progress and lowering global carbon emissions.

Green activists do not realize that the reason for increased global carbon emissions is that the Third Energy Transition has not been completed. And the single biggest reason why it has not been is because of Green political opposition.

So why have overall global carbon emissions increased so much during that period? There have been a few counter-veiling trends over the last two centuries:

1. Rapid population growth (which has been slowing and is projected to reverse later in this century).

2.   Even more rapid economic growth, powered largely by fossil fuels.

3.   Economic growth has spread to new geographical areas, particularly Asia. Those regions have largely adopted coal, the most carbon-intensive fuel, for geographic and economic reasons.

Developing nations in Asia have not yet reached the level of development where they can participate in the Third Energy Transition under current price structures. Wealthy nations have failed to make those energy sources affordable enough for them to want to do so.

Natural Gas

The cornerstone of the Third Energy Transition is natural gas. While a few nations have abundant hydroelectric resources or a robust electrical grid powered by nuclear power, most nations do not. Unfortunately, nuclear power is currently too expensive in most countries, and it can only generate electricity, so another energy source is needed.

For the United States in particular, successfully making a Third Energy Transition will require a large increase in natural gas production. For a long time, doing so appeared to be geologically impossible, but the dramatic increase in shale gas estimates has shown that it is not only possible, but it is inevitable if government policy does not stand in the way.

Natural gas has an extraordinary number of advantages over other energy sources:

1.   The world has 188 trillion cubic meters of proven natural gas reserves, while United States alone has 12.6 trillion (Our World in Data). Given past results, it is extremely likely that actual recovery will be far beyond those amounts.

2.   We have enough natural gas to last for generations. Because of constant technological innovations in exploration and drilling, proven natural gas reserves in the United States and the rest of the world keep growing despite constant extraction.

3.   American natural gas is affordable, and, thanks to the Shale

Revolution, has stable prices (Our World in Data).

4. Natural gas can be used in every sector of the economy: electricity, industry, commercial and home appliances. While 78% of petroleum is used for the transportation sector, and 90% of coal is used for electricity, gas is far more flexible. Gas is commonly used in residences for heating, air conditioning, heating water, cooking and refrigeration. Only within the transportation sector is natural gas less than ideal due to its gaseous form (EIA 2021).

5. Natural gas is the only energy source that can cost-effectively replace coal in industrial uses, for example in metal production (EIA 2021).

6. Natural gas is the only energy source that can cost-effectively replace crude oil in the production of petroleum byproducts (Zeihan 2016).

7. Natural gas emits much less carbon and dramatically less pollutants than coal (Smil 2015).

8. Whether burned directly or consumed via electricity, natural gas is constantly available and easily modulated with little human labor.

9. Natural gas is extremely convenient and clean to use both at home, at commercial sites and within industry.

10. Though pipelines occasionally explode due to poor maintenance, natural gas is extremely safe (Smil 2015).

11. Modern gas turbines offer the most energy-efficient means of converting chemical energy into electricity (EIA).

12. Gas-powered electrical plants have the lowest construction costs and are the quickest to build of any utility (EIA 2018)

13. Natural gas drilling and combustion sites use very little land, although pipelines are fairly land intensive (Zeihan 2016).

14. Gas-powered electrical plants can be run constantly to produce base load electrical power, and they can also be rapidly cycled to produce peak electricity. With the exception of hydroelectric dams, no other energy source can do this (Smil 2015).

15. Natural gas is cost-effective to store and transport via pipelines. It is, however, much more difficult to transport over deep waters (Smil

2015).

16. Natural gas pipelines can transport far greater volumes of energy (10-25 GW) than electric lines (2-3 GW). Energy losses during transmission are also far lower than for electricity (Smil 2015).

For all the reasons listed above, natural gas is an irreplaceable energy source given the current technology. No other energy source comes even close to all the advantages that natural gas possesses. Particularly if you are concerned about lowering global carbon emissions while maintaining economic growth, natural gas is a no brainer.

Despite the enormous subsidies for solar and wind, natural gas is far more widely used. Natural gas made up 24.4% of global energy usage in 2021. In Europe, gas made up 33.6% to total energy usage, while in North America it made up 32.8%. The continent with the lowest natural gas usage is Asia, with 18.4% (Our World In Data).

The Shale Revolution

A rapid transition from coal to natural gas has occurred in the United States over the last 15 years. In 2007, the United States consumed enough coal to produce 2 trillion kilowatt hours of electricity. By 2020 this amount had been cut by almost two-thirds to 773 billion (EIA). Meanwhile, natural gas consumption almost doubled (from 897 to 1624).

The result was a dramatic decline in American carbon emissions. Of the 819 million metric tons decline in CO_2 emissions between 2005 and 2019, a full 65% of that decline was caused by replacing coal plants with natural gas plants. Only 30% of the decline was due to renewables (EIA).

While increasing energy efficiency and increasing solar/wind output played some role in lowering coal combustion, it was the Shale Revolution that was the main cause.

In the early 2000s, many energy experts and virtually all environmental activists were sure that the United States was running out of crude oil and natural gas. Since the early 1970s, domestic production had been gradually declining, while imports were increasing. The same was happening to oil-producing countries all over the world. "Peak oil" had supposedly been reached not just in the United States, but also in the rest of the world.

Then the Shale Revolution hit, and everything changed.

Until about 2005, natural gas came almost exclusively from conventional fields. In conventional fields, natural gas and crude oil migrate upward to a basin until they hit a cap rock. This creates a large underground reservoir. Drillers can then drill down into that reservoir, and the underground pressure pushes the oil and gas up to the surface.

Shale oil and gas are very different. Shale is a common rock formation that often holds large amounts of oil and gas. Shale oil and shale gas consist of individual molecules that are trapped within the rock. Twenty years ago it was thought to be impossible to liberate the oil and gas from its rock and then force it up to the surface.

Shale oil and gas is so different from conventional oil and gas that they require fundamentally different technologies. While conventional drilling goes straight down through a formation, shale drilling goes horizontally along the formation. It was only with the technological innovations of horizontal drilling, multilateral drilling, hydraulic fracturing, micro-seismic imaging, sliding sleeves, and 3D computer modeling that this became possible (Zeihan 2016).

Hydraulic fracturing, often called "fracking," consists of pumping a mixture of 90% water, 9.5% sand, and a few other chemicals under high pressure to crack the shale rock and release the trapped oil and gas. The sand holds the microscopic cracks in the shale rock open so that the oil and gas can then be pumped to the surface. At first, drillers used water from the surface, but they later learned that brackish underground water found during the drilling process is far cheaper. So the process no longer consumes large amounts of surface water.

A typical shale drilling pad consists of one small cement pad with one drill rig on the surface and dozens of miles of drilling pipes all going to different depths and in different directions. This means that shale pads have a very small land footprint while gathering a large amount of oil and gas. Micro-seismic imaging enables drillers to drill exactly where the oil and gas is located, drastically lowering the failure rates.

Conventional drilling for oil and gas typically requires decades of exploration, drilling, and extraction, particularly if the site is offshore. Shale sites typically take less than a month, perhaps two for very difficult sites. This drastically reduces capital costs, time delays, and risk. Shale production is onshore, so it is nowhere near as vulnerable to hurricanes, storms, and spills. All of the above reasons make it much easier for shale sites to keep energy abundant, affordable, and secure.

Whereas conventional drilling leads to large amounts of oil and gas as soon as the well is drilled, with declining output over time, shale gas extraction can be modulated. Drillers can cap the well so they can strategically release the oil and gas when the price is high, and each of the separate pipes can be capped and uncapped separately. This helps to keep energy prices steady over long periods of time. As the technology improves, drillers can go back to previously-drilled holes and extract oil and gas that was unreachable just a few years before.

All of these technological innovations have drastically cut the cost of oil and natural gas in the United States. Shale oil prices dropped from $90 per barrel in 2012 to $40 per barrel in 2017. The United States can now produce oil almost as cheaply as Saudi Arabia, the lowest-cost producer in the world, and cheaper than Russia and other OPEC nations. Even lower prices seem very achievable. These prices would have seemed like science fiction back in 2000 (Zeihan 2016).

Shale gas is now so inexpensive that it is driving American and Canadian conventional gas producers out of business. The *sale* price of shale gas is now one-third of the *production* costs of conventional gas. There is no way that conventional producers can compete with such a price discrepancy.

As of today, shale gas is almost exclusively an American phenomenon. If the Shale Revolution spreads to the rest of the world, it would be one of the most important energy revolutions in world history. It would complete the Third Energy Transition. The only force stopping this revolution are Green policies that make the exploitation of shale gas illegal, or at least very expensive.

Shale gas is a revolutionary energy source because it is so widespread globally. The known shale deposits are already greater than all conventional deposits in Saudi Arabia and Russia combined. The main problem with shale fields is that each has individual characteristics that require high levels of expertise to locate and extract oil and gas. Currently, only American companies have that expertise (Zeihan 2016).

Ironically, shale gas is a byproduct of the production of shale oil. Many shale fields, particularly in the Dakotas, are venting off shale gas because there are no gas pipelines in the region via which to transport the gas to markets. Not only is this bad for the environment, but it is also failing to capture highly profitable energy resources. Completing pipelines to shale oil and gas fields should be a national priority.

Combined-Cycle Gas Turbines

Shale gas is a revolutionary new energy source, but another technological innovation makes gas perfect for generating electricity: combined-cycle gas turbines (CCGT). Invented in 1961, the technology has undergone constant improvement since that time. CCGT plants now generate more electricity in the United States than any other source, and their total production capacity is growing fast (EIA 2019).

CCGT plants generate energy via a two-step process. First, gas turbines burn natural gas directly, to generate electricity. Then the heat recovered from this process is used to boil water to create steam. That steam then powers a more traditional steam turbine.

Because they are a two-step process, CCGT plants are extremely fuel efficient and they emit far less carbon per unit of energy. A new CCGT plant emits one-third of the carbon per unit of energy (752.3 pounds per MWH) compared to an existing coal plant (2162.6 per MWH) (Frank).

Better yet, the efficiency of CCGT technology keeps improving. The most recent versions of General Electric H-class CCGT plants

PROMOTING PROGRESS

convert energy with 64+% efficiency. Even more impressive, H-class plants can start up in less than 30 minutes, so they can modulate with customer demand (General Electric website). This makes CCGT far more useful for generating electricity than coal, nuclear, oil, solar, wind, or biomass.

The combination of cheap shale gas and CCGT plants enabled the United States to rapidly replace aging coal power stations that were at the end of their life cycle with brand-new hyper-efficient power plants. Best of all, doing so actually reduced the cost of electricity. Unfortunately, Green renewal mandates and subsidies are sabotaging the complete phase-out of coal in the United States.

Renewables Need Natural Gas

The second type of natural gas power plant is a conventional power station. Rather than going through two separate electricity-generating steps, conventional stations only burn natural gas to spin a steam turbine. Unfortunately, this type of power plant is far less energy-efficient than CCGT: only about 30-40% of the energy in natural gas is converted into electricity.

If it were not for Green energy policies, conventional gas power stations would largely have been phased out in favor of more energy-efficient CCGT plants. Conventional natural gas plants are very important because they take much less time to warm up and operate at peak efficiency. This makes them excellent "peakers." Peakers generate electricity for very short periods to even out short-term variations in electricity production and consumption. Because natural gas peakers are less efficient than CCGT, they burn more gas, cost much more to run, and emit more carbon.

Natural gas peakers play a crucial role in supplementing intermittent solar and wind power. Without natural gas peakers, short-term variations in wind and solar power would constantly collapse the electrical grid. So Green energy policies that force utilities to use solar and wind unintentionally also force utilities to construct and run

| 130 |

less energy-efficient natural gas peakers. This makes no sense from an environmental or economic perspective.

Two Separate Energy Infrastructures

The need to use natural gas peakers alongside solar and wind means that Green policies require us to build two separate energy infrastructures: solar/wind plus a completely redundant natural gas peaker infrastructure. Since there are times when neither wind nor solar is available, the second natural gas peaker infrastructure must be able to generate as much power as solar and wind combined. Virtually all the cuts to carbon emission from running solar and wind are being made up by running carbon-producing gas peakers.

This leads to a fact that Green activists cannot seem to grasp. Solar and wind *require* additional usage of natural gas. That is one of the many reasons why solar and wind can *supplement* fossil fuels, but they cannot *replace* them, as is their stated goal. Note that biomass or batteries can also perform this peaking role, but as we will later see, those energy sources are definitely not Green.

A far better option would be to eliminate subsidies and mandates for renewable energy sources and let utilities phase out natural gas peakers in favor of CCGT. If done in combination with a phase out of coal plants, this would reduce electricity costs and lower carbon emissions and pollution.

Successful Third Energy Transitions

The United States is not the only nation to make rapid progress in the Third Energy Transition. A large part of the reductions in European carbon emissions occurred in the 1980s and early 1990s, long before there were any serious investments in Green energy. During that time period, a huge number of coal power plants that had been built decades earlier reached their age of retirement (fossil fuel plants typically last 40-50 years). These obsolete coal plants were largely replaced by natural gas, nuclear or hydroelectric plants.

For example, coal consumption in the United Kingdom peaked in 1956, decades before we knew anything about climate change. Between 1956 and 1999 coal consumption declined steadily, long before Green energy policies were introduced.

How did the UK achieve this decline? Mainly by radically increasing the use of natural gas and nuclear power. Declining coal usage fits in nicely with the concept of the Third Energy Transition, as opposed to Green energy policies.

France and Belgium achieved the Third Energy Transition in electricity via nuclear power. Coal production in those two nations peaked in 1957. Both nations initiated a massive nuclear construction program, which made phasing out coal relatively simple. Finland, Sweden and Switzerland followed less aggressive nuclear programs, but they also exploited their local hydroelectric resources.

Norway achieved the Third Energy Transition in electricity by focusing almost entirely on hydroelectric dams. Brazil and Canada did much the same. Again, the Third Energy Transition at work.

Germany is another example, at least for a while. German coal consumption peaked in 1958 and then slowly declined. Germany's steepest declines in coal usage occurred between 1989 and 1999, when East Germany's obsolete coal stations were taken offline and replaced with of natural gas plants. Again, this was the Third Energy Transition at work.

Since Germany announced its famous Energy Turn in the early 2000s, coal consumption has actually declined at a slower rate than during the previous period. Rather than eliminating coal, which was entirely feasible, Germany tried to eliminate natural gas and nuclear production.

For this reason, coal still makes up about 30% of electrical power generation in Germany (more than in the United States). Just as importantly, coal is still the backbone of Germany's famous export industries.

Even worse, Germany did not really cut natural gas consumption. Instead, it cut natural gas *production* and made up the difference by importing gas from Russia. This made Germany dangerously dependent upon an aggressive, authoritarian power. The dangers of this policy were fully exposed when Russia invaded Ukraine in 2022.

When one adds in the Shale Gas Revolution in the United States, we can see many examples where nations radically lowered their carbon emissions while maintaining abundant, affordable and secure electrical grids. They did so not with Green energy policies, but through the Third Energy Transition (switching from coal to a blend of natural gas, nuclear, and hydroelectric). Each nation did so in a different way due to geographical, economic and political factors, but they all succeeded.

Norway's Third Energy Transition in Transportation

Norway is the first nation to push the Third Energy Transition into the transportation sector. With a combination of subsidies, discounts and mandates, sales of new electric vehicles in Norway have jumped from virtually zero in 2011 to 54% of sales in 2020. Most of the remainder of new cars purchased are either plug-in hybrids or hybrids. Greens have rightfully cheered this transition and claim that Norway is an example of a nation where their policies have succeeded.

But what made the rapid transition to electric vehicles possible is that the Norwegian electrical grid is 95.3% powered by hydro-electric dams, a power source that Greens oppose. An entire electrical grid based upon hydroelectric dams is a dream scenario. Hydroelectric dams can offer very cheap carbon-free base-load power and the ability to modulate with demand. No other power source offers this combination.

More to the point, Norway has been able to fund the transition to a large extent because it has a massive oil and gas industry. The Norwegian fossil fuels industry generates 49% of all government revenue. It also makes up 33% of the Norwegian economy and 64% of its exports (Norsk Petroleum).

Fossil fuel production makes Norway one of the few nations in the world with a higher per capita GDP than the United States. This huge economic boon, combined with an abundant, affordable and stable electric grid powered by hydroelectric dams makes their electric vehicle policies economically sustainable.

Norway has been able to radically increase electric vehicle car sales, while the rest of Europe has not done so, precisely because Norway did not follow Green policies in the rest of their energy system. The Third Energy Transition enables the electrification of transportation, while Green energy policies do not.

Fossil Fuels Power Economic Growth

Long periods of affordable fossil fuels are closely aligned with long periods of economic growth. The periods of 1950-1970, 1983-1989, and 1992-1999 all saw energy prices at historically low levels. Those same periods experienced strong widely-shared economic growth.

In addition, the timing of past economic recessions points to the importance of affordable fossil fuels. Almost every economic recession since 1970 was preceded by a spike in energy prices. This does not mean that energy was the only cause of each recession, but in every case, energy crises were clearly an important contributing factor.

From 1900 to 1973 energy spending accounted for 2-3 percent of the American economy. This affordable energy is a key cause of strong economic growth throughout much of this period. Then in 1973 energy prices skyrocketed causing a series of global recessions (Thunder Said Energy).

The recession of 1973-75 was preceded by the Arab oil embargo against Western nations that supported Israel. During that time energy spending shot up to 8-12% of global GDP. The recession of 1980-82 was preceded by the Iranian revolution and the Iraqi invasion of Iran. Those two events removed Iranian oil exports from the world and drove up oil prices. The 1990-91 recession was preceded by a smaller oil price shock caused by the Gulf War.

The 2001 recession was preceded by a more than doubling of world oil prices in the preceding two years. The 2007-2009 recession was preceded by an almost quadrupling of world oil prices in the preceding few years. During that period energy spending was 8-10 percent of the global economic GDP.

It is quite possible that the energy crisis of 2021-22 will also lead to an economic recession. As of 2022 energy spending has shot up to 13% of global GDP, among the highest on record. What is worse, this is not just an oil shock. Today we are experiencing a drastic increase in the prices for all energy sources (Thunder Said Energy).

Now I am not claiming that there would be no economic recessions if we had affordable energy. A market-based economy seems to have a boom-and-bust cycle built into the system. I claim that with affordable, abundant, and secure fossil fuels, we can create long-term economic growth interrupted by milder recessions. This produces far better results for the working class and poor in wealthy nations and developing nations.

Affordable Fossil Fuels Help the Poor

In addition to a growing economy, the poor and working class need affordable prices above all else. Affordable energy is the basis of affordable prices for all other goods. Expensive energy drives up the cost of manufacturing, transportation, education, health care, housing, and virtually every other good or service.

Lower-income households spend a significantly larger share of their income on energy than middle- or upper-income households. On average low-income households spend 8.1% of their income on energy, compared to only 2.3% for the rest of the nation. A full 40% of those households spend more than 10% of their income on energy. High energy prices function as a regressive tax that punishes the poor and the working class far more than the professional class (Drehohl).

Fossil Fuels Power Manufacturing

Viable manufacturing in wealthy industrialized nations requires abundant, affordable, and secure energy systems. Seen from a high-level perspective, a nation can choose one of two paths to becoming a manufacturing power. For low-value-added manufacturing, a nation needs cheap labor and the necessary skills to run factories.

For high-value-added manufacturing, a nation needs skilled labor plus abundant, affordable, and secure energy. Wealthy nations do not have local supplies of cheap labor, so they must substitute cheap energy and sophisticated technology to dominate high-value-added manufacturing. Otherwise, they risk having little domestic manufacturing. Energy is what powers all the technology that allows for highly-paid workers to compete with cheap labor.

China, India, Mexico, and Southeast Asia have the cheap labor required to manufacture low-value-added goods. These nations are seeking to gradually work their way up the value-added chain to reach more profitable types of manufacturing. The higher they go, the more important abundant, affordable, and secure energy becomes.

Wealthy nations, such as the United States, Europe, and Japan, simply do not have the vast amounts of cheap labor to compete in low-value-added sectors of manufacturing. These nations desperately need abundant, affordable, and secure energy systems so they can manufacture high-value-added products. This generates wealth that can then be used to purchase imported cheap goods from poorer nations.

Green policies that drive up energy costs, make the grid less stable, and lower energy use seriously hamper the ability of wealthy nations to compete in manufacturing. A shift to natural gas, nuclear and hydroelectric will enable wealthy nations to rebuild their manufacturing sectors.

Reshoring American Industry

Over the last few generations, American manufacturing dominance has been eroded. During the 1980s and 90s, new manufacturing plants were more often located in Japan, Germany, Taiwan, or South Korea. Since 2000, China has become the dominant manufacturing power in the world.

Just a few years ago China seemed unrivaled as a low-value-added manufacturer and was rapidly moving up the value chain into high-value-added manufacturing. With the disruption of global supply chains by Covid lockdowns, tensions with the United States, more expensive labor, technology theft, and slowing economic growth, American companies are increasingly looking to relocate out of China.

At the same time, European and particularly German manufacturing are being undermined by Green energy policies. It is unclear if European manufacturing will be able to compete globally any longer. Now manufacturers in both China and Europe are looking for another region to which to relocate.

While low-value-added manufacturing will probably relocate to Southeast Asia, South Asia, or Mexico, the United States has a real chance to become a high-value-added manufacturing power once again. The key to doing so is affordable, abundant, and secure energy. Fully exploiting shale oil and gas is by far the best means to rebuild the American manufacturing base.

Feedstocks

Fossil fuels are not only an irreplaceable energy source, they are also an essential material. In addition to powering our energy system, fossil fuels are also essential feedstock for many of the materials that we take for granted. Virtually every new material invented over the last two centuries partly or entirely derives from petrochemicals.

Petroleum byproducts have a huge number of uses. Methane is used as a chemical feedstock to produce hydrogen gas, and as a fuel additive. Ethane is also used as a pigment for paint. Propane is used as an adhesive. Butane is used as a refrigerant and solvent. Octane is used as an additive in fuel and paint. Hexadecane is used as an absorbents (Zeihan 2016).

This is just a tip in the iceberg of products created entirely or partly from petroleum byproducts. To list just a few in no particular order: ink, upholstery, floor wax, sweaters, boats, soccer cleats, tires, nail polish, fishing lures, shoe polish, tool boxes, caulking, tool boxes, soap, antihistamines, purses, deodorants, putty, dyes, refrigerant, life jackets, skis, tape, maps, insect repellent, fertilizers, toilet seats, fishing rods, linoleum, synthetic rubber, trash bags, water pipes, toothpaste, dentures, bandages, shaving cream, mobile devices, DVDs, heart valves, tents, and sun glasses (IAG). To the best of my knowledge, Greens have not even attempted to explain how they would manufacture any of these products without fossil fuels.

Paying Off the Federal Debt

Promoting exploration and drilling of federal lands and offshore is likely to lead to massive economic benefits. The taxes generated from the activity also give us the ability to significantly shrink the federal debt, to get it to a sustainable size. Elsewhere in this book, I propose constitutional amendments to strictly enumerate the powers of the federal government and impose balanced budget requirements. These two steps will go a long way to stabilizing the growth of federal debt, but we need to go further.

To promote long-term economic growth, we need to reduce the size of the federal debt relative to the overall economy. This will in turn reduce the interest payments that federal taxpayers pay with each annual budget. The most effective means of doing so will be to maintain robust economic growth with the policies that I propose in this book. Economic growth will lead to greater tax revenues without having to raise tax rates. Increased revenue with flat spending will enable the federal government to gradually shrink the size of the federal debt relative to the economy.

We should also pay off some of the national debt directly using revenue derived from drilling for natural gas and petroleum on federal lands and offshore. Federal lands, including the off-shore area, have massive reserves of fossil fuels, worth over $50 trillion as of 2011. As energy prices have increased since that date, the total value of reserves is probably higher (Coleman).

Even if we focus exclusively on direct federal revenues, the total amounts that drilling on federal lands can raise are breathtaking. Direct federal revenues from royalties and corporate income tax receipts from producers alone come to over $12 trillion. And this does not include the indirect revenues caused by greater economic growth (Coleman).

Norway has leveraged its oil and gas drilling industry to create a sovereign wealth fund that is currently valued at over $1.2 trillion. Given that the United States has far larger oil and gas reserves than Norway, there is no reason why we cannot lower debt levels as a percent of the economy back to what they were in 2000.

Energy Austerity in Europe

Climate activists claim that European energy policies prove that their pro-renewable strategy is working. Green energy just needs more public-sector investment to succeed, they claim.

Unfortunately, this is far from the case. As I will explain in the *Cutting Global Carbon Emissions* chapter, Green energy policies have failed to lower global carbon emissions, nor can their policies appreciably lower future temperatures. While it is true that many European nations have been able to reduce carbon emissions over the last 40 years, it is not a clear success. While we need abundant, affordable, and secure energy, the Green energy policies have created expensive and insecure energy through policies of austerity.

Much of the reduction of carbon emissions in Europe since 2007 has been due to *a stagnant economy and very high energy prices*. The European economy has essentially not yet recovered from the 2008 recession (unlike the United States). In most European nations, per capita GDP is virtually the same in 2022 ($38,231 for the EU) as it was in 2007 ($37,050) (World Bank).

Meanwhile, electricity prices have sky-rocketed. While household electricity prices in the United States are around 12 cents per kilowatt hour, they are double and triple that in Europe. Even before the current energy crisis, Denmark had electricity prices at 36 cents, Germany at

35 cents, and the UK at 28 cents. This is hardly reassuring evidence of the low cost of renewable electricity. Such electricity prices impoverish working-class and poor families and undermine the competitiveness of industries that they rely upon for employment (ElectricRate).

Over the last 20-30 years European NATO members have practiced unilateral energy disarmament. Northwest Europe and parts of Eastern Europe have huge natural gas reserves in the form of traditional gas fields in the North Sea, as well as shale gas fields in many parts of the continent.

Despite these vast fields of low-carbon natural gas, most European nations have essentially refused to use them. The UK, France, Germany, Spain, Netherlands, Ireland and Bulgaria have banned hydraulic fracturing. Then most of these nations imported huge amounts of natural gas, coal and petroleum from Russia. This does nothing for the environment, and seriously undermines peace and national security.

Even worse, European nations tried to decommission nuclear power plants, which emit no carbon emissions at all. Unsurprisingly, this forced many European nations to keep coal-burning power plants going to avoid a total collapse of their energy grid. As of 2022, Germany is bringing their coal power plants back online.

Starting in the summer of 2021, the situation got much worse. While, in 2020, the maximum EU wholesale electricity price was around 50 Euros (already very high compared to the US), it suddenly jumped to 275 Euros by December 2021. Minimum prices were now almost three times the price of what maximum prices had been just one year previously. Note that this was *before* the Russian invasion of Ukraine, not afterward. The maximum price then doubled after the invasion (Ember).

The result of these sky-high energy prices has been declining energy usage. In fairness, some of the credit should go to investments in renewable energy, but the bulk of the contribution goes to lower energy usage. This is not an energy transition. *This is energy austerity induced by high prices*. The inevitable result was economic stagnation.

Putin Loves Green Energy Policies... Overseas

Green energy policies have fundamentally undermined European security and empowered Russia. Green energy policies deliberately cut back on domestic gas production. In particular, Greens are opposed to hydraulic fracturing, which enables the drilling for shale gas.

The United Kingdom, France, Germany, Poland, Ukraine and other European nations have substantial shale gas fields, but they are not being fully exploited due to government regulations. While the mineral rights to American shale gas fields are owned by private land owners, mineral rights in Europe are owned by the government. So while the United States has experienced a Shale Revolution, European governments have deliberately chosen not to exploit this valuable resource.

Unfortunately for Europe, natural gas is so essential to their energy system that they filled the void with imports from Russia. Gradually, over the last 20 years, Central and Eastern European dependency upon Russian imports increased.

Not surprisingly, Russia is strongly against fracking in the West and mobilizes propaganda sources to constrain its use as much as possible. While we have no way of knowing if this propaganda has changed public opinion, the desired results have transpired either way.

Green Energy Policies Built Nord Stream

One of the many negative unintended outcomes of Green energy policies in Europe was the Nord Stream 1 and Nord Stream 2 gas pipelines. European countries quickly learned that it was impossible to substitute solar and wind for fossil fuels and nuclear. Rather than choose to produce domestic Shale Gas, Europeans instead chose to import Russian gas. Why they view Russian gas as more Green than European gas is not clear. It seems very likely that Europeans can drill for natural gas in far more environmentally-friendly ways than Russia does.

The two Nord Stream pipelines enable Russia to pump natural gas from Siberia directly to Germany while avoiding eastern Europe. The two pipelines are owned by Nord Stream AG, a holding company owned jointly by Gazprom and four European energy firms. These energy firms then sell Russian gas at marked-up prices to the rest of Europe.

Gazprom is largely owned by Russian oligarchs and is closely aligned with the Putin regime. Indeed, Gazprom is the most important weapon in his fight for domination of Central Eurasia. Just as important, state oil and gas revenues amount to as much as 45% of Russia's annual budget. Without energy exports to Europe, the Putin regime would have a hard time surviving (Hersh).

So in the name of saving the environment Greens are subsidizing an aggressive authoritarian regime and enabling energy companies to sell gas at a nice markup. This does not sound very Green, or very sensible, to me.

Ukraine Paid the Price for Green Energy

Putin correctly interpreted European energy dependency as a sign of weakness and invaded the country that was most vulnerable because it was not in NATO: Ukraine. The result was a threat to European stability and massive human rights violations.

Vladimir Putin saw Green energy policies in the West as a tremendous opportunity to be exploited. His calculations prior to invading Ukraine were probably heavily influenced by the belief that Europe would not intervene. He assumed they might protest diplomatically, but they would not intervene with hard power. Nor did Putin think that the United States would intervene, because they were also deliberately constraining its natural gas production. Ukraine was ripe for the picking, and then afterward, who knows...

Fortunately, Putin was wrong. The surprise invasion of 2022 failed to conquer Kyiv, and the Ukrainian army fought back much more fiercely than anyone had expected. Once a quick military defeat seemed unlikely, the United States and many European nations donated large amounts of precision weapons that give Ukraine a fighting chance of winning the long war.

As of 2023, the outcome of this war is unclear, but the war in Ukraine displays how energy power translates into geostrategic power. Without oil, gas, and coal, Russia would be just another European nation. As Europe is unwilling to exploit its own fossil fuels, Russia is a regional power. In the Cold War 2.0 that appears to be starting, energy will be critical. In such a conflict, Green energy policies are virtually unilateral disarmament.

Green Policies Benefit Russia and China

The Russian invasion of Ukraine in 2022 and the potential for a Chinese invasion of Taiwan show that geopolitical competition between the Great Powers has not been banished from the planet.

We appear to be moving into a period of history that we might call Cold War 2.0. Once again, Russia and China are loosely aligned against the United States and its European and East Asian allies. The outcome of this global struggle will play a huge role in determining the future of human progress, at least in the short term. The radical centralization of power that these two regimes represent will fundamentally undermine the Third Key to Progress (decentralized power).

A Warmer Earth Is Not the Biggest Risk

Disastrous climate change is not the worst possible outcome. Far more terrifying than higher global temperatures, and far more likely, is the possibility that the West incapacitates its economy and its military by abolishing fossil fuels, while Eurasia, particularly China and Russia, keeps increasing their usage of coal and other fossil fuels.

Communist China and Russia will able to greatly strengthen their military power if they continue using fossil fuels, while the Western powers abandon them. Then we have two existential problems rather than one: climate change plus two totalitarian world powers.

And **Green energy policies make this worst possible outcome far more likely**.

We need the wealth of the West to adapt to a warmer world, and economic prosperity gives us the resources to do so. If progress is killed, then we will have less wealth. Less wealth means less technological innovation, less ability to adapt to the climate, lower standards of living, and weaker military power.

When I first started writing this book, the threat of Green energy policies undermining the West and enhancing Russian and Chinese power seemed remote. Then in 2021 and 2022, the threat became very real.

In the summer of 2021, European energy markets had a meltdown. The prices of both electricity and natural gas increased to levels never seen before. While electricity and natural gas prices were already very high compared to the United States before the summer of 2021, they more than quadrupled in 2021 and 2022.

Unlike previous energy crises, such as 1973 and 1979, the cause is not external. The causes were largely driven by European energy policy: simultaneously trying to abolish nuclear, natural gas, and coal power while substituting solar, wind, and biomass.

Much has been made of European NATO members not honoring their pledge to spend at least 2% of their GDP on the military. Since the Russian invasion of Ukraine, fortunately, many European nations are now scrambling to make up the difference. But energy security is just as vital to European security, and perhaps more vital than military spending for maintaining an effective deterrence against Russia.

The Russian attack on Ukraine also suddenly highlighted the possibility of China invading Taiwan. In both fronts of the battle between authoritarian powers in Eurasia versus the democratic powers in the West and their allies, energy is crucial.

If, in 30 years, the United States, Europe, and Japan have abandoned nuclear power and fossil fuels, while Russian keeps producing fossil fuels and China keeps constructing coal-burning power plants, the entire balance of world power will be altered. The military of the United

States and its allies simply cannot function without huge amounts of fossil fuels. Nor can their civilian economies.

The idea that the United States Army, Navy, and Air Force can run on electricity produced from renewable resources is preposterous. Armored vehicles, ships, and airplanes cannot function purely on electricity, and the technology to do so is probably many generations away (if it ever comes). Manufacturers of weapon platforms and munitions also need fossil fuels to maintain production at scale.

The Russian invasion of Ukraine also brought home how vulnerable the world is to famine without exports from nations with highly-productive agriculture. When Russian blockaded Ukrainian agricultural exports, many developing countries were threatened with malnutrition and perhaps even famine. Global food production and distribution powered by fossil fuels are essential for world food security.

A world dominated by authoritarian China and Russia is much worse than a world that is a few degrees warmer.

Energy Security for Europe

Increased drilling for natural gas in the United States can help save Europe from itself. This would be the fourth time that the United States has rescued Europe in a little over one century. The first three times were World War I, World War II, and the Cold War.

This time the United States is rescuing Europe with LNG (liquefied natural gas) exports to Europe. This is as it should be, but these natural gas exports must be in tandem with Europe dropping its Green policies that sabotage domestic natural gas exploration, drilling, and distribution. Rather than sabotaging such activities, Europe must support these essential activities to maintain continental security.

For 70 years, NATO has been essential to European security. It is commonly thought of as a military alliance for national security, but it also needs to be seen as an energy alliance for energy security. To be strong allies that can resist Russian aggression (or any other nation), Europe must have a strong military as well as a strong energy sector.

Energy is so essential to national security and economic vitality that it can never be fully replaced by military power. Over the last few decades, Russia has been the master of leveraging domestic energy sources to increase military power and national security. Europe must learn to do the same.

Europeans Need to Allowing Gas Drilling

The United States should assist Europe in transitioning away from Russian oil and gas, but, in return, the United States must insist that Europe increase domestic natural gas production. Just as NATO nations are required to spend a certain percentage of their economy on the military (which unfortunately most are not doing), they should also be required to promote energy security through natural gas, nuclear power, and hydroelectric dams.

The problem for the United States is that LNG exports, while profitable, greatly increase the cost of natural gas in North America. Ten years ago natural gas exports from the United States were illegal. This created a North American natural gas market that was isolated from the rest of the world. Once the ban on natural gas exports was lifted, the natural gas markets of North America, Europe, and Asia started to be integrated together. The result was a marked increase in the price of natural gas in North America.

Increased natural gas production in Europe is essential for stable and affordable natural gas prices in North America. Massive American LNG exports will lead to a convergence of prices between very low prices in North America and very high prices in Europe. So Green energy policies in Europe also hurt North America by making its energy prices higher.

Crude Oil Exports

So far, I have focused largely on natural gas. We cannot forget crude oil, which is still the energy backbone of modern transportation. Very few transportation devices are not powered by gasoline, diesel, or jet fuel.

In the *Cutting Global Carbon Emissions* chapter, I will advocate the gradual electrification of transportation. Electric cars have made major advances over the last 15 years, and I expect that trend to continue. It will be generations, however, before electricity will fully replace crude oil for powering transportation. In the meantime, we still need abundant, affordable and secure sources of crude oil.

From 1970 to the early 2000s, the United States imported increasing amounts of petroleum. Just as with natural gas, it seemed like "Peak Oil" had already hit us and that energy seemed to be on a long downward trend. Then the Shale Revolution transformed the industry.

The United States is now the leading oil producer in the world and imports are dropping rapidly. Because the technologies that increase shale gas production are essentially the same as the technologies that increase shale petroleum production, there is every reason to believe that the supply of both energy sources will increase in tandem.

Many Greens want to drive up the price of crude oil by creating artificial scarcity. This is misguided. Until electric cars and trucks become the dominant form of transportation, we need abundant, affordable and secure crude oil. That oil will come from the United States, Canada and Mexico, or else it will come from a host of authoritarian regimes overseas.

If the United States deliberately curtails crude oil production and exports, as Greens propose, this will drastically increase the price of oil and divert trillions of dollars to authoritarian regimes such as Russia, Saudi Arabia, Iran, Venezuela, and the Persian Gulf nations. There is nothing Green about that.

Affordable crude oil would not only boost Western economies, but it would also be disastrous for those authoritarian regimes. This will help to constrain their negative influence on the global balance of power. This is particularly important in the case of Russia. Affordable crude oil will also be a great boon for wealthy Western allies such as Europe, Japan, South Korea, and Taiwan.

In the long run, I believe that electric vehicles will drastically reduce our need for crude oil, but in the meantime it is far better to use affordable American crude rather than expensive crude from other regions. Affordable gasoline may slow the transition to electric vehicles somewhat, but prosperous consumers are far more likely to be able to afford new electric cars if our economy keeps growing.

Inventing New Energy Sources

In the *Technological Innovation* chapter, I will argue that we should transition away from fossil fuels over a much longer time period than Greens claim is necessary to avoid climate change. I believe that a Fourth Energy Transition will come, but it will not be based on solar and wind. I also believe that the transition will take place over generations. The long-term trend of technological innovation makes a new energy source inevitable, but it will not come tomorrow.

However, waiting 100 years for a new energy source does seem a little too mild. There are some policies governments can implement to speed up this process. By far the most important policy to promote global progress would be drastically increasing funding of research into and development for new energy sources.

A far more achievable means of lowering carbon emissions while promoting progress would be to invent a new carbon-free energy source that is significantly cheaper than fossil fuels. This energy source must be extremely dense and either have 24/7/365 output or controllable output.

In other words, it must be better than fossil fuels in almost every way. And it is difficult for me to see how solar or wind can possibly meet the challenge, even if we add on much cheaper batteries. I will go into more detail how we can achieve that energy breakthrough in a later chapter.

Focus on Results

In this chapter and following chapters, I recommend policy reforms that I believe will promote future progress. Each of my proposals is associated with concepts that I developed in my first book in this series:

- The Five Keys to Progress
- How Progress Works

I believe that these two concepts are fundamental towards understanding progress and for developing policies that will promote future progress.

Because my proposed policies resemble policies and practices that worked to promote progress in the past, there is reason to believe that similar policies will promote progress in future. But logical consistency is just a starting point. Many seemingly great ideas do not work, and some even lead to very undesirable outcomes. We must subject our ideas to the test of reality.

A key principle of a Progress-based reform agenda should be to focus on results. No matter how confident that we are that a policy will be a success, we must keep our minds open to the fact that the results might not be so positive in the real world. The modern world is very complex, and policy outcomes are always uncertain.

Because of this uncertainty we should carefully monitor real-world results of policy reforms. At the end of most chapters I will add a *Focus on Results* section that lists metrics that will measure the success or failure of my proposals.

Supporters of progress should monitor these metrics, so we can gradually improve the effectiveness of our policies. Programs that achieve positive results should be expanded, while programs that achieve poor results should be reformed or eliminated. Only in this way can we show positive results for humanity.

As much as possible, I use metrics that are already widely available. Unless otherwise noted all costs should be indexed for inflation and not include government subsidies.

Key metrics for measuring the success of energy policies should be:
- Energy spending as percent of GDP
- Cost of electricity ($/KWh)
- Cost of natural gas ($/thousand cubic feet)
- Cost of gasoline ($/gallon)
- Average interruption duration of electrical grid per year
- Average energy costs per vehicle mile driven
- Average HVAC costs for homes and commercial buildings
- Percent of energy produced domestically (or in North America)

Conclusion

The single greatest threat to continuing economic growth in wealthy nations are Green energy policies. Because it is impossible under current technology to substitute fossil fuels, nuclear and hydroelectric power for solar and wind, these Green policies have only resulted in energy austerity and economic stagnation. Moreover, they have not even successfully reduced global carbon emissions.

My proposed Progress-based energy policy would accelerate the Third Energy Transition to build an abundant, affordable, and secure electrical grid based on natural gas, nuclear and hydroelectric power. In a later chapter, I will proposed a policy to extend the Third Energy Transition into the transportation sector and lower global carbon emissions.

A Progress-based energy policy will:
- Accelerate economic growth in wealthy nations
- Lower energy prices
- Enable export manufacturing to return to the United States
- Increase the standard of living of the working class and poor
- Lower air pollution
- Help to pay off the federal debt
- Create energy security for the United States, NATO and their allies
- Undermine the influence of totalitarian powers, such as Russia

and China.

AFFORDABLE CITIES

The Second Key to Progress: Trade-based cities packed with a large number of free citizens possessing a wide variety of skills. These people innovate new technologies, skills and social organizations and copy the innovations made by others.

Wealthy nations currently have very high urbanization rates. They also have robust infrastructures in the domains of water, sanitation, electricity, transportation, communication, police, and fire. On the face of it, it is difficult to see how the issues addressed by the second Key to Progress could be improved.

One very bad trend within cities in wealthy nations, however, is unaffordable housing. Affordable prices are one of the key foundations of prosperity. Nowhere is this truer than in housing.

In general, change in per capita GDP is a useful high-order measurement of progress. Per capita GDP measures the amount of money that people have, but what is far more important is *what people can buy with that money.* Affordable prices, particularly for necessities, are also a key metric for measuring progress. Nowhere is this more important than housing. Without housing, cities simply cannot exist.

The Importance of Affordable Housing

Housing is crucial to people's overall standard of living, because it takes up such a large portion of their budgets. According to the Consumer Expenditure Survey in 2019, the typical household spends around 19.3% of their spending on mortgage or rent. They spend another 13.5% on other housing-related expenditures, such as utilities, maintenance, and furnishing. In all, just under one-third of a typical household budget is spent on housing. This is far more than any other category (CES).

Housing prices particularly impact lower and middle-income households. Low- and middle-income households spend a significantly higher proportion of their income on shelter than upper-income households. Households in the lowest 10% of income spend 25.8% of their income on mortgage or rent, while the top 10% spend only 17.7%. Middle-income households range between 19 and 23%.

This figure understates the significance of housing to monthly budgets. Many retirees have paid off their mortgage, so, for the remaining citizens, housing makes up a higher proportion of their spending. Some people are still paying off a mortgage for a house that they purchased when housing prices were more affordable, but many have bought more recently at higher prices.

Housing Affordability Before 1970

Housing inflation is a relatively new phenomenon. Until 1970, housing prices did not vary much from the core rate of inflation. This made housing affordable across the nation.

A useful means of measuring housing affordability is the ratio between the median cost of a house and the median family income within that metro. In 1969, virtually every metro in the United States had a ratio of 3.0 or less. The national average was 1.8 (Antiplanner, 2020).

At that point, housing in the United States was affordable everywhere, even in the wealthiest cities. Though we do not have good housing price data from before that time, there is every reason to believe that this had been the case throughout American history.

Then, in the 1970s, something began to change radically. In a few key metro areas, housing prices began to increase far more rapidly than median family incomes.

The affordability numbers were quite similar in Europe, Canada, Australia, New Zealand, and Japan. It was partly down to simple supply and demand. When the population grew in a metro area, builders built more houses. And they typically built single-family residences on the outskirts of the metro area, where land was relatively cheap. Housing prices would vary with the level of income for the metro, but housing affordability would stay roughly the same.

Failure Since 1970

Government policy over the last 50 years has been an abysmal failure at promoting affordable housing. In fact, government policy has been extremely effective at making housing unaffordable in many metro areas.

Since the 1970s, many metro areas have experienced inflation of housing prices that have been far beyond the base rate of inflation. More accurately, it is an inflation of the price of land under those houses. The actual houses themselves are not increasing in cost at anywhere near the rate of land prices. Almost all geographical variation in housing prices is due to the price of land, while variations in labor and materials are not very large in comparison (Antiplanner, 2020).

People living in these metropolitan areas take it for granted that home values will continually move upward, as if by magic. Few stop to think about what causes this inflation. Far more people just enjoy the rapid increase in their wealth that is a result of this land inflation.

This housing inflation has impacted the large urban areas of the Northeast and Pacific coast of the United States, Europe, Canada, Japan, Australia, and New Zealand. Housing inflation has become such a part of modern life that we take it for granted as if it is normal. It is anything but normal. It is caused by very bad government policies.

New Deal Democrats Promoted Sprawl

Today, "sprawl" is perceived as a bad thing, particularly by those on the Left. Sprawl is typically defined as the spreading of urban developments onto undeveloped land near the city. This trend is almost universally derided by those on the Left as a bad thing that undermines our quality of life and our natural environment. Promoting density and limiting sprawl is now considered one of the most critical goals of urban design.

Ironically, we forget that it was Democrats who actively promoted the very suburban developments that are so derided today. In the 1940s, 50s, and 60s, New Deal Democrats actively promoted home construction and ownership on the outskirts of urban regions. They also founded institutions – the Federal Housing Administration (FHA), Fanny Mae, and Freddy Mac – that made it easier for working-class families to purchase those homes. The federal government allowed (and still allows) workers to deduct the interest on their mortgage payments from their taxes. This is a substantial stimulus on home ownership. Most importantly, the federal, state, and local governments erected few barriers to building homes.

These policies were particularly important because America was experiencing a post-war Baby Boom. All these new families needed someplace to live, and new housing construction on the outskirts of metro areas was deemed the best solution to the problem.

During the 1940s, 50s, and 60s, the suburbs popped up like mushrooms in the forest. The result was a fantastic increase in the standard of living of the American working class from the late 1940s to the early 1970s. Certainly, a growing economy, strong trade unions, and limited foreign competition played important roles, but one should not underestimate the importance of affordable housing.

Rather than being cramped up in small, urban apartments, young working-class families could buy new, much larger single-family residences in brand-new suburbs. The government encouraged suburbanization by constructing new freeways to make transportation to and from those suburbs easier, faster, cheaper, and safer.

Suburbanization played a key role in promoting ethnic and religious integration. Before World War II urban working-class neighborhoods were typically very segregated. There were WASP neighborhoods, Irish Catholic neighborhoods, German neighborhoods, Polish neighborhoods, Jewish neighborhoods, and Italian neighborhoods. Everyone typically kept to their own kind. Local toughs enforced rigid ethnic and religious segregation at the neighborhood level.

After World War II, though, young people from those neighborhoods moved to the new suburbs. All the people from those segregated urban neighborhoods suddenly lived together in the same suburban neighborhood. Not surprisingly, many of them fell in love with each other, got married, and had children.

Genetic and cultural mixing meant that all these ethnic and religious minorities fused until they became what we now call "Whites." American unity and integration were stronger than ever. Without the growth of the suburbs, ethnic and religious segregation would have persisted.

Tragically, in most parts of the country, Blacks were left out of this process of integration, so legal and cultural racial segregation remained (while Asians and Hispanics were still relatively small in number). Only with the passage of the Civil Rights Act of 1964 and the Voting Rights Act of 1965, did racial segregation begin to diminish.

For all Americans, though, the period between World War II and the early 1970s was one of widely-shared prosperity. Affordable housing played a key role in that widely-shared prosperity.

Housing Is Both a Product and an Investment

Housing is unlike any other type of market. In most markets, if prices become more affordable, everyone benefits (except for producers). In housing, however, prices are more of a zero-sum phenomenon. Some people benefit from affordable housing, while other people lose (at least in comparison to the current situation).

Housing is unusual because it is both a consumer product and an investment. Most products that you buy on the market depreciate rapidly after the initial purchase. This makes them extremely poor investments.

When a person buys a home, however, they are not only purchasing a place to live. They are also purchasing an investment that can potentially accrue more value over time. For many homeowners, their house is their most substantial investment. For some, it is their only investment.

This places the financial interests of homeowners in direct conflict with those who do not own homes. When the price of housing goes up, rents go up with them. So renters have to spend an increasing portion of their income on rent. Aspiring homeowners also have to save up a larger deposit and pay higher prices for the same house. Meanwhile, homeowners are making money (though, of course, they do not fully realize the increased value until they sell their house).

When housing prices stay affordable, homeowners fail to gain wealth from their most important investment. While renters and young people need affordable housing, homeowners want a steady upward trend in the value of their houses. Such a situation is vulnerable to political influence.

Urban Containment Zones

Take a look at a list of metro areas that have seriously expensive housing in the United States: San Francisco, San Jose, Los Angeles, San Diego, Portland, Seattle, Boston, New York City, and Washington DC. All of these cities have two things in common: robust economic growth and urban containment zones. Most people are very aware of the first factor, but they have never even heard of urban containment zones.

Urban containment zones (sometimes called "green belts") are areas immediately adjoining metro areas where builders are placed under serious restrictions on building new homes. Often these zones completely encircle entire metro areas, effectively prohibiting builders from expanding outward as demand for housing increases. Sometimes urban containment zones work in conjunction with natural geographic barriers, such as oceans, lakes, or mountains, to have the same effect.

Ironically, the walls that surrounded cities during the medieval period have been reconstructed as green walls today. While these green walls are pleasant respites from urban congestion for a lucky few who live near them, the negative consequences for the rest of society are massive and widespread.

The world's first urban containment zone was created in London in 1947. The area immediately outside the edge of the London metro area is called the Metropolitan Green Belt. The idea spread rapidly through the community of urban planners because it appeared to protect natural habitats and farms while having no costs to society.

Hawaii enacted the first urban containment zone in the United States in 1961. The state designated all land in the state as either urban or rural. Land designated as rural had serious restrictions on development enacted.

In 1963, California enacted strict growth-management laws, followed rapidly by Oregon, New Jersey, Maryland, Washington, and all the New England states. Florida did the same but then repealed those laws in 2011. Some cities, such as Minneapolis, Denver, and Salt Lake City did so at the local level. In total, about 45% of the nation's population lives in cities or states with strict growth-management laws (O'Toole, Eicher).

Take a look at a satellite photo of any of these urban areas. You will notice very abrupt changes between dense urban development and green, blue or brown areas with very limited development. Sometimes this will be due to oceans, lakes, or mountains, but often it is not. This is the urban growth boundary.

The long-term negative consequences that these laws created for housing affordability as the economy grew were hidden for decades. Now, everyone can see the symptom of the problem, unaffordable housing, but they cannot all see the cause of the problem itself.

Of course, having parks and wildlands in and near urban areas is a valuable amenity. No one, least of all myself, wants to do away with them. The issue here is not whether cities should have parks and wildlands. Of course, they should.

The issue is whether we should deliberately construct green walls to *entirely encircle urban areas* and cut off all future home construction on the outskirts of metro areas. The greenery of these belts was an accidental side-effect of the main urban planning goal; to build walls around cities outside which houses cannot be constructed.

Housing Affordability Ratings

The Urban Reform Institute and the Frontier Centre for Public Policy releases an annual Demographia report that calculates housing affordability in various metros throughout the Western world. Their study includes 56 metros in the United States, 21 in the UK, five in Australia, six in Canada plus Hong Kong, Auckland, Singapore, and Dublin. In all Demographia tracks 92 different metros in seven different nations.

Their Housing Affordability index compares the cost of the median house compared to the median pre-tax household income. They rate 3.0 and under as affordable (i.e. the median house is three times the median household income) and anything over 5.1 as Severely Unaffordable (Demographia).

Unfortunately, in 2021 only one metro area rates as Affordable, while 55% rate as Severely Unaffordable. Another 21% rate as Seriously Unaffordable. Demographia does not track a broader range of European housing prices, but there is no reason to believe that the overall trend is any different.

And remember that, until 1970, virtually all metro areas had scores of 3.0 or less (though data for earlier periods is relatively sparse). This is a remarkable, and probably unprecedented downturn in housing affordability.

Sprawl Is Not Bad

A big part of the problem is the goal of urban planners. While we might consider urban design to be a pure type of engineering, urban design has always gone through wild swings in design philosophy.

Today, virtually all urban planners regard "sprawl" as something that cities desperately need to avoid. These urban designers view the dense metro areas in Europe and the United States of the late 19th and early 20th Century as the ideal urban form. They effectively view "density" as one of their prime design goals, though they also often use the term "livable" and "walkable" in its place.

Urban planners also regard "affordable housing" and "government-subsidized housing" as synonymous. The idea that builders should be free to construct homes on the outskirts of a metro area as it grows in population is entirely foreign to their worldview.

Sprawl, or the geographical expansion of urban areas, is critical to keeping land prices affordable. And when land is affordable, housing is affordable. The actual cost of materials and labor varies relatively little between metro areas. It is the cost of land and government regulations that varies. And it is the working class and lower class that pay the price for these policies.

These urban growth boundaries force builders to construct houses and rental units inside the boundary, where land is artificially expensive. These boundaries and other regulations force builders to build up. This sounds good until one realizes that this dramatically increases the cost per square foot. These additional costs effectively make it illegal to build housing that can be sold on the market for affordable prices. Even with heavy government subsidies, the higher construction costs guarantee unaffordable selling prices (Arenson).

Metro areas with urban containment zones sort people into "Haves" and "Have nots." These regions have a professional class that owns homes that are rapidly increasing in value. The value of their home allowing for their mortgage balance often reaches hundreds of thousands of dollars. Forced density subsidizes the investment portfolio of the professional class.

Metro areas with urban containment zones also have youths and renters who are struggling. Some older members of the working class were fortunate enough to have bought into the market when prices were lower, but younger members of the working class are priced out of the market.

It should not be a surprise that the very same people who object so vehemently to sprawl are homeowners in affluent neighborhoods in cities with highly expensive housing. Sprawl is not a fundamental threat to the environment; sprawl is a fundamental threat to their investment portfolio.

The goal of these urban design policies was to increase density, but as Shlomo Angel's major work on the subject shows, they failed in that goal. In all nations, cities are becoming less dense, not denser, despite every effort from urban planners. Unfortunately, all these urban designers succeeded in doing was creating dangerous distortions in our economy (Angel).

We Are Not Running Out of Land

It is often claimed that we need urban density because we are running out of land. Many people claim that containing the spread of urban areas is the only way to preserve what little wild habitat and agricultural land we have left. In reality, the United States is not running out of land for cities any time soon.

Few Americans realize just how little land is devoted to cities. Satellite data and GIS mapping show urban areas, including their transportation infrastructure, take up only about 3.2% of the land within the United States excluding Alaska (Fischel). Even doubling the urban land area, which is not very likely under any scenario, would lead to little change in the balance between urban areas and wildlands. Any expansion of urban areas would likely come at the expense of agricultural land, either for farming or ranching.

Professor William A Fischel, an expert in the field, routinely presents his students of urban economics with the following thought experiment: Divide the current U.S. into households of persons and house them on plots of land equal to one acre per household (a size of land plot that is much higher than most Americans own). What percentage of the total land area of the United State would be covered? Virtually no students guess under 10%, while the median answer is 30-40%. Even urban planners at conferences are just as far off in their estimates (Fischel).

If affordable housing at market prices were widely available, then I could see the argument for constraining urban expansion. But with urban housing becoming less and less affordable, these constraints are a very bad trade-off.

Slower Economic Growth

There is clear evidence that government-forced density is seriously hurting material progress. One study estimates that, because high-productivity cities such as San Francisco and New York City adopted stringent restrictions on housing supply, overall U.S. economic growth was lowered by 36% between 1964 and 2009. Another study came to the conclusion that these housing regulations in California and New York substantially lowered overall national productivity, causing lower economic activity. Presumably, those lower levels of economic growth disproportionately hurt the working class and the poor (Hsieh and Moretti; Herkenhoff).

Increased Inequality of Wealth

This widespread inflation of land values within cities that have urban containment zones has had a huge effect on the distribution of wealth. Indeed, Matthew Rognlie makes the compelling argument that increased inequality in wealth over the last few generations is *entirely* due to housing inflation (or more accurately the inflation of the cost of land under that housing). Ironically, the liberals who complain the most loudly about inequality are the ones who created the problem and are the main beneficiaries of this trend (Rognlie).

Because residential real estate makes up a very substantial portion of all wealth in American society and variations in the value are largely determined by policy, homeowners in metro areas on the Pacific coast and Northeast have enjoyed huge increases in personal wealth over the last few decades. And they have enjoyed those increases of wealth, not by increasing their wealth via work or innovation, but by extracting wealth from land ownership.

While some of this wealth goes to members of the working class and retirees who were lucky enough to purchase homes before the big inflation started, the benefits overwhelmingly go to the professional class. And the pain goes overwhelmingly to the poor and young people who cannot afford to buy houses.

The professional class in these metro areas is strikingly similar to the old extractive elites of Agrarian regimes. For both of those classes, their primary source of wealth comes from owning very expensive land and government policies that drive up the value of those lands. While they each use different methods and the old elites were far more deliberate in their extractions, the results are the same.

Both groups are what economists call "rentiers." Rentiers are persons who gain wealth, not by creating it, as people who work in free markets do, but by extracting wealth created by others. Government policies are what enable them to do so.

Geographical Mobility

This massive inflation in land prices has fundamentally changed the nature of geographical mobility in the United States. Until 1970, the general trend of migration was for people to migrate away from rural areas toward the largest and most productive cities. For two centuries, the trek from depressed rural regions to large growing cities was a rite of passage for young people.

Today, however, internal migration patterns are overwhelmingly away from the most productive cities. While there are many reasons for this new migration trend, the most important is housing prices. People want to live in an area where they can afford to purchase an affordable single-family residence. And they are willing to pay the consequences of a lower income to do so.

Economists who study agglomeration effects have noted the tremendous benefits of people migrating to high-value-added cities. These cities are typically the headquarters of one or more high-value-added industries that export to the rest of the nation and the world. Ideally, those high-value-added industries include a gaggle of large, medium, and small companies all competing against each other for market share within that industry.

By combining more and more people into small geographical areas, high-value-added industries have access to skilled workers. This enables them to grow with demand. As those workers move from company to company, they share ideas of what has worked and what has not worked. This spreads important skills and processes throughout the industry.

These high-value-added cities also tend to attract capital for investment in those industries. Employees can leave established companies to found their own companies based on new technologies or business models. This keeps the industry agile and potentially leads to new spin-off industries.

All of these agglomeration factors led to the growth of American cities. Some of these cities experienced their boom decades or even centuries ago and are now a shadow of their former selves: consider Baltimore, New Orleans, St. Louis, Cincinnati, Cleveland, Buffalo, Pittsburgh, and Detroit. Other cities grew early and remain large metro areas: New York City, Chicago, San Francisco, Los Angeles, and Boston. More recently, a new generation of mega-metros has exploded in growth: Phoenix, Dallas, Houston, Miami, and Atlanta.

Today, however, domestic migration patterns in the United States are overwhelmingly away from the most productive cities. What is most unusual is that the population decline is not due to the decline of specific industries as with past urban declines.

The metro areas with the most expensive housing prices are all seeing net outward migration: San Francisco, Los Angeles, New York City, and Boston. Virtually every one of the metro areas that has net negative domestic migration has housing affordability rates well above average. And virtually every one of the metro areas that have net positive domestic migration has housing affordability rates that are average or better (O'Toole, Eicher).

Of course, Americans are still moving out of economically depressed rural regions and toward economically growing metros, but now high housing prices are warping the overall trend. Cities with expensive housing are being abandoned, even if they have dynamic economies. As far as I know, this is unprecedented.

Economic Instability

In addition to warping patterns of geographical mobility, housing unaffordability also creates serious distortions to the economy. In their breakthrough book, *This Time Is Different: Eight Centuries of Economic Folly* Reinhart and Rogoff examine 66 nations across five continents to determine what financial crises of the past had in common. They give strong evidence that real estate prices have played a key role in previous financial crises. Indeed, current real estate prices are the most accurate predictor of future economic crises.

Ironically, Reinhart and Rogoff published their book just before the crisis of 2008, which was linked to housing. While the American economy has recovered from the resulting recession, the European economy has not. Per capita GDP in most Western European nations has been flat for the last 15 years.

Perhaps part of the reason why the American economy recovered much faster is that, unlike European cities, many American cities lack urban containment zones. This at least leaves Americans with the option of migrating to metro areas with far more affordable housing. And they have taken advantage of those opportunities with a vengeance. Like feudal peasants of yesteryear migrating to lands not controlled by extractive nobles, so Americans today migrate to avoid the negative consequences of urban containment zones.

The recent 2008 crisis is far from the only example of housing inflation triggering financial crises, which undermine long-term economic growth. Japan's super-inflated housing prices in the 1980s immediately preceded the financial crisis in the years around 1990. This crisis caused a dramatic shift from decades of rapid economic growth to tepid growth over the last thirty years.

There are also eerie resemblances to this problem in China today. Reinhart and Rogoff point out that housing prices in China are now more inflated than Japanese housing prices were during the extreme inflation in the 1980s. If their theory is correct, a financial crisis caused by housing inflation leading to far lower rates of economic growth is a real possibility in China.

Western nations need to wake up to the massive unintended consequences of current policies on the economy, wealth inequality, the poor, and future generations. These policies are completely unsustainable, and, until we come up with a better way to reverse the increasing inequality of wealth, young people and the poor will feel left out of the American Dream and economic crises will continue.

In-fill Is Not Enough

Currently, there is a YIMBY movement that seeks to eliminate policies that restrict new housing construction. YIMBY stands for "Yes In My Backyard," an obvious dig at the NIMBYs ("Not In My Backyard") who oppose many construction projects.

The YIMBY movement strongly believes in in-fill development. In-fill development is adding new housing on plots of land clearly within the urban footprint. This includes developing isolated plots of agricultural land, subdividing large plots of existing residential housing, and building rental units on owners' land.

Anyone in favor of material progress should favor all that, but I think it is naïve to believe that in-fill development will be enough. The major focus should be on constructing new housing on the outskirts of the metro area where land is affordable.

It Is All About Land Prices

Currently, property taxes are a major source of revenue for local and state governments. Property taxes are based on the assessed value of both the land and all structures on that land. This means that owners of empty plots of land pay much lower taxes than owners with buildings on their land. In metro areas where the price of land is going up, landowners increase the value of their portfolio by doing nothing. This creates a strong incentive for land speculation.

What is effectively happening in many major metro areas is that entrepreneurs, engineers, and other workers create wealth that benefits all of society. Unfortunately, because of the artificial scarcity of land in that metro area, a highly significant proportion of the wealth creation goes to those who own land near those industries. Those rentier landowners need to do absolutely nothing to experience massive increases in wealth. Meanwhile, the young, poor, and working class must deal with ever-increasing housing costs, which sap their ability to enjoy the benefits of living in a productive economy.

If you do not believe me, check out the housing prices in California, Hawaii, Seattle, Portland, New York City, and Boston. Expensive houses, right? Well, no: expensive land under the housing!

Take a look at the American Enterprise Institutes Land Share Indicators for 2012 and 2020. The share of the cost of land in all those cities listed above is over 60% of the total cost of houses. For Los Angeles and San Francisco it is over 70%. In comparison, most metro regions have land shares of 25-53%.

And the overall land share is increasing over time. In 2012, land made up 38.2% of the total value of all residential real estate. In 2020, land made up 54.7% of the total value. Given that real estate values increased overall during that period, this is an enormous increase in the cost of land. And that land inflation is concentrated in a few dozen expensive metros.

Supporters of in-fill development do not realize two key facts. The first is the cost of land, which is the fundamental problem, not the cost of the housing on that land. You could pitch a tent in those places, and it would not be affordable because the land under the tent is so expensive (AEI Land Price Indicators).

Building Higher Increases Cost

Many YIMBYs attempt to overcome the high cost of land by promoting construction upward, not outward. This keeps them in alignment with the overall philosophy of promoting density and opposing sprawl.

YIMBYs do not seem to realize that building upwards increases housing unaffordability. The more vertical stories that housing consists of, the higher the cost per square foot (Arenson).

Single-family residences of one or two stories are economically feasible without government subsidies in virtually any location, which is exactly why you see them all across the nation. Because relatively cheap wood construction can be used for the first and second floors, the second floor is only slightly more expensive than the first floor.

Once you start building the third floor, however, this forces builders to shift away from wood construction and towards using concrete. Such changes in materials increase costs by 30-50%. This makes three-floor housing feasible without government subsidy only in wealthy metros on the Pacific Coast and Northeast.

A fourth story requires the addition of an expensive elevator system, which doubles the construction costs per square foot compared to the first two stories. This makes them economically feasible without government subsidies in only a few housing markets.

As you build more stories, the costs just escalate further. The fifth story triples or quadruples construction costs so they require some type of government subsidy except in the most expensive areas. Once you get to eight or more stories, the construction cost per square foot is five to eight times the price of single-story construction (Arenson).

Yes, you can construct tiny apartments and call them "affordable," but those apartments are very expensive per square foot. You cannot get around the economic disadvantages of vertical construction. Worse, as the housing size per unit shrinks, fewer and fewer people actually want to live there. So you are stuck with very expensive housing that few people want to live in, given a choice.

Density Creates Unaffordability

The fundamental intellectual problem with much of the YIMBY movement is that they still have not overcome their desire to promote density. Both YIMBYs and NIMBYs agree that sprawl is bad.

But government-enforced density is the major cause of housing affordability. Until we realize that density is a major driving factor in unaffordable housing, then we cannot truly bring down housing costs.

Those on the Left in general also need to overcome their prejudice against single-family residences. Both by their buying behavior and poll responses, it is clear that Americans want to live in single-family residences. The drive by urban planners to force Americans to live in much denser housing than home-owners prefer is a big part of what got us into this problem in the first place.

The reality is that any housing built within expensive metros will be expensive regardless of the type. That is why the construction of one- or two-story housing on the outskirts of the metro area is the only real solution to housing affordability.

Affordable Housing Isn't

Some housing advocates try to break this conundrum by advocating for affordable housing. One of the biggest oxymorons in housing policy is so-called "affordable housing." In our current political lexicon, affordable housing is government-mandated or government-subsidized housing that is sold for prices below market value. When constructed in metro areas with unaffordable market housing, such housing is generally nowhere near being truly affordable.

In many regions, in order to get approval to construct new housing developments, builders are forced to build a certain number of "affordable housing units." Because it is impossible to sell or rent these units at market value while complying with the regulations, builders are forced to increase the prices of other houses within the same development.

Because the type of urban planners who favor such "affordable housing" also favor density, those units are typically multi-story and built well within the urban area. The result is highly expensive housing.

In reality, current "affordable housing" means unaffordable housing where someone else pays the bill. That bill is either being paid by other homeowners in the same development or by taxpayers. I define affordable housing as houses or rentals that have an affordable cost per square foot on the open market without subsidies. An affordability index of 3.0 or lower is a good place to start.

The current affordable housing policy is simply not sustainable. Housing prices in metro areas will continue to mount, forcing greater and greater subsidies, which in turn drive market-based values even higher. Affordable housing is a great business model for some developers, but it is a losing proposition for everyone else.

Multi-Family Housing Does Not Help

Some claim that, by constructing multi-family residences, such as condominiums and apartments, we can address the housing shortage while lowering the urban footprint. I am in favor of building more condominiums and apartments to lower rent prices, but I seriously doubt that it will have any effect on housing prices.

Single-family residences and condos/apartments are effectively two separate markets, like cars and pickup trucks. The kind of people who want one are unlikely to want the other unless they are given no choice.

Most Americans appear to view living in rental properties as a temporary solution, not the desired lifestyle for the long term. Rentals are also popular for families who have recently moved to a new metro area and want to take their time to purchase the right house. And condominiums are a niche market reserved for the most affluent metro areas.

Generally, families with children want single-family residences, though they cannot always afford them, while singles and couples without children prefer multi-family residences. Once those same people have children, their preferences change to favor the other market.

The size of a typical multi-family residence aligns with this perception. While the average new single-family residence is 2,350 square feet, enough room for a family with children, apartments average 1,065 square feet, while condominiums average 1,400 square feet. Those sizes are sufficient for young singles but quite cramped for families with children. Very few condos or apartments are as big as modern houses (2019 American Community Survey).

This is not due to bad urban planning, but due to consumer preferences. Developers could build larger condos or apartments, but they do not do so due to a perceived lack of demand. Nor is there much of a market for very small single-family residences. The two markets do not overlap much.

Now, it is true that many lower-income families are forced to live in smaller multi-family residences because they cannot afford to buy a house, but that is because of a shortage of housing. Very few residents of single-family residents would actually prefer to live in condos or rentals for a long period of time.

High-rise Rental Dystopia

If we do not rethink our current attitudes towards sprawl, we could unintentionally create a dystopian society. About 83% of single-family residences are owned by live-in residents who accrue the increased value of their house and the land that it rests upon. Meanwhile, a full 87% of multi-family residences are rentals (2019 American Community Survey).

If housing construction focuses on multi-family residences to increase density, wealthy landowners and developers will be the only people who can afford to purchase most real estate. Those landlords will receive all of the increased value of the land and still be able to extract higher rents from tenants. Everyone else without a high income will be forced to be a renter their entire lifetime. None of those renters will receive any additional wealth from housing inflation.

Such a society is destined to be highly unequal, with the benefits of economic growth and progress going to a small class of landowners. This is not the type of society that I want to live in. Nor can it be defined as progress in any way.

Historic Preservation

One reasonable argument against widespread housing construction in the urban centers is the desire to preserve historically important buildings. As a history buff, I love to visit historical buildings where famous people lived or that represent architectural designs from bygone eras. I would hate to see all of these treasured buildings bulldozed in the name of progress.

I do believe, however, that we have expanded the definition of historic importance to such an extent that virtually all older buildings apply. This makes it very difficult for older metropolitan areas of the Northeast to construct new buildings. Historical preservation must be balanced with promoting housing affordability.

Fortunately, historic preservation is rarely relevant to housing construction on the outskirts of metro areas. Historical buildings largely tend to be clustered in older urban centers, while more modern construction has proceeded outwards. In fact, sprawl tends to preserve historic buildings as the focus shifts outwards. Historical preservation is really only a strong argument against in-fill development, which I believe is a less effective solution to the problem of housing unaffordability anyway.

What to Do

We desperately need to come up with a new urban planning paradigm that puts affordable market prices for housing as its centerpiece. This strategy must not include urban containment zones, excessive zoning rules or excessive environmental regulations.

Unwinding the current system that promotes unaffordable housing will be a serious challenge. It is not due to one policy on one level of government. Unaffordable housing is due to building restrictions by local, country, state, and federal governments.

Peeling back each layer of regulation will take many years, if not decades. And many if not most homeowners will be opposed to them because these reforms will reduce the value of their largest single investment. Realistically, it will be hard to make progress within the next few decades.

I believe the proposals made by Shlomo Angel in his book, *Planet of Cities* is a great starting point for a new paradigm. Angel argues against land use policies that force density and gives clear evidence that those policies are not only failing in their main goals but also driving up housing costs.

Instead, Angel advocates for a "Making Room" paradigm which he describes thus:

• *The Inevitable Expansion Proposition: The expansion of cities that urban population growth entails cannot be contained. Instead, we must make adequate room to accommodate it.*

• *The Sustainable Densities Proposition: City densities must remain within a sustainable range. If the density is too low, it must be allowed to increase, and if it is too high, it must be allowed to decline.*

• *The Decent Housing Proposition: Strict containment of urban expansion destroys the homes of the poor and puts new housing out of reach for most people. Decent housing for all can be ensured only if urban land is in ample supply.*

• *The Public Works Proposition: As cities expand, the necessary land for public streets, public infrastructure networks, and public open spaces must be secured in advance of development.*

Until Angel's paradigm gains traction among urban planners, the simplest policy, for now, is for urban planners to "tear down the wall" or at least major portions of it and let metro regions grow where land is cheap. Florida did this in 2011 (or, more accurately, the state removed the requirement that cities had to implement these policies). We need to go much further, and we need to do so across the nation, particularly near the Northeast and Pacific Coasts.

Affordability Trigger

We should also establish the general principle: if an urban area has an affordability index of 3.0 or higher, urban planners should modify their plans to enable affordable housing construction on the outskirts of the metro region where land is cheap. Even just eliminating one-quarter of the green belt to give cities growing room would make a huge difference in the long run.

We need to let housing markets work on the outskirts of metro areas where land is cheap. While some might be horrified by the idea of promoting "sprawl," it is unavoidable if we want to keep housing affordable.

We Need to Rethink Zoning and Building Codes

Shlomo Angel primarily researches high-level urban design and the negative effects of urban containment zones. We also need to focus on the lower level of individual plots of land. This brings us to the world of zoning and building codes.

Our current paradigm of zoning and building codes were designed by an earlier generation of urban designers who believed that quality of life can be improved by separating incompatible land uses from each other. Ironically, these urban designers were an earlier generation of progressives whose ideas are now roundly rejected by the newest round of progressive urban designers.

Typically, zoning segregates residential, commercial, industrial and retail activities from each other. Residential zones also typically define lot sizes and height limits, which have a major impact on density. Typical zoning rules also include parking requirements, soil quality, shapes of lots, the number of unrelated people who share the same home, and a myriad of other restrictions (Fischel).

Ordinances cannot mention the income, ethnicity, or race of occupants, but they can mention age to allow for retirement communities. Many communities abuse the original intent of these restrictions by minimizing the number of schoolchildren to stop local housing construction (Fischel).

Building codes also prescribe certain regulations regarding materials and procedures to be used in new structures. These regulations include material for water and sewage pipes, insulation standards, fireproofing and sprinklers. While these regulations add to the cost of housing construction, those costs seem to be modest in comparison to zoning (Fischel).

When done in a limited way, zoning and building codes make complete sense. Few people would want to buy a house, only to have a large-scale industrial plant or mining operation as a next door neighbor just a few years later. The plant would probably ruin one's quality of life while also ruining the property values making it difficult to sell. We also do not want to create incentives for builders to use shoddy materials that save a few dollars, but then force the owners to pay for expensive rebuilds afterwards. And few people want to live on land without access to open space, transportation rights-of-way, schools and other public buildings.

The New Urbanist planning movement advocates mixed-use zoning, where residential, retail, and commercial buildings are all allowed on the same plot of land. In many cases, this would mean that all three types of land use would be spread vertically throughout a single building. Such a type of land use is common in Europe, with retail shops on the ground floor, commercial offices on lower floors and residential housing on the middle and upper floors. I see no reason why this should not be allowed throughout a metro area.

The prime goal of zoning and building codes should be:

1. Affordable housing, as measured in cost per square foot on the open market without public subsidies.

2. Cost-effective construction standards that minimize the total cost of ownership, including both the construction cost and long-term maintenance and energy costs.

3. Cost-effective safety and health standards based on the most common and most dangerous hazards in the local region: fire, floods, hurricanes, tornados, and lead or mercury poisoning. Since these hazards vary greatly by region, this is likely to lead to great regional variations in regulations.

4. Reasonable access to ground transportation, open spaces, and public buildings.

I believe that our current system has strayed from these fundamental goals, particularly the first. Building mobile homes, renting out rooms within a private residence, establishing businesses within a private residence, and building detached or attached AUDs (Accessory Dwelling Units) should all be encouraged. Landowners should also be able to build duplexes, small apartments, or condominium complexes on land that is currently zoned for single-family residences. In many localities, however, these desirable practices are illegal.

Environmental Impact Is Secondary

Since the 1960s, state and federal governments have adopted a myriad of environmental regulations to protect wild habitats and the plants and animals that live on that land. Many of these regulations have been successful, but we need to factor in housing affordability first. Far too often, environmental regulations are used as a means to hold up vital housing construction.

Required environmental impact statements make sense in rural or wild areas that are far from metro areas, particularly for large-scale industrial, timber, or mining operations. Near metro areas, however, the priority should be keeping housing affordable.

Local governments should instead set aside open spaces in sensitive local habitat so that they can be used for both outdoor recreation and wild habitat protection. It is important, however, that open spaces and wild spaces do not completely or mostly encircle entire metro areas.

Nor should environmental impact statements be able to hold up the building of residences in or near a metro area. If a metro area has unaffordable housing, then local, state, and federal governments should favor housing construction, not hold it up. If the area already has large-scale housing nearby, then we have already drastically changed the natural environment.

A Typical House

Let me give an example with which I am intimately familiar. My house is a two-story single-family residence consisting of 2,430 square feet. It includes 3 bedrooms and 3 bathrooms plus an oversized two-car garage. Those statistics make my house almost exactly the average size of new homes built in the United States.

My house is located in a relatively new housing development on the outskirts of my metro area, so the purchase price was much more affordable than other houses of a similar size. My lot is just over 7,000 square feet, while the footprint of the house is only 1,660 square feet of land (or 23% of the total plot). I am pretty confident that all but the wealthiest Americans would consider it a "nice house." Most young families would be ecstatic to be able to afford to purchase such a house.

Now, some urban designers may insist that such a big house on the outskirts of the suburbs is a clear example of sprawl. If we are trying to reduce the impact of housing on wild habitat, however, we should be concerned primarily with the size of the lot, not the size of the house.

So to be more environmentally sensitive, let's shrink the lot down to 5,000 square feet (or 33% of the total plot). By shifting the house forward on the lot, you can still have a nice backyard, which most American families want.

One might argue that my plot of land is a bit too large or a bit too small, but this is exactly the type of housing that we should be building at scale on the outskirts of metro areas. Of course, any good master plan should also mix in denser duplexes and small apartment complexes to increase affordability, but urban designers should do so because of customer demand, not to conform to an ideal of fighting density.

Just as in my housing development, any good urban design should mix open spaces, public buildings, as well as access to streets, arterials, and highways into the plan. When done at scale in every metro area that is seeing population growth or experiencing a problem of housing unaffordability, we could at the very least keep housing prices from rising faster than incomes. Over the long run, we could even make housing more affordable.

Unfortunately, with current land use regulations, we cannot possibly develop at the necessary rate.

Geographical Mobility

I will delve into this issue in much more detail in future books in this series, but geographical mobility is a key weapon against unaffordable housing. Being blessed with a huge geographical footprint, the United States has hundreds of metropolitan areas. Many of them have relatively affordable housing.

In most of the rest of the Western world, there is nowhere to migrate to, as all major cities within those countries have the same problem. This is unacceptable for the many different reasons that I mentioned previously.

In the short term, moving to another metro area with affordable housing is the preferred solution. Already there is a big trend in the United States of young, poor and working-class people migrating to different cities to seek more affordable housing.

Urban containment zones lead to unsustainable housing price increases, so eventually the policy must come to an end. We need to find better options that allow the building of affordable houses in what are now protected green belts.

Working from Home

Another major trend that will both help and hurt housing affordability is working from home. Before Covid-19, working from home was relatively rare. Most businesses actively discouraged their employees from working from home. Many had strong rules against it. Employees who worked from home typically had a long tenure at their company and had earned the respect of their employer.

Suddenly, with the Covid lockdowns of 2020, that all changed. Particularly in the sectors of digital technology and finance, working from home suddenly became the standard. While many employers are still eager to return to all employees working in one building, many employees want working from home to remain the norm. It is not clear how this will all work out in the long run, but I seriously doubt that working from home will now return to the low pre-Covid levels.

Because working from home is becoming a new norm, many employees who work for companies based in the major metropolitan areas on the Pacific Coast and the Northeast are moving to areas with more affordable housing. The financial incentive to sell their overvalued house, and then purchase a larger and cheaper house elsewhere is just too enticing for older workers. The financial incentive for younger employees to own a house at all is even more enticing. Making this trend even stronger is the pending retirement of Baby Boomers, who also want to retire to an area with a more affordable cost of living.

If this trend continues, they will probably push housing costs down in the most expensive metro areas, while driving housing costs up in the destination cities. While the housing affordability crisis has until now been largely restricted to about a dozen metro areas, it is now expanding much further.

It is vital that these newly growing metro areas do not repeat the same mistakes that the metro areas of the Pacific Coast and the Northeast did. They must avoid implementing policies that will make their housing unaffordable in the long run.

Land Value Tax

We also need to change the incentive structure of local landowners.

In the late 19th Century, Henry George was one of the most influential men in America. His political views were what appear today to be a bizarre blend of left-wing radicalism and right-wing libertarianism. George believed that industrial progress and capitalism are good things, but the benefits of that progress were overwhelmingly going to landowners who contributed little to economic growth. We seem to be in a very similar situation today.

To solve the problem, Henry George advocated a land value tax. A land value tax is similar to a property tax, except that it only taxes the value of the land. Land value taxes do not tax the value of any buildings on that land. The logic behind George's proposal is that landowners did not create the land, but they did create the buildings on that land. George believed that we should not tax productive assets created by human beings, only land created by God.

While a property tax seems similar to a land value tax, it creates radically different incentives for landowners in or near metro areas. Currently, a landowner has a strong incentive to hold onto empty plots of land as long as possible to get the maximum possible amount of money at the point of sale. They can do this because their property taxes are relatively low.

The land value tax, however, gives landowners a strong incentive to develop or sell their empty plots of land. If landowners decide to lease their land, they have the incentive to develop the land as much as possible to maximize their returns. The more the development benefits society, the more valuable the land becomes, so the incentives of the landowner are aligned with societal interests.

What is even better is that increasing the value of that single plot of land will also increase the value of the surrounding land. So, if a metro area has a high-value-added export industry that creates wealth for the city, landowners will have a strong incentive for building the infrastructure to house workers for that industry and others. This will increase the value of the land and the taxes raised from that land.

In the *Decentralizing Political Power* chapter, I made the case for radical decentralization of political power from federal government to the state governments and the creation of new states. If this were implemented, this would require a massive new funding source for states to fund programs that are currently being run by the federal government.

I believe that this new tax should be a land value tax. While most taxes directly or indirectly undermine progress by taxing productive wealth or income, the land value tax creates incentives to build infrastructure that helps to create progress. This makes a land value tax far superior to property taxes, sales taxes, state income taxes, and state corporate taxes.

Ideally states would abolish all their state and local taxes, except for user fees, and replace them with one, simple land value tax. Less radical would be to replace current property taxes with land value taxes that raise a similar amount of revenue.

An even much more targeted strategy would be to replace the current property tax with a land value tax in states and metro areas that have an Affordability Index of over 4. This would mainly be in states in the Northeast and Pacific coast. Implementing a land value tax would not immediately lower housing prices, but it would give a strong incentive for landowners to construct some sort of housing on their land.

There are good reasons for liberal Democrats to favor a land value tax. They want a progressive tax system that taxes high-income earners at a higher rate than either the middle class or the poor. They also want to tax wealth.

Most proposed wealth taxes are completely unworkable because most wealth is so mobile. A sizable wealth tax would only drive capital out of an area, causing the economy serious damage. Land, however, is a unique source of wealth that is not mobile. And the total value of land is highly concentrated.

There are also good reasons for conservative Republicans to favor a land value tax. Republicans have long wanted to decrease or eliminate income taxes, property taxes, corporate taxes, and sales taxes. They are also opposed to taxing the kinds of wealth and income that generate economic growth. Land value taxes give them an option to do so.

Republicans might also enjoy the fact that the increased tax bill would be largely paid by property owners in the wealthy neighborhoods of metro areas in the Northeast and Pacific coast, all of which are liberal strongholds. Rural and metro areas in the Midwest and South would see little change in their tax rates. If liberals want to increase taxes, conservatives might say, let them pay the bill themselves.

In general, there is a pretty close association between geographical areas that want a more expansive welfare state and those areas that have over-priced land. It makes sense to tax that land to pay for these expansive social programs. Land value taxes in other geographical areas would generate fewer revenues, but those areas also tend to have less of a desire to tax and spend in the first place.

I believe that the combination of a land value tax, the abolition of urban containment zones, and a radical streamlining of zoning and building codes would have a profound effect on land usage in and near major metro areas. Landowners with empty lots, lightly developed or agricultural land would have a strong incentive to develop it. And they would have a strong incentive to choose the types of development that are most valued by society. In particular, empty lots on the outskirts of metro areas would be rapidly developed.

Granted, it will take a long time for the price of land to fall enough so that housing becomes affordable in the major metro areas in the Northeast and Pacific Coast. However, in combination with domestic migration to more affordable cities, particularly by youths, we can mitigate the problem quickly and bend the housing curve to greater affordability.

A New Homestead Act

Even with all of the proposals mentioned earlier, this may not lead to affordable housing being constructed in enough volume to meet the needs of young people. Government policies are difficult to change, and housing construction takes long periods. Unless the land value tax is implemented quickly, which is unlikely, landowners will have the incentive to wait out housing inflation so that they can make more profits at a later date.

To radically boost home construction, we may need a new Homestead Act. The Homestead Act was passed in 1862 by Abraham Lincoln and the Republican party to encourage westward expansion. It was one of the most important Congressional acts in American history. The Homestead Act divided western lands owned by the federal government into 160-acre plots and made them subject to sale for only $10 as long as the owner lived on that land for 5 years and developed it into a viable home or farm.

While virtually all federal land in the Midwest has been sold off, huge tracts of federal land remain. Where the geography allows and where there is no unique wild habitat, the federal government should seriously think about founding new cities for settlement. This may seem unusual in the 21st Century, but it is a time-honored American tradition.

Because federal lands are largely in the Mountain West, that is where the new cities should be sited. Fortunately, the Mountain West has seen a massive increase in domestic migration from the unaffordable cities on the Pacific coast. Arizona, Nevada, Idaho, Utah, and Colorado are already some of the fastest-growing states in the Union.

In line with the original Homestead Act, the new act should enable people who could not otherwise afford land to purchase it for a reasonable price. The federal government should subdivide land into small parcels, just large enough for a single-family residence or duplexes. All purchasers of that land must:

1. Be an American citizen.

2. Have never owned a house previously.

3. Pay $10,000 for the land in equal payments over the next 5 years (or $166 per month) to the federal government.

4. Promise to pay for the construction of some sort of permanent habitation on their land within the next 5 years. Construction costs can be paid for in the form of a traditional mortgage.

5. Physically live in that permanent habitation for at least 5 years after the construction is complete.

6. Not sell the land to another party until after they have resided on that land for the full 5-year residence period.

7. Not own another house while residing on the land.

An overall urban design in line with Shlomo Angel's guidelines could be developed for each Homestead city. While some of the lands would be zoned for transportation corridors, open spaces, industry, and denser urban centers, the bulk of the land could be sold in 5000-square-foot plots.

An initial trial run of the concept could involve selling a large amount of the federal land that surrounds the existing metro area of Las Vegas. As far as I know, Las Vegas is the largest metro area in America that is largely surrounded by federal land. The boom-bust nature of the Las Vegas real estate market due to it being a tourist city makes this a little tricky, but it seems to be the best location to start.

If the Las Vegas experiment works well, then actual Homestead cities could be founded elsewhere. The exact location of the Homestead cities would be dependent on plenty of water, relatively flat ground for construction, and access to interstate highways.

To focus resources and limit the chance of financial boondoggles, the federal government should only establish one Homestead city at a time. Federal lands along the route of Interstate 80 in Nevada would make a good location to start, as it is the biggest single transportation corridor in the region. This land is overwhelmingly sparsely populated range land with little vital environmentally-sensitive habitat. The key constraint would be water, but the area does have large underground aquifers.

The future growth of these new urban areas would suffer from "the chicken or the egg" problem. People would not want to live in these new cities without jobs and basic amenities. Businesses would not want to expand to the area without a strong local market and a reliable pool of labor.

To encourage private investment, businesses, employers, construction companies and residents should be completely exempted from federal taxes and all but the most essential federal regulations for a period of time. This would effectively create opportunity zones like those that proved so successful in China and other developing nations. Once a city has built its key urban infrastructure, has a solid population base, and is financially sustainable, then a new Homestead city could be founded along the same Interstate 80 corridor.

With a large portion of American employees working from home, it would not be necessary for large businesses to relocate to the metro to create initial employment opportunities. Of course, there would still need to be a substantial number of workers to construct water, sanitation, ground transportation, airports, electrical, and gas infrastructures. Perhaps any worker that agrees to work for five years on construction sites in a Homestead city would be allowed to purchase their own plot of land. All of this construction of infrastructure would take time, but, with the incentive of cheap land and no taxes, the new cities would probably grow rapidly once the design had been completed.

Owners could choose to pay for the construction costs for any type of permanent structure on their plots of land: single-family residences, duplexes, AUDs, or mobile homes. They could also be allowed construct retail and commercial space on the land, as long as they maintained their primary residence on the land. Most likely, owners would hire professional construction companies to do the actual construction.

One of the great benefits of my Homestead city proposal is that it would not cost the federal government any money (just like the original

Homestead Act). The system would be self-financing by settlers and private businesses that seek to profit from new markets.

Focus on Results

Key metrics for measuring the success of housing policies should be (all costs should be indexed for inflation and not include government subsidies):

- National home affordability (median cost of a house /median family income)
- Home affordability for each metro area
- National housing units under construction per capita
- Housing units under construction per capita for each metro area
- Time necessary to acquire housing construction permits
- National construction cost per housing unit ($/square foot)
- Construction cost per housing unit for each metro area
- Percent of renters who say that they want to purchase a house but cannot afford to do so
- Percent of adult children living with parents who say that they want to purchase a house but cannot afford to do so
- Percent of domestic migrants who give housing costs as a major reason for relocation.

Conclusion

To promote progress and upward mobility, we should embrace a radical increase in new housing construction. This construction should take place mainly on the outskirts of existing metro areas where land is cheap, but also in new Homestead cities founded by the federal government. To encourage landowners to develop their land, we should replace existing property taxes with a land value tax.

TECHNOLOGICAL INNOVATION

How Progress Works:

Technological innovation. This includes radical innovations such as the railroad, electrical grid, computers, and the internet, as well as the ongoing incremental improvement and differentiation of thousands of other existing technologies.

Once the Five Keys to Progress come into existence in a society, the rate of technological innovation in that society increases. This technological innovation is the immediate driving force in material progress. Without technological innovation, material progress is impossible to imagine.

Today there is a crucial discussion on whether or not the rate of technological innovation is slowing down. Some researchers make the credible case that the rate of innovation was actually faster a century ago than it is today (Cowen).

Starting around the year 1867 until about 1914, there were an enormous number of critical technological and organizational innovations. The breakthrough innovations of the period include:

• Energy: internal combustion engine, dynamos, generators, transformers, steam turbines, electric motors, dynamos, transformers, generators, steam turbines, pipelines, hydro-electric dams and the electrical grid.

• Agriculture: mechanized tractors and synthetic nitrogen

fertilizer.

- Materials: cheap steel, cheap paper, reinforced concrete, and aluminum.
- Transportation: the automobile, trucks, and airplanes.
- Communication: telegraph, phonograph, photography, radio, movies, linotype, typewriters.
- Housing: electric lights, electric appliances, refrigeration, air conditioning, elevators and skyscrapers.
- Organizations: the modern corporation.

And this list is just a snapshot of the most important innovations during this period. Many smaller and lesser known technologies were also invented (Smil 2005).

These innovations were so fundamental in nature and so numerous that it took the United States, Europe and Japan over a century to fully exploit them in the marketplace. Even today, major corporations are still making incremental improvements to many of these technologies.

With the exception of the domains of digital, medical and genetic technology, the vast bulk of subsequent innovations have effectively been spin-offs or improvements on the inventions made between 1867 and 1914. While the digital world is populated by techno-enthusiasts, the rest of us still live in the world of atoms. And the bulk of the technologies that were invented to manipulate those atoms stem directly or indirectly from the innovations made between 1867 and 1914.

So does that mean that we have picked all the low-hanging fruit and we are doomed to slow technological innovation and economic growth going forward?

I do not believe so.

While it is true that the period between 1867 and 1914 saw an unprecedented number of transformative innovations that may never be repeated, technological innovation is still rapid and ongoing. Among the technological breakthroughs in the century following 1914 have been gas turbines, jet engines, rockets, plastics, container ships and ports, oil tankers, robots, nuclear energy, television, transistors, satellites, space probes, computers, mobile phones, the internet, genetic engineering, antibiotics, and x-ray imaging. While this list is not quite as impressive as the previous one, it is hardly testament to technological stagnation.

Rather than debating whether innovation is slowing or not, I think the real question that we should be asking is: how can we implement policies and practices that improve the rate of technological innovation?

Funding for Science

One of the most popular strategies for improving the rate of technological innovation is funding scientific research. This strategy has a very old pedigree going all the way back to Francis Bacon, the English philosopher and statesman who lived from 1561 to 1626; he is known by many historians as the founder of the scientific method.

Since Francis Bacon, the dominant paradigm for understanding technological innovation has been what one might call the "linear model." The line of reasoning is that government-funded academic research leads to:

1. Breakthroughs in Basic science, which leads to:
2. Breakthroughs in Applied science, which leads to:
3. Breakthroughs in Technological innovation, which leads to:
4. Economic growth

To be clear on terminology, Basic science is the pursuit of knowledge without any specific desire to apply that knowledge to solve a specific problem. An example would be exploring Pluto, documenting the mating habits of lemurs or investigating the origins of the Universe. Basic science is knowledge for its own sake.

Applied science is where scientists who are extremely knowledgeable in a specific domain of science apply that knowledge to solving a specific problem. Typically, this solution does not include technological innovation (at least, not immediately).

A real-world example of Applied science would be scientists studying Asian bees, an invasive species which have recently been detected in Australia. The scientists want to learn about their mating and feeding habits in order to understand why they are driving out native bees. This might give governments insights on how to fight back against the invasive species.

Obviously, to conduct their work, these scientists need to be very knowledgeable about insects, particularly bees, and their interactions with the natural environments within Australia. Because there is no way to make a profit solving this problem, private industry has no interest in getting involved. Only government or non-profits could provide the funding to undertake this research project.

The third step of the linear model is when the technological innovation is turned into a viable product that can be used at scale to solve a problem. This is where the linear model ties into promoting long-term economic growth.

Technological innovation involves the combination of multiple existing technologies to create a new technology that is advantageous in some way. Here we leave the world of science and enter the world of engineering and entrepreneurship. Because technological innovation leads directly to products that can potentially be sold to customers at scale, private industry has a vested incentive in funding these type of projects.

As I said earlier, technological innovation is the most immediate driving force of progress and economic growth. So I agree with the second half of the linear model. I also have no doubt that government funding of Basic science and Applied science can promote the advancement of scientific knowledge. So I also agree with the first half of the linear model. The problem with the theory is with the supposedly tight linkage between science and technological innovation.

I have worked in the technology sector for over 20 years. During that time I interacted with a wide range of experts in the field of business, technology, customer service and production. Most of my work has been in the digital technology sector, but I have also worked for hardware companies.

During that time, the subject of new scientific knowledge has never come up. In my experience engineers, who do the bulk of technological innovation, are no more informed about science than a typical college graduate. Nor do they spend any significant time keeping abreast of scientific developments. While I have no doubt that it would be different in the fields of medicine, materials or chemicals, I do not think my experience has been unusual.

The worlds of business/technology and science interact very little with each other. While it is true that entrepreneurs and engineers rely on scientific knowledge, it is overwhelmingly scientific knowledge that has been in existence for decades, not recent discoveries. For this reason, I am skeptical that increasing funding for scientific research, whether basic or applied would have much effect on technological innovation, economic growth or progress.

In reality, Basic science, Applied science and engineering are three separate worlds that rarely interact with each other. Progress within the field of technology comes from recombination of existing technologies, not breakthroughs in science. For much the same reason as mentioned above, I do not like the term STEM (Science, Technology, Engineering and Math), because it lumps together two or three very different domains.

The key domains of knowledge and skills that promote progress are technology, engineering, entrepreneurship and venture capital. The worlds of science and mathematics are important, but separate domains, which have far less impact on progress.

The greatest cross-fertilization among Basic science, Applied science and technology goes in the opposite direction; technological innovations make scientific research more productive. Where would science be without the inventions of the telescope, microscope, books, the printing press, computers, and the internet? Yes, each one of those inventions relied on exploiting some phenomena that was discovered by scientists, but none of them followed hot on the heels of new scientific discoveries. They all came from the tinkering of craftsmen, engineers and entrepreneurs.

Rather than being a cause of progress, scientific learning is one of the many *results* of progress. Most importantly, long-term economic growth gives societies the resources to fund scientific inquiry even when it has no tangible economic benefits. Scientific knowledge is just one more reason why we should be wanting to promote progress in the first place.

Let me be clear. I am not arguing that we should cut government funding for Basic science or Applied science. Both are an inherent good, and the private sector is unlikely to fund this domain for the reasons that I listed above. Nor am I arguing that scientific breakthroughs never lead to technological innovation. I am arguing that government funding of scientific research is not a cost-effective means for promoting technological innovation or promoting progress.

My sense (and I must admit that I have little to back this up) is that scientific knowledge has already expanded far beyond what engineers can possibly develop into technologies for many decades, perhaps even centuries. Even if there was not a single scientific breakthrough going forward, engineers and entrepreneurs would have plenty of new technologies to innovate for the foreseeable future.

I would add that the extent to which government does promote scientific research, it should be towards fixing a specific problem, as in my earlier example with Australian bees. Regardless of whether the resulting solution involves innovating a new technology, Applied science can help to fix societal problems. For this reason, government funding still seems appropriate.

Private-Sector Innovation

First, we should acknowledge that the vast majority of technological and organizational innovation takes place in the private sector. Large companies are experts at squeezing every last bit of innovation from established technologies within their market. Entrepreneurs establish new companies that invent new technologies and business models that are missed by larger, more established companies.

We should also acknowledge the fact that government policies have typically done more to stifle innovation than foster it. I have discussed the need to decentralize and deregulate elsewhere in this book, so I will not dwell on it here. Regulations, even when they are initially cost-effective, become outmoded very quickly in the face of technological innovation.

For these reasons, I believe that government policies to promote technological innovation should focus on leveraging the power of both the private-sector and society in general to do the heavy lifting. In most cases, private industry is already on the path to do so, so government should stay out of the way. In other cases, private industry does not have the incentive to take on the problem, so government should change the financial incentives so that private actors take on the challenge.

The Precautionary Principle

Supporters of strict government regulations promote the concept of the Precautionary Principle. Supporters of this principle correctly point out that we do not fully understand the implications of new technologies, so we should proceed with caution. They effectively argue in favor of "when in doubt, regulate." This principle has been particularly influential in the European Union.

While the logic of this argument makes some sense, I would argue that the Precautionary Principle should lead us in the opposite direction. The Precautionary Principle as currently interpreted assumes that we do not know if a new technology is good for society, but that we do know that new government regulation is. In reality, we are just as unsure about the relative benefits of both new technologies and new regulations.

I would argue that the overall track record of technological innovation is overwhelmingly positive. There are very few technologies for which we would better off as a society if they had never existed. Nuclear weapons might be one example that many would point to, but nuclear weapons also played a key role in averting World War III during the Cold War.

More to the point, the track record of government regulation is nowhere near as positive as the track record of technological innovation. While there are clearly some important regulations that have benefitted society, it is hard to argue that the overall results of government regulation are anything like as positive as technological innovation. The history of government regulations stifling innovation and driving up costs is so clear and broad-reaching that we should not implement regulations until we have solid evidence that the regulations' benefits outweigh the costs.

I would argue that the correct interpretation of the Precautionary Principle for regulations should be: "when in doubt, do not regulate."

Alternative Strategies

Governments have a wide variety of strategies through which they can stimulate desired innovation:
1. Direct government research and development
2. Tax exemptions for private-sector research and development
3. Funding of university research
4. Purchasing large amounts of a new technology from the private sector
5. Regulations and mandates⊠

For the sake of brevity, I do not want to go into details on all of these strategies. I will, however, go into one key weakness that all of them share.

Centralization of Funding

All of the innovation strategies that I mentioned above involve a centralized government directly or indirectly funding research and development. They all involve elected officials or policy experts choosing which projects to fund. This inevitably means that other potential solutions are starved for funding.

The problem is that, when technology does not exist, it is very difficult to know which ideas can lead to useful technologies and which ideas will lead to dead-ends. We need a method for funding technological innovation that does not pick potential winners up front and hope that, with the proper funding. they can be turned into cost-effective solutions. We need a funding solution that only spends taxpayers' money when the problem is solved. Fortunately, there is such a method.

Innovation Prizes

I believe that the most cost-effective means of stimulating socially-desirable innovation is via innovation prizes. An innovation prize is where an institution promises to pay a cash prize for any individual or group of individuals who solve a specific problem.

Innovation prizes have a long, but not so famous, history. One of most famous examples was the Longitude Prize in 18th Century Britain. To promote the power of both the Royal Navy and merchant shipping, Parliament offered a prize of £10 million to the first team who offered a practical method for the precise determination of a ship's longitude at sea (Sobel).

A more recent example of an innovation prize has been XPRIZE Foundation, which has offered substantial prizes for radical breakthrough innovations that benefit humanity. XPRIZE started in the field of space exploration and has subsequently branched off into the fields of super-efficient vehicles, oil clean-up, health care sensing, ocean acidification, education, literacy and pandemic mitigation.

Ideally, an innovation prize:

1.   Identifies an important problem that the government or private sector is not solving or cannot solve.

2.   Sets a specific amount for the prize to be awarded in the future.

3.   Establishes very specific, transparent and verifiable metrics for earning the prize.

4.   Is open to as broad an audience as possible.

Advantages of Innovation Prizes

Innovation prizes have many advantages over the other strategies that I mentioned earlier. The single biggest advantage is that, if the proposed solution does not meet the criteria, innovation prizes cost the taxpayers almost no money. Most of the other strategies require the government to spend significant amounts of money or defer on raised revenue regardless of result. This alone is a huge advantage that prizes have over all other strategies.

Innovation prizes are the perfect method for leveraging the efforts of a constellation of individuals, start-ups and established companies. Rather than creating a large centralized bureaucracy to solve a problem, prizes promote a large number of small-scale experiments by different organizations.

In other words, just like progress itself, prizes work on evolutionary principles. Prizes encourage decentralized experimentation and allow the best solution to survive. If all attempts fail, then no money is lost, but if one succeeds, it will be an important step forward for society.

Innovation prizes also offer the advantage of focusing on outputs (i.e. results), rather than inputs (i.e. how those results are achieved). All of the other strategies for promoting innovation focus on inputs. Innovation prizes, when correctly designed, focus exclusively on outputs. And it is outputs that matter, because that is what affects society.

Because innovation is focused on the unknown, it is not clear how a problem should be solved. There are typically many potential pathways to doing so, and all institutions and individuals have different ideas as to which pathway is preferred.

An incorrect decision on the best pathway early in a project is likely to lead to a dead end. And it may not be clear that a dead end has been hit until after an organization invests millions or even billions of dollars. Ideally, governments should encourage all of those potential pathways to be fully explored, while only rewarding the groups that followed the correct path.

Most government subsidies for technological innovation favor one or a small number of established institutions to the exclusion of the rest of society. Prizes enable a single individual or a small informal group to compete on equal terms with giant established institutions. This dramatically increases the potential number of proposed solutions. The greater the number and the wider the diversity of solutions, the more likely that the problem will be solved.

Innovation prizes also encourage experts in completely different domains to get involved. While experts in a certain domain often have a knowledge advantage, that advantage is often undone by a group-think mentality. Often the best solutions come from applying slight variations on tested solutions in one domain into a different domain. Prizes make that much more likely.

Prizes also encourage outsiders and iconoclasts to get involved. While scorned by experts, these people often offer simple solutions that are missed by experts who are so immersed in their field that they get tunnel vision.

Prizes encourage individuals with contrarian ideas within established institutions to quit, form their own institution and test their ideas in the field. Rather than being stymied by bureaucratic politics, prizes can enable iconoclasts to put their potentially revolutionary ideas into practice.

Prizes do not require the government to found new institutions and ramp up the hiring of experts. One of the major problems of direct government research projects is that they require established institutions and expensive, long-term funding streams. The method also requires hiring a large number of experts in their domain. If those institutions already exist, this is less of a problem, but funding is always a problem. And remember that all this funding is required, even if the institution fails to achieve its goals.

Prizes also have zero costs in the short run, so it is possible for the government to create a large number of prizes very quickly. The new prize system would then compete with already-existing government research institutes. If the prizes yield better results than existing models, then funding could shift away from government research institutes to more prizes. If the prizes fail to produce results, then there is no financial loss.

For all of the reasons above, innovation prizes should become the default method through which the government and other institutions promote technological innovation. If we take advantage of the unique benefits of innovation prizes, we can also leverage in other institutions that have already contributed heavily to innovation.

Innovation prizes also have some disadvantages. One of the biggest is that they do not provide funding for individuals and organizations while they are working to solve the problem. For governments and society in general, this is a huge advantage, but for those who are trying to solve the problem, it is a huge disadvantage.

Innovation prizes encourage individuals and organizations to devote years of their lives and vast sums of money to solving a problem knowing full well that they will most likely fail. They might fail because the problem is unsolvable with current technology, or they might fail because some other group can implement a better solution.

For innovation prizes to work, we need a set of mediating organizations between the prize itself and the people who work to solve the problem. This set of institutions would provide funding for those individuals and organizations before they actually win the prize. Presumably they would do so in return for a share of the prize. Given that so many different groups would be trying to solve the problem, this would be a high-risk, high-reward financial industry.

We have a word for that: venture capital.

Expanding Venture Capital

Venture capital is a critical financial institution that specializes in high-risk, high-reward loans to entrepreneurs. As any entrepreneur knows, raising capital is one of the key challenges to scaling up a new business.

With the right amount of funding, "crazy ideas" can grow into major sectors of the future economy.

Venture capitalists in the private sector are experts at vetting new, untested ideas and deciding which ones should be funded. The field is particularly active in the digital technology industry.

Today, the single greatest geographical concentration of venture capital firms is on Sand Hill Road in Menlo Park, California. Menlo Park is on the edge of Silicon Valley, the heartland of the digital technology industry. Sequoia Capital, Kleiner Perkins, Andreessen Horowitz, Lightspeed, IVP, GCV and Greylock are just a few of the legendary venture capital firms concentrated in one very small geographical area.

Ironically, I lived most of my childhood just a few blocks away from the headquarters of all of these legendary venture capital firms, and this was just as they were getting started in the 1970s. Many of my relatives were indirectly involved in the early Silicon Valley technology sector. I have since followed up with more than 20 years in my own career in the field.

Venture capital is so critical to technological and organizational innovation, and innovation is so critical to material progress, that we should look for ways to grow the field to solve a broader range of problems. Such expertise deserves to have a broader impact on society.

My hope is that, once innovation prizes become a standard practice of governments, an entire new sector of venture capital will spring into being. Today venture capital is associated with digital technology because that is where investors have the best opportunity to make huge returns. But there is no inherent reason why venture capital should be restricted to that domain. With the right incentives, we could get venture capital to spread into entirely new domains.

Obviously, the amount of the prize and the total number of prizes will play an important role in determining whether venture capitalists find the potential pay-offs enticing. My guess is that current venture capitalists will stay away from innovation prizes, so they can focus on their current field of expertise. My hope is that a whole new generation of socially-conscious venture capitalists will found new institutions that focus largely on innovation prizes.

A new generation of venture capitalists would have a strong incentive to contact individuals and organizations who are attempting to win a specific innovation prize. They might even recruit individuals and institutions to start working on the problem. These venture capitalists would then use their skills to identify which individuals or groups stand the best chance of winning the prize. They could then offer them capital in exchange for a promised percentage of the prize earnings. Since the amount of the prize is known, this is a fairly easy calculation.

Crowd-Sourcing

It is also not too difficult to imagine something like Kickstarter springing up around innovation prizes. Kickstarter is a crowd-financing website where individuals or companies can list their proposed products and request donations to help them design and produce their ideas. Usually, people who donate larger amounts get something in return, such as the actual product when it is completed.

Something similar could emerge for innovation prizes. Anyone who is attempting to win a prize could create a page via which individuals could donate to the cause. Depending upon the desires of the individual, a donation might give them a small portion of the earnings. Or it might just give them the satisfaction of knowing that their money is going towards a good cause. The site might also include a way for venture capitalists to easily contact the individual.

Social Entrepreneurs

Because innovation prizes are focused on socially beneficial solutions, an entirely new type of person might get involved. When prizes are focused on solving important societal problems rather than just creating a new product, "do-gooders" get into the action. When people can combine technical expertise with a desire to change the world for the better, they can achieve impressive results.

The combination of bettering mankind and being able to earn lots of money is a potent combination. If dozens of innovation prizes in the amount of billions of dollars went public, this would attract a great deal of attention from people wanting to make money and also those who want to help humanity.

Between a large prize, an emerging venture capitalist sector and Kickstarter-like crowd-financing, it is not difficult to imagine a Silicon-Valley-like culture emerging around solving important social problems via innovation prizes. The more prizes, and the greater their amount, the more likely such a culture is to emerge.

There is absolutely no reason why innovation prizes should be restricted to the U.S. federal government. Foreign governments, state governments, local governments, non-profits and billionaire philanthropists could also get in on the action. They could either create separate prizes with different goals and criteria, or they could pool their resources together to increase the total amount of the prize.

Successful Prizes

It is important to note that many innovation prizes fail to achieve results. If implemented incorrectly, prizes might not achieve positive results that exceed their significant pay-out cost. Some of this is due to the prize itself, and other failures are due to the inherent riskiness of innovation. We can, however, increase the likelihood of a prize inspiring success by creating innovation prizes with the following characteristics:

1. The prize should be focused on an important problem that current market incentives are not able to solve in the desired timescale. Prizes should not be subsidizing normal private-sector research and development. Nor should they focus on trivial issues that few care about.

2. The goals of the prize should be relatively uncontroversial politically. If either party or substantial sections of American society

think achieving the goal is inherently bad, this will tend to undermine the political legitimacy of all prizes.

3. The amount of the prize should be substantial enough to motivate people, but not more than the actual benefits to society.

4. The criteria should be focused on the desired outcome, not how it is achieved or a certain technology or method. Ideally, the criteria should be about solving a problem and not a specific solution, though this can be hard to achieve in practice.

5. The criteria should be very specific, measurable and potentially achievable. This is probably the most important characteristic. The criteria must be very well designed.

6. The prize should be as available to as broad a demographic as possible. It should not be restricted to government agencies, established institutions or credentialed experts. Even supposed crackpots should be eligible. Earnings should also not be restricted to any one nation.

7. The prize and its criteria should be transparent to all of society on the internet. Ideally, the prize would also be widely advertised by media and social media.

8. The government should follow through on delivering the prize as stated in the criteria. Obviously, this is critical. If the government gets a reputation for reneging on its prizes, trust will collapse and so will the entire prize system.

Prize-generation process

Successful prizes are more likely to come out of a solid process. The prize-generation process should go something like this:

1. Individuals and groups identify a societal problem that currently does not have a profit incentive that enables the private sector to solve it. They pressure elected officials to establish a prize.

2. Elected officials negotiate amongst themselves for the overall amount of money that should be devoted to the prize.

3. Experts in the field both in the government, academia and non-profits recommend criteria that an innovation must meet or surpass.

4. The prize along with the amounts and criteria are published on one highly-visible government website.

5. Individuals, informal groups and formal institutions launch projects to earn the prize. Some may do so publicly to acquire financing, while others might do so quietly.

6. Government or independent third-party institutions validate the fact that the criteria have been fulfilled.

7. Once the criteria are met, the prize is paid out to the inventors.

8. The inventors then pass part of their earnings to venture capitalists and donors who helped them finance their efforts (if they agreed to do so beforehand).

9. The solution is then implemented at scale by either the inventor or an organization that has purchased the rights.

An Energy Prize

Since I wrote the *Energy Abundance* chapter, arguing that government should stimulate research into new energy technologies, I will focus on that domain here. A new energy source that is cheaper and denser than fossil fuels, that is widely available across the nation and the globe and also has little or no radiation, pollution or carbon emissions would be one of the greatest technological breakthroughs of the 21st Century.

Energy technologies are second only to food production technologies in their importance in promoting progress. A new abundant, secure, carbon-free energy source that is significantly cheaper than fossil fuels would fundamentally change the world for the better.

If such a technology existed, wealthy nations would receive a far better energy system than the one that currently exists. Both fossil fuels and renewable energy sources would become obsolete, once such a system could be widely rolled out.

Wealthy nations would no longer have to spend trillions to import fossil fuels. Carbon emissions and pollution would drop like a rock. It is difficult for me to conceive of innovation as profound as this for the next century.

A far superior source of energy would lower the cost of living and greatly boost economic growth, while having a positive impact on the natural environment. The new energy source would also create a new high-value-added industry to create jobs and exports.

If this energy source were far better than coal China, India, Indonesia and the rest of Asia would immediately stop building fossil fuel-burning power plants and purchase this new technology. In the long run, they would likely decommission all or most of their existing coal-burning power plants.

Poorer developing nations in Africa and Latin America could also build an energy infrastructure far more easily than with current technology. In the same way that mobile devices enabled these countries to avoid the enormous cost of building a landline infrastructure, the equivalent might happen in the energy sector.

Such an innovation would also be devastating to the authoritarian regimes of Iran, Saudi Arabia, Russia and other oil- and gas-exporting nations. Without huge export earnings from fossil fuels, those nations will be forced to reform their economic and political structures. More importantly, their regional influence would be seriously curtailed.

For this reason, I believe that the government should offer a $100 billion prize for the first individual or group who can design it and produce a working prototype. This may seem like a huge amount of money (and it is), but the amount is trivial in comparison to the trillions of dollars and Euros spent thus far on fossil fuels and Green energy systems.

More to the point, the benefits of such an energy technology to society would be hundreds of times greater. $100 billion, while a huge incentive, would be a bargain price for such a technology.

In order to win a prize, the individual or group must do all the following:

1. Must have design specs and a working prototype that is fully testable.

2. Must offer a total cost of operation per unit of energy that is significantly lower than coal, natural gas or petroleum. This total cost

should include the cost of construction, fuel, operations, maintenance and decommissioning.

3. Must output its energy in the form of electricity or be easily capable of being transformed into electricity, so it can be easily integrated into an electrical grid.

4. Must output energy as either a steady 24/7 stream for months at a time, or be capable of being fully modulated (i.e. the energy output can be cranked up or down) with little effort.

5. Must have a capacity factor of at least 80% (i.e. it can actually produce at least 80% of its theoretical output over the course of the year).

6. Must rely on materials that are widely available in North America and preferably the rest of world.

7. Must not be more land intensive (the total area of the plant) than a standard fossil fuel power plant.

8. Must produce little or no radiation, carbon emissions, pollutants or other known threats to human health and safety.

9. Must be capable of being manufactured or constructed at scale. Ideally, this would consist of a mass production plan.

10. Must be capable of being safely manufactured, transported and constructed in close proximity to major metropolitan areas.

This energy prize should not choose technologies, but I want to single out one with particular promise to illustrate the possibilities.

Nuclear fusion has the potential to revolutionize our future. It creates energy by fusing simple atoms together to create more complex atoms. The reaction creates very little radiation, no carbon dioxide, and no pollution. Most importantly, the net energy created far exceeds any current energy source, including fossil fuels and nuclear fission (the type of nuclear energy currently being produced).

One specific type of nuclear fusion is particularly promising: hydrogen-boron fusion. It creates energy by fusing hydrogen and boron (two very common elements) into lithium, and it creates electricity directly without the need for steam turbines. The lithium could then be used as a raw material for the construction of batteries.

Nuclear fusion is not in any way theoretical, as it relies on proven physical reactions. Nuclear fusion is the process that makes the sun work. There is no reason why it cannot be made to work on Planet Earth.

For decades, nuclear fusion seemed more like science fiction than science fact. However, in December 2022, scientists at Lawrence Livermore lab finally achieved net energy. They created an extremely short fusion reaction in a lab that generated about 50% more energy than was input into the system.

This is a major milestone in nuclear fusion research. It not only proves that we can create energy with nuclear fusion, but now we can constantly run experiments to make the reactions last longer and generate more net energy. The only problem is that we do not know if the technology can cost-effectively produce energy.

We have already seen that the wealthy nations have gone through two Energy Transitions and are currently in the middle of a third. Nuclear fusion might well be the Fourth Energy Transition that would be at least as important as the first three.

Current energy companies have no incentive to create such a transition. The research costs are too high and the pay-offs seem too remote, as they are possibly decades in the future. Meanwhile, governments are largely ignoring the possibilities because of their fixation on solar and wind.

The dominant government research program in the field, ITER Tokamak, has placed all its bets on a different type of fusion energy that is probably far more expensive. So far, the project has consumed over $14 billion of government funding, and the likelihood that it will produce energy that is cheaper than fossil fuels is very low. At the same time, governments around the world have funded trillions of dollars in renewable energy.

Meanwhile, a gaggle of small companies are building prototypes for other, more promising types of fusion technologies with little or no government funding. Many of them claim that they can produce energy far more cheaply than fossil fuels. That remains to be seen, but not following up on this possibility seems foolhardy.

A large prize would enable energy scientists to go in completely new directions that are currently impossible due to the centralized "put all your eggs in one basket" approach that is typical of government projects.

With the enactment of a $100 billion research prize, venture capitalists would come out of the woodwork to fund those companies and create new ones. If that is not enough money to provide strong incentives, we can increase the amount. The wonderful thing about prizes is that, **if they do not produce results, it does not cost the taxpayers any money.**

So what exactly is the downside?

To be clear, I do not predict a nuclear fusion breakthrough within the next 10 years or even 100 years. Many companies do, and I am optimistic that one will achieve a breakthrough, but it remains to be seen.

I do however predict that, with the right incentive structure, we can at least find out if nuclear fusion or some other energy technology is a potential replacement for fossil fuels within 20-30 years. With the proper funding, we can probably create a working prototype within a decade.

And nuclear fusion may not be the energy source that triggers the Fourth Energy Transition. Perhaps it is a fundamental breakthrough in solar, wind, geothermal or other renewable resource. Perhaps it is small modular nuclear fission reactors. Or perhaps it is an energy source that only a few supposed crackpots are currently dreaming about.

Geothermal energy, in particular, is a renewable energy source that has not been fully explored. For some reason, Greens are far less enthusiastic about geothermal energy than solar, wind and biomass.

Geothermal energy exploits intense underground heat caused by radioactive decay in the Earth's mantle. Current geothermal energy only exploits the very few geographical areas where heat plumes penetrate upward through the crust, so it is near the surface. Drilling deep into the mantle, however, may unlock massive amounts of renewable, high-capacity energy. A $100-billion innovation prize may create the economic incentive to fully exploit this vast energy resource.

Other Innovation Prizes

Once one starts thinking about scaling up innovation prizes, the true possibilities emerge. What about better insulation for walls, doors and windows, electric airplanes, or solar-powered cars?

Nor is there a reason not to expand the idea to solving difficult social problems. What about cures for mental illness or substance abuse, the best means to teach reading to children, low-cost housing for the homeless, using digital technologies to isolate non-violent criminals and parolees in their own homes rather than in prisons? These are just a few ideas that I came up with off the top of my head. There are thousands more problems that can potentially be solved by innovation prizes.

We have become so used to the idea that government needs to solve a problem directly that we ignore the possibilities of other sectors. The private sector is extremely good at solving problems, far better than government in most cases. Unfortunately, there are many domains where there is no profit incentive. Rather than give up on the private sector and assume that government can solve the problem itself, we should reformulate the problem. Innovation prizes would enable us to do that.

Focus on Results

Key metrics for measuring the success of technological innovation policies should be (all costs should be indexed for inflation):
- Estimated benefits to society per dollar of prize money
- Duration between prize being established and prize being awarded.

Conclusion

By leveraging the power of innovation prizes, we can increase the rate of technological innovations, particularly in the domains that are most able to bring great benefits for humanity. Energy, in particular, is a field where a breakthrough innovation might bring benefits for humanity as astounding as the original Industrial Revolution.

MERIT-BASED INSTITUTIONS

How Progress Works:

People learning new skills to support those technologies. Without these skills, technologies are not useful, a fact that is often forgotten.

The Importance of Skills

As I argued in the first book in this series, *From Poverty to Progress*, technological innovation is just one of the factors that cause a society to experience long-term material progress. Skills and organizations are also critical factors.

While biological organisms can survive and reproduce without human intervention (except for some domesticated plants and animals), technologies cannot exist without human intervention. Technology requires humans to possess highly specialized skills for it to survive and reproduce (by getting widely used by humans).

Even the simplest technology requires some amount of skill to use. In addition, conceiving of the technology, designing it, building it, and repairing it are important related skills. Until people possess these skills, a specific piece of technology cannot come into being; or, if it does, it would not last very long. It will certainly never spread far enough to become an important part of a society's technological suite.

The collective skill set of even the simplest Hunter-Gatherer band, while very simple compared with other types of human societies, dwarfs the skill set of any non-human animal. As a society acquires more complex technologies, its collective skill set increases even more rapidly. This is because each technology requires a host of related skills. The more complex the technology, the greater the number of required skills.

While the total skill set of a society has no upper limit, there is an upper limit on the number of skills that one person can acquire. Learning a skill requires large amounts of time to practice it, and time is finite.

Cesar Hidalgo has developed the concept of a "personbyte" to denote the total amount of knowledge and skills that one person can possess. This concept is important, because it shows that the only way for a society to increase the number of skills beyond a personbyte is for individuals to specialize in one skill or a small number of related skills. Fortunately, the more a person specializes in a skill, the greater the frequency of the repetitions and the more opportunity to get better at that skill. With an incentive to improve, and actionable feedback, humans can become extraordinarily good at one skill.

As the number and complexity of technologies accelerate, people need to specialize in a small number of skills. So technological innovation and progress fragment us into more specialized professions, each with clusters of related skills. But something more is required to knit these specialized workers into a team that can produce a technology or service.

The Importance of Social Organizations

That something more is a social organization. Social organizations have existed throughout human history. The family, bands, tribes, and nations are just some of the social organizations that humans have lived within. In modern times, social organizations have formalized into institutions, for example governments, corporations, labor unions, churches, militaries, non-profits, and many more.

For progress and technological innovation, corporations are the most important institution. Corporations knit together people with many different skills into one organization based on a business model designed to sell a small set of products or services to a specific customer base. Because each corporation has different technologies and different customer bases, each corporation evolves its own business model to succeed in that environment. Because customers have a limited amount of money, corporations are forced to compete with other corporations to survive.

In this way, a corporation, like all social organizations, is much like a biological organism. While biological organisms compete for energy and nutrients, corporations and other institutions compete for revenue.

To survive this competition for revenue, corporations must adopt technologies, employ people with skills appropriate to those technologies, and adopt processes that organize those people toward a common mission. Corporations that do this successfully will tend to acquire increased revenue. Those that fail to do so will tend to acquire less revenue. The worst will go bankrupt.

As technologies become increasingly complex, requiring a greater number of specialized skills, corporations and other institutions must also become more specialized and complex. Traditional societies have a relatively small suite of technology, so they require only a few small organizations. Modern societies, however, have an enormous suite of technologies. This requires a vast number of complex social organizations, each specialized in a narrow domain of technologies or services.

Importance of Merit-Based Decisions

For organizations to deliver the benefits of progress to the people, they must make hiring, firing, and promotion decisions based on merit. This ensures that the people with the skills most relevant to a job will be hired and gradually filter up the organization. Just as importantly, merit-based decisions give all employees and potential employees the incentive to keep learning new skills and improving the skills that they already have.

Skills relevant to success in a modern organization largely consist of the ability to understand and use technology, as well as "soft skills" that enable them to cooperate effectively with others in the organization. To fulfill its chosen method, it is vital for all organizations in society to make hiring, firing, and promotion based upon those two categories of skills.

Defining Merit

Before going further, I want to define what I mean by "merit." Unfortunately, the word has been somewhat conflated with the term "virtue" to imply that a person with merit is a more virtuous person than one with less merit. This meaning of merit implies a moral judgment about an individual.

I do not use merit in that sense. I would argue that merit is highly specialized to a specific domain, so that a person with a great deal of merit in one domain is very unlikely to have merit in other domains. These domains are typically very specialized occupations.

I use the term "merit" to mean having demonstrated an ability or accomplishment that is related to the decision at hand, typically hiring, firing, and promotion. In other words, merit is using a person's past results in a specific field to attempt to predict the likelihood that they will show similar results in a related field. In practice, this means using job experience, educational credentials, and test results for hiring, firing and promotion decisions.

A person can have a great deal of merit in one field and very little in most other fields. In practice, this is usually the case. As I mentioned, we live in a highly specialized world, in which few people are good at doing many different things.

For example, if I am looking for an electrician to wire my house, I am only interested in the qualifications that are directly related to that task. I might ask how many years the applicants have been working as an electrician, what type of jobs they have done that are similar to my house, and whether they are licensed contractors. I might also ask other electricians or construction workers if they know anyone who would be good for the job.

By hiring a specific electrician, I am not saying that this person is a better person than all the others. I just perceive them as the best person for that specific job at that time and location. In practice, of course, I will also ask how much they want to be paid and disqualify any excessively high bids. I might even accept a very low bid from a lesser candidate to save a few bucks, depending on the work I need performed.

I have been on both sides of the hiring process in digital technology. I have directed or assisted in looking for candidates, typically software engineers or designers, and I have applied and interviewed for positions on many occasions. My overall sense is that most job search processes are relatively merit-oriented, but that corporations focus more on avoiding hiring a bad candidate than on identifying the best candidate.

So if a person looking for a job is above average in qualifications, they will eventually find a job, but it will probably not be on the first attempt. In times of great demand, that person will be hired quickly, while in times of slow demand, it might take significantly longer. Merit-based decisions are about playing the odds wisely, not about getting the perfect results for each individual case.

Meritocracy

One of the greatest benefits of material progress has been the creation of the most meritocratic societies that have ever existed. Today, an individual's position in a society largely depends upon their skills and effort to deploy those skills over the long run.

A meritocratic society is one where the bulk of the decisions made by institutions for hiring, firing, and promotion is based on merit (as I defined "merit" above). In his book, The *Aristocracy of Talent*, Adrian Wooldridge states it well:

"A meritocratic society combines four qualities which are each in themselves admirable. First, it prides itself on the extent to which people can get ahead in life on the basis of their natural talents. Second, it tries to secure equality of opportunity by providing education for all. Third, it forbids discrimination on the basis of race and sex and other irrelevant characteristics. Fourth, it awards jobs through open competition rather than patronage and nepotism. Social mobility and meritocracy are the strawberries and cream of modern political thinking, and politicians can always earn applause by denouncing unearned privilege. Meritocracy's success in crossing boundaries – ideological and cultural, geographical and political – is striking."

Life Before Merit

Today we take our relatively meritocratic society for granted. For virtually all of history, humans were born into a certain position in life and most were trapped in those circumstances for their entire life. Agricultural societies were stratified by ranks, orders, or castes into which all people were born. No amount of effort would fundamentally change one's circumstances. Occasionally, some extraordinarily talented person could break into the upper classes, and, presumably, some people with mental or physical disabilities would plummet, but these were rare exceptions.

In traditional agricultural societies, everyone understands that only the children of aristocratic families can fill the leadership positions in political, economic, religious and military institutions. While there was often intense competition between members of the upper class, no one believed that members of the lower classes could enter that competition. This kept the talent pool very small and undermined the effectiveness of all institutions in society.

In traditional agricultural societies, patronage (support from your superiors) was far more important than merit or achievement. The political, economic, military, and religious elites usually lived in national or regional capitals. Those living in rural areas would strive to find favor from those above them so they could move to regional capitals. Those living in regional capitals strove to find favor from those above them so they could move to the national capital. Those lucky enough to live in the national capital found that they still had to get by mainly upon political patronage from their superiors, rather than their skills and achievements.

The royal court was the center of most agricultural societies. The court consisted of the monarch, his advisors, and an entire entourage of hangers-on. The court functioned not only as the political center, but it also functioned as the economic, cultural, artistic, and social center.

This forced almost everyone who wanted to excel in a domain to focus a great deal of time on currying favor from the royal court. This meant that no one was ever truly independent. The opinion of the royal court always trumped competence.

In traditional agricultural societies, the key question was not "What can you do?" It was "Who is your family or patron?" It was only when you gave a satisfactory answer to the latter question that anyone would bother to think about the first question. Few questioned the natural order, and those who did were not invited into the halls of power.

Rise of Meritocracy

Meritocracy evolved over centuries as a means to take advantage of people's talents for the benefit of rulers. Kings, nobles, and the church were all bastions of the established order, but they also needed more talented workers than the upper classes could provide. Because they were in military competition with other kingdoms, they could not afford to completely ignore talent as a criterion. Each found ways of promoting especially talented members of the lower classes to leadership positions.

Meritocracy Is Revolutionary

Political revolutions also played an important role in creating meritocracies. The Dutch Revolt against the Spanish Empire, the American Revolution, the Puritan Revolution against the British Crown, and the French Revolution all destroyed an old regime based upon titled privilege.

The new revolutionary regimes needed men of talent to staff their government, military, and other institutions, so they opened up hiring to the lower classes even further. Each revolution undermined the moral legitimacy of the established order and expanded the role of merit in organizational decision-making.

Britain, France, Prussia, and the United States, at different times, overhauled their educational system to provide greater opportunities for the lower classes. This included reforming the admissions system, and lowering tuition costs, as well as overhauling the curriculum.

Those same nations also overhauled the way they staffed government institutions. Blatant political patronage and aristocratic privilege were gradually replaced by rigorous entrance exams and educational credentials. These reforms enabled each of these societies to compete better in both economics and the military domain.

For much of the 19th and 20th centuries, the political Left championed the ideal of meritocracy and saw it as the key to building a more just society. The Left realized that giving an upward path to talented members of the working class would benefit society as well as building leaders for the future of the party. The opponents of meritocracy were primarily conservatives who tried to defend the established order by supporting the privileges of the upper class. In the long run, the conservatives lost the fight, as meritocracy kept expanding.

The Triumph of Merit

Gradually the concept of meritocracy spread throughout most institutions in society. Particularly in the United States, a four-year college degree is today regarded as the bare minimum for getting a high-paying job. Many positions now demand a master's degree or even higher.

Today, merit-based decisions are far more widespread than they were 200 years ago. Whereas title and family connections used to dominate organizational decisions, now education, skills, and accomplishments do. All Western countries embrace the ideal of meritocracy, even when they do not totally fulfill it. Just as strikingly, so do Asian nations. Even Communist China, which promotes an ideology completely alien to meritocracy, embraces the concept within the party (although the current leader seems to value personal loyalty as a higher goal).

Opponents of Meritocracy

Recently, a number of books have been written that have been strongly against the concept of meritocracy. Daniel Markovits' *The Meritocracy Trap* and Michael Sandel's *The Tyranny of Merit* are two of the most important examples. Markovits focuses largely on college admissions, a topic that I will cover later. Sandel criticizes the concept of merit because he believes that the concept assumes that those with less merit deserve their fate of having less. Sandel also claims that those with merit congratulate themselves on their efforts and on moral virtue that they do not really possess.

The problem with all of these criticisms and others is that none of them offer a viable alternative. Of course, meritocracy has its faults. People with greater merit than others in a specific domain are fallible, and sometimes catastrophically so. But what is the real alternative? Do we want to go back to a world of rigid orders, classes, or castes? Do we want institutional decision-making based on family title, patronage, or purchase of office? No, obviously not.

The only cure for the failings of our current meritocracy is to apply merit-based decisions in a fair and transparent way. Meritocracy is much like democracy. They are each flawed because humans are flawed, but they are still better than all other alternatives that humans have yet come up with.

Critical Theory and Meritocracy

The only critics of meritocracy that have a clear counter-proposal are Critical theorists (more commonly known as the "Woke."). Because Critical theory sees all intellectual concepts as means by which powerful groups oppress marginalized groups, they see merit as just another tool of oppression. Critical theorists believe that they have a moral obligation to stand up for the oppressed by deconstructing the moral underpinning of merit so that the entire system comes crashing down.

While many Critical theorists have been entirely vague about what comes after merit, Critical race theorists mostly see systematic discrimination against powerful groups as the only other option. They essentially argue for radically expanding affirmative action for marginalized groups into all organizational decisions. They want to substitute "What can you do?" with "What group do you belong to?"

Affirmative action started in the early 1970s and, until recently it has largely been restricted to universities, governments, and government contractors. Early in my career in the digital technology industry, I worked in Apple Computers' Department of Multicultural Affairs. While the department had many tasks, monitoring the racial and gender characteristics of employees and pushing managers to "do better" was a key task.

When I first started working there, I accepted the goal of affirmative action, but as I began to see how it worked in practice, my support waned. At the time, managers had a huge financial incentive to hire the most qualified person, and begging and pleading for them to do otherwise was pointless. In the 1990s, the Department of Multicultural Affairs was swimming against institutional incentives. Unfortunately, since that time institutional incentives have changed radically.

Diversity, Equity and Inclusion

Particularly since 2020, institutions of all types have accepted (or at least pretended to accept) the rationale of making hiring, firing, and promotion decisions based on race, gender and other characteristics. While I do not believe that corporate executives and managers actually believe that this is good for society or the corporation, they promote the practice in order to maintain public relations.

The DEI industry has convinced corporations to pretend that they believe that only discrimination against the oppressors can compensate for past discrimination by oppressors. They cover up the intent using words such as diversity, equity, and inclusion (DEI), but deliberate discrimination is clearly their goal.

Particularly toxic is the way that executives tie the performance reviews of managers to the racial and gender representation of their hiring, firing and promotions. This enables executives and HR departments to pretend to support merit-based criteria while forcing hiring managers to deliberately discriminate.

Any manager who believes that these practices are unethical or even bad for the company risks termination. Managers in many corporations now have a career incentive to discriminate, stay quiet, and pretend that nothing unusual is happening.

Also toxic to progress has been the radical expansion of racial sensitivity training that is effectively promoting Critical theory. These training sessions actively (but privately) promote racial discrimination, racial stereotyping, and racial segregation. Employees are forced to sit and listen to left-wing agitators lecture them on race, while pretending to agree.

The evidence from these racial-sensitivity training sessions is clear. They do not work to lower racial tensions or elevate racial minorities. They only inject racial tension, anxiety, and left-wing ideology into the workplace (Harvard Business Review).

A lack of transparency and the fear of being fired play a key role in the continuation of these policies. Employees know that they will be at best stigmatized, and at worst endanger of being fired. And since all the training and policy are done in secret, it will be difficult to acquire the evidence necessary to prove discrimination and harassment.

Supporters of DEI also conveniently ignore the fact that affirmative action has been widely used in many sectors of society for over 50 years. By their own claim that the United States is a racist society with unfair outcomes, they prove that previous affirmative action was a failure. Rather than accept the failure of past policies, they chose to double down on them. This, unfortunately, has been a consistent pattern on the Left.

Patronage 2.0

What is shocking is the way that liberals who used to believe in integration, merit, non-discrimination, and getting beyond race now support imposing policies that are the complete opposite. However, when seen from another perspective, it may not be so surprising.

When you get past all the ideological rhetoric, the new DEI regime looks remarkably similar to political patronage. Patronage was the fuel that supported American political parties in 19th and early 20th century politics. While the practice was widespread, it was particularly prevalent in the Democratic party in the large cities of the Northeast and Midwest. This style of politics is often called "urban political machines."

These urban political machines traded votes for jobs and money. Political candidates and local party leaders promised various ethnic groups in the city that they would hire them as government bureaucrats or party activists and focus government funding in their neighborhood if the group supported the Democratic party. These urban political machines also frequently stuffed or dumped ballots to win elections. Systematic corruption was the lifeblood of these urban political machines.

While the proponents of DEI use rhetoric to create the impression that their goals are based upon moral principles, they apply their concepts selectively. Institutions that embrace the concepts of DEI do not seem too concerned about professions where Blacks are heavily over-represented: athletics, music, and entertainment. Nor are they particularly worried that women are increasingly over-represented as students in universities. Nor do they care too much about the under-representation of religious or ethnic minorities who happen to have white skin.

The new DEI regime is a means by which the Left rewards groups who support the Democratic party. Those rewards come in the form of government benefits and jobs. Just like the machine politics that the same party practiced in big cities in the past, they have a clear message: vote for the Democrats, and you will be rewarded with money and jobs.

The goal becomes particularly clear when it is combined with attempts by stifle conservative Blacks, Hispanics and women who speak up. If you do not toe the party line, you are still at risk of being fired. Your demographic group will not save you. Only your partisan alignment will.

The Merits of Merit

I believe that supporters of meritocracy have not done a very good job of selling the principle. Despite the principle being widely viewed as positive, few people can clearly articulate why an individual decision in the workplace should be based upon merit instead of equity.

Every institution in society exists because it helps to solve a problem for the rest of society. Organizations that do a good job of solving a specific problem acquire more resources from customers and investors, and they can attract the best talent with higher pay.

It is a fundamental truth that no organization can be good at everything. For this reason, it is critical that all organizations specialize in the specific domains that are necessary for solving a specific problem. This leaves space for other organizations to specialize in different areas.

By focusing on one clear organizational goal, an organization is far more likely to achieve its goals. When one adds additional goals into a business model, this undermines the ability of that organization to achieve socially desirable results. This is particularly true when the additional goals fundamentally conflict with the ability of an organization to hire, fire and promote people who possess the necessary skills to pursue organizational goals.

Everyone Wins

Critical theorists and many others on the Left see hiring, firing and promotion as a zero-sum game of distribution. For them, this game is something like divvying an economic pie that is of a fixed size. One person's gain is another person's loss. As they see it, the person who gets the job is a winner in the game, and everyone else is a loser. The job itself and what that person does in it after winning is incidental. This is completely wrong both factually and morally.

When the best person for that job gets the job, everyone wins. When the best person for the job gets the job, their co-workers win. They have a greater ability to accomplish their own tasks because all work is at least somewhat interdependent. It is demoralizing for co-workers when the efforts of the entire group are undermined by one incompetent or disruptive co-worker. This is even more true if that co-worker is given a free pass because they happen to share demographic characteristics with under-represented groups.

It is particularly bad when that person is a manager. There are few things worse in employment than having a bad manager. I have been pretty lucky in my career. Most of my managers were competent enough, but I have had a few that were… not. Employees have little recourse against a bad manager other than quitting or suffering in silence while waiting out the manager.

Hiring the person most qualified for the job also benefits the customers and shareholders of the company. When everyone in a company is qualified and believes that they are honestly being graded on their performance, customers will receive a better product, and stocks are more likely to rise in value. Of course, all companies have bad employees, but when the dominant hiring ideology is the theory that diversity, equity and inclusion are more important than merit, this guarantees a much higher proportion of bad employees.

While it is true that the person who does not get a job is a short-term loser in the transaction, there are still very real benefits for that person. I see merit-based decision-making as a way of guiding people toward the position where they can make the greatest contributions to the organization and society in general. So someone may fail to get an individual job, but this may benefit them in the long run.

The feedback from the job search process helps people, particularly young people, to get real feedback on where their talents would best be applied. Assuming the job market is not too bad for job-seekers, numerous job rejections over a long period of time sends a clear signal that another career path may be a better choice.

Far too many people struggle for decades to launch careers in extremely competitive fields, such as athletics, music, acting, art, politics and academia, without being willing to confront the possibility that they are not good enough. In many of these desirable professions, a lucky few make the cut and earn huge amounts of money, but so many cling to unrealistic hopes for too long.

A person who is a very bad lawyer or doctor might be a very good mechanic. While there are some people who truly cannot support themselves with employment, the vast majority of people can. The hard part is finding a match between what one is good at, and what society wants sufficiently enough to pay money for.

And if an unqualified person gets a job, they are most likely moving their careers in a direction that will create dead-ends. Supporters of DEI seem to believe that no one will notice the results of employees who are not hired based on merit. While there might be some jewels that rise to the occasion, everyone will notice if employees of certain demographic groups perform worse as a whole compared to other demographic groups. They may be too scared to say anything, but everyone will know.

DEI sets favored demographic groups up for long-term failure. Sadly the entire regime of diversity, equity, and inclusion has hugely stigmatized all employees in the very groups that its supporters claim to want to help. People will immediately assume that a person was a diversity hire based upon their physical appearance — *even when it is not true.* This forces them all into a position where they have to prove their worth even after they are hired. No amount of protestation that they were not a diversity hire will persuade some of their fellow employees.

When DEI hires reach a certain critical mass, it is likely to seriously undermine employee morale. No one will believe that decision-making is ever based upon merit. Why put in the extra effort for the company, when you know that it will not change who gets hired, fired, or promoted, or who gets a pay raise?

The concept of intersectionality is particularly toxic in an organization. While most ideologies focus on one division within society, for example, class, race, ethnicity, religion, or gender, intersectionality uses all of them at once to create a hierarchy of oppression. Worse, supporters of intersectionality keep inventing new supposedly oppressed groups.

Everyone can game the system to identify a characteristic that they have that is under-represented in the company overall. Everyone can also game the system by identifying characteristics of other employees that make other people less deserving of favors.

This transforms organizational decisions into pure politics, where all resources are divided into different groups and everyone thinks that their group is deserving of more. Because Critical theory rewards those who side with the oppressed, regardless of logic, and so many individuals can find a criterion that explains why they are being oppressed, organizations are doomed to everyone fighting everyone in a never-ending zero-sum conflict.

Contribution, Not Distribution

A fundamental problem with ideologies on the Left is that they focus exclusively on the distribution of the gains from progress. The Left wants to achieve a fair society, which they define in terms of equal outcomes, and they bridle at any deviations from that outcome. They see political activism to create demand for redistributionist social programs and regulations as being the way we need strive for a better society.

Instead of focusing on the *distribution* of the gains of progress, we should primarily focus on the *contributions* that individuals make to progress. Progress is not an inevitable outcome of forces; it is the outcome of human activity. And some people can contribute to progress far more than others.

We need to ensure that people who have won the genetic lottery and have lucked out on other non-genetic factors are put into a position where they feel an obligation to contribute as much to society as possible. Part of that incentive comes from economic incentives to learn skills and perform in the workplace. Part of that incentive comes from meritocratic decisions within organizations. When the most talented succeed, everyone wins.

Living in a society experiencing material progress benefits everyone, not just the most fortunate. Long-term economic growth pays for all the social programs that the Left supports. It pays for our food, energy, housing, transportation, health care, entertainment, and virtually every other thing that can be purchased on the market.

This is why meritocracy works. It is not because of social mobility, although that plays a role. *Meritocracy works because it places the people who have the ability to contribute the most to society in a position where they are best able to do so.*

Focus on the Individual

A fundamental concept of a Progress-based reform agenda should be to focus on the individual, not on the group. Institutions make hiring, firing, and promotion decisions about an individual, not a group. Each person is hired, fired, or promoted based upon their own unique characteristics, which cannot be defined by which demographic groups they happen to fall into.

A person is not defined by their race. A person is not defined by their gender. A person is not defined by their nationality, religion, ethnicity, age, marital status, sexuality, or any other characteristic. Nor is a person even defined by all of those characteristics in combination (as in the theory of intersectionality).

Each person is unique. Only the people who interact with them regularly within the context of their workplace can make judgments about their merit. Of course, those persons will have biases, self-interest, and personal goals. That is why we need to focus on merit so that we have a principle that limits the impact each of those biases plays in the decision-making of organizations.

And of course, even if the process is perfectly merit-based, some will make judgments in error. Others will make decisions because they have inaccurate stereotypes about a person because of their demographic characteristics. Others will make decisions based on accurate stereotypes that do not happen to apply to that individual. Some will make blatantly discriminatory decisions.

The antidote to all these poor decisions is organizations competing against each other in the marketplace, and the ability of the talented to create new organizations based upon new models of operation. It is this competitive process that forces organizations to overcome their prejudices and hire the individual with the most merit for that specific position.

Individuals Do Not Represent a Group

An implicit assumption of many on the Left who criticize the unequal outcomes among different demographic groups in a meritocracy is that an individual "represents" a group. In politics, the concept of representation makes sense. We elect leaders to represent us: i.e. to make decisions on our behalf so we do not have to. In that sense, political leaders can be judged by how much they represent voters.

In most institutions in society, however, representation is not a useful concept. A corporate CEO or manager who happens to have identical demographic characteristics to me does not represent me in any way. Nor does a corporate CEO or manager with differing demographics fail to represent me.

It is not and should not be the goal of individuals in an organization to represent anyone. They should be applying their skills, time, and energy to solving a specific problem for the organization. Doing this has nothing to do with representation.

I want to work for a great CEO, a great manager, and co-workers who have the right technical skills, people skills, integrity, and work ethic to perform their job. I win, and all the other employees win when the staff possess those characteristics. My guess is that the vast majority of people want the same for their employment.

Inequality is Inevitable

Virtually all ideologies on the Left have a goal of equality. I would argue that they are trying to achieve an impossible goal and their unwillingness to acknowledge that 200 years of effort have been wasted on this goal undermines the entire movement. At some point, the Left must look at the actual results of their policies and acknowledge that they have not been able to achieve their goal of equality.

Inequality is an inevitable outcome of living in a human society that has evolved past a Hunter Gatherer lifestyle. Even among Hunter Gatherers, there were important biological inequalities based on strength, speed, charisma, beauty, intelligence, and charisma. Inequality is part of the human condition.

Diversity inevitably leads to inequality. Different types of people have different preferences. Those preferences lead to different choices. Those choices lead to different outcomes. Different outcomes piled on top of each other lead to inequality. Over generations, those inequalities will tend to be reinforced until people's fundamental preferences change.

In every society that has ever existed, there have been different outcomes between different ethnicities, religions, races, and genders. There is no reason to assume that discrimination always is the cause. In some cases, it has been, but differing outcomes are not evidence of discrimination per se. And when those inequalities reproduce themselves even when individuals migrate to different societies, it is safe to assume that discrimination is often not the cause.

Inequality is inevitable, but it really matters what type of inequality exists in society. An inequality where a handful of titled families rule through expropriation and pass those titles onto their children is not a just society. Nor is a society where rank in the ruling party determines outcomes a just one.

A meritocratic society with a high material standard of living leads to the most just form of inequality that we can probably ever achieve. We want a society where the most talented work hard to better themselves and in the process improve society. Such a society creates the incentive for individuals to innovate new technologies, learn new skills, cooperate in groups to solve common problems, and outcompete other organizations trying to do the same.

Yes, such a society is inevitably unequal in income and wealth distribution. It seems only fair that such individuals have more income, wealth, and status than the rest of us. And once society reaches a certain material standard of living, those inequalities will be about luxury items, not the necessities of survival.

The inequalities of a meritocratic society are fair because those inequalities are largely due to the contributions that individuals make to society. As long as a society maintains the Five Keys to Progress, meritocratic decision-making will lead toward good ends.

Merit Is Not Social Mobility

Some people mistakenly conflate merit and social mobility. These people start with the "blank slate" assumption that all persons are born with the same inherent characteristics, so the outcome of a meritocratic society will be high levels of social mobility.

When a society transitions to being relatively merit-based, rates of social mobility typically increase, but after a few generations, the overall levels of social mobility decline. In social mobility research, this is often operationalized by comparing the income and social status of adult children compared to their parents.

In fact, a meritocratic society is a sorting process. Meritocratic societies sort people based on socially beneficial factors, the most important of which are intelligence and conscientiousness. Because intelligence is closely related to genetic factors, meritocracies indirectly sort by genes. Because members of the same class tend to intermarry and have children, that genetic sorting moves on to the next generation. This is why meritocratic societies tend to have lower rates of social mobility than the ideal of social mobility would imply.

Nepotism

One of the principal objections to meritocracy is that influential and wealthy parents often game the system to the benefit of their children. Whether it is getting their children into the best schools, taking them to SAT test prep schools, paying for tutors, or bribing college deans, there is certainly no shortage of parents gaming the system.

But we need to be clear that much of this gaming of the system is *against* the concept of meritocracy, not in favor of it. And, more importantly, much of this behavior is desirable for society.

We want parents to give their children the best. The fact that parents have differing abilities to do so should not undermine this goal.

I could think of no better definition of a dystopia than a society where parents do not care about their children more than others. Passing on the values, skills, and habits that are necessary to thrive in a modern society typically happens via direct interpersonal exchange. Parents are in by far in the best position to do this. Most do an adequate job of it.

We want parents who invest in their children's education, comfort them in their failures and push them to succeed. We want parents to care about the quality of their children's teachers and schools and, if necessary, to relocate to find better options. We want parents to invest in their children's health and cultivate interests in different fields.

What we do not want is for parents who contributed to society in their lifetimes to give their below-average children a better shot than lower-income children with greater potential. Their personal interest in wanting the best for their children cannot distort the meritocratic decision-making of our institutions.

In short, we want parents to invest in their children without being able to cheat the process in their favor. We should not expect the children of wealthy parents to have the same outcomes as the children of poor children. But we do not want a system where the children of wealthy parents can coast to success with very little effort, while the talented children of poor parents are unable to succeed despite their inherent talent.

The fact that some parents attempt to game the system on behalf of their children should not be used as an excuse for moving our society away from meritocracy. The proper response should be better enforcement and transparency so that we can have more meritocracy.

Credentialism

Another argument used against meritocracy is that it has degenerated into a veneration of academic credentials that does not accurately reflect the ideal of meritocracy. I will deal with four-year college degrees in much more detail later, but here I will say that the opponents of credentialism have a strong point.

The goal of a meritocracy should be encouraging people who have the ability to contribute the most to society to find a position within institutions to do so. Educational credentials were an important means for breaking down non-meritocratic decision-making in past generations. However, we must never forget that educational credentials are just one means of measuring merit, and they are not very focused on the specific skills needed for a specific job.

Academic credentials were an important step forward toward a more merit-based society, but today we can do better. In an era of computers and the internet, there are far more ways to learn new skills and knowledge. There are also far better ways of validating the fact that a candidate has mastered those skills and knowledge. Having a specific degree, no matter how prestigious, should not be enough.

Expanding Meritocracy

We should strive to replace academic credentials with exams that measure specific skills and knowledge relevant to the job. In the internet era, there should be no reason why we cannot do so.

Supporters of progress need to simultaneously:

1. Make overt discrimination, particularly as practiced by DEI advocates, illegal.

2. Allow individual non-government organizations to make hiring, firing, and promotion decisions free from government interference as long as they are transparent, objective, and merit-based.

3. Encourage private industry to develop very specific exams that more objectively measure job-based skills than current educational credentials do.

To support goals #2 and #3, Congress should pass legislation that any employer who requires a specific educational credential for a job must also accept:

• Job experience that typically demonstrates that the necessary skills for the job have already been acquired, or:

• Exam results that demonstrate that the candidate acquired

the necessary skills and knowledge via a method other than formal education.

Rather than focusing excessively on educational credentials or previous jobs, employers should be encouraged to make hiring, firing, and promotion decisions solely based upon:

1. Demonstrated skills and knowledge that are relevant to the job.

2. Previous job performance, including the ability to work cooperatively with co-workers and customers.

3. Living in a geographical area that enables working for the company (to the extent that the position cannot be remote).

4. Salary and compensation demands.

5. Being an American citizen, legal resident, or having a work visa.

Companies should be required to allow potential job-seekers to replace academic credentials with online exams or physical demonstrations that show the degree to which the candidate has mastered the necessary skills for the job. Physical demonstrations might be more appropriate for working-class jobs, while online skills and knowledge exams might be more appropriate for professional jobs.

Imagine a new credential system where university degrees were replaced by formal exams that were very focused on the skills and knowledge necessary to master a specific job. In such a system, all college graduates would have the incentive to take the exam, as proof that their education fulfilled the requirement. However, contrary to today, a degree would not be the only way to learn the necessary skills and knowledge.

All job seekers would then be able to acquire the necessary skills and knowledge via:

- Online learning
- Community college
- Working on the job
- Company training
- Reading books or watching videos
- Informal teaching from family, friends, or co-workers

- Personal projects

This would create an even playing field on which college graduates would have no advantage over those who learned via other paths. It would also have the advantage of giving universities a strong incentive to increase the quality of their education in order to justify their tuition. If, for example, all university engineering programs received test scores for how well their students did on online engineering exams after graduation, then they would be forced to compete on more than their amenities and finding the best students.

Ideally, these exams would be very specialized, so that, for every job position, there would be different exams and the higher someone went in their career path, the more challenging the exam. Individuals could retake the exams periodically over the course of their careers so they could demonstrate their actual skills learned via employment. Rather than one exam per job position, there could be a menu of smaller exams the employers could choose between for a specific job.

Such exams could also be useful for immigration rules and enabling online foreign workers to compete on equal terms with American citizens. All exam results could be entered into a database that is fully searchable by employers. In the event of alleged discrimination, the results should also be available to the courts.

Of course, no exams or demonstrations can fully account for all the soft skills that are required in many jobs, but exams can help to create a more objective and well-rounded assessment compared to a resume, degree, and job interview. All races, ethnicities, genders, classes, ages, religions, and nationalities would be judged based on the same criteria.

Employers Will Benefit

The government should not tell employers what type of employee to hire, but the government should force them to make their hiring, firing, and promotions process objective, transparent and merit-based. I believe that corporations in the same industry can come together to define:

1. What job skills and knowledge are necessary for a specific position.

2. How to develop exams that more objectively measure those skills and knowledge.

3. How to enable all potential job seekers to take a test in a simple way that doesn't enable cheating.

4. How to establish third parties to deliver and store test results in a transparent manner.

This process should not be seen as an undue administrative burden on corporations. Perhaps the most significant problem for any employer is finding qualified candidates who fulfill the specific requirements of a job. By forcing themselves to come up with objective criteria for what is needed for a job, companies will make it much easier to cast a broad net that covers the entire nation and even the entire world.

Employees will also benefit. If employees know what the standards are, they will have a strong incentive to learn the skills and knowledge and then take the test before even applying for a specific job. Just as resumes today always list previous jobs and educational credentials, they would also add their test results.

As someone who has been involved in corporate hiring on both sides, I would love to have had some objective data that ranked candidates on specialized skills relevant to that specific job position. Unfortunately, those rarely exist, so I was forced to try to interpret the skills of a candidate from their educational skills and past employment. We can do better.

Employers focus on educational credentials and past job experience largely because it is an easy way to filter out poor candidates from their HR database before interviews take place. If employers were forced to develop more meaningful exams that better measured merit, they would still be able to do so, but the filtering process would be less arbitrary.

The database of test results would also make systematic discrimination by employers obvious. Particularly for large companies with big sample sizes (which encompasses most of the job market), any major deviations in test scores based upon race, gender or other factors would be difficult to explain away. Some companies might also realize that they were unintentionally passing over qualified candidates.

Intelligence Tests

Because intelligence tests are very good at predicting long-term career success, some have suggested that they be used for employment. The rationale is that, since intelligent people tend to perform better, it would be a simple universal employment test. Such an exam was, in fact, used by Duke Power, in the scenario that provoked the landmark Supreme Court affirmative case ruling, Griggs vs. Duke Power.

I do not believe that general intelligence tests should be allowed for employment because they are too general and a person can do little, if anything to change their score. I think such tests are far more useful for education. In fact, the SAT, ACT, and other academic exams are actually intelligence tests although they are not marketed as such.

Let me give an extreme example to illustrate why I oppose general intelligence tests by employers: imagine the smartest person in the world graduating from college. He takes an intelligence test and gets the highest possible score. He then applies for a job, and of course, he gets the job. Being intelligent, he realizes that he should not wait any further and then applies for a more prestigious job. He keeps doing this over and over again. Within a few months, he is CEO of the largest corporation in the world even though he has no clue how to do any of the jobs he got hired for! Such a system would be unacceptable.

We need a system of exams that encourages people to learn the valuable skills and knowledge that employers covet. Those skills and knowledge are very specific to a job. Such skills and knowledge cannot be identified by a general intelligence test. The most intelligent person in the world knows little about the specific skills and knowledge required for most jobs, so that person is not qualified to do them.

Obviously, a more intelligent person will have an advantage in learning those skills and knowledge at a faster rate than a less intelligent person. However, less intelligent persons can make up the gap through hard work and dedication, just as they do in the workplace.

Banning Intentional Discrimination

The critics of meritocracy are wrong. We need more meritocracy, not less. We also need less discrimination, not more. Hiring, firing, and promotion processes based on merit help the nation, employers, the employee, their co-workers, shareholders, and customers.

Diversity, Equity, and Inclusion is an intellectual rationalization for systematic discrimination based on race, gender, and other characteristics. It will not help Blacks, Hispanics, or women. It will only elevate a few lucky individuals who hold those characteristics above their demonstrated level of competence. Those lucky winners in no sense represent their demographic groups. Most importantly, DEI will sabotage future progress.

Supporters of progress should introduce legislation that specifically states that all governments, businesses, or non-profits must abide by the following:

1. A disparity of outcomes is not in itself evidence of discrimination. Nor is it even evidence that there is a problem.

2. Any corporate policies that intentionally hire, fire, or promote based on race, gender, ethnicity, religion, age, etc. violate the Civil Rights Act of 1964. The supposed quest for diversity, equality, inclusion, or social justice does not override the illegal nature of this act.

3. Any training or organizational practices that attempt to categorize or label employees based upon those criteria are also illegal. These policies encourage discrimination in the workplace, which violates the Civil Rights Act.

4. Any promotions, bonuses, or financial rewards to managers for preferentially hiring, firing or promoting individuals from certain demographic groups are also illegal.

5. We will establish an anonymous hotline to enable employees to report any suspected violations.

Federal, state, and local governments should be held to a higher standard than private enterprises. So should any companies or non-profits who accept government contracts or subsidies. Such organizations must make all internal training transparent to all by posting on the internet all training handbooks, syllabuses, presentations as well as videos of the trainers in the classroom.

Focus on Results

Because the policies in this chapter relate to the internal decision-making processes of institution, it is not easy to identify key metrics for measuring success. The entire concept of merit is based on allowing the people who worked most closely with a person to make decision on their individual merit. This is very difficult to capture in aggregate statistics.

Some metrics that might be useful are:

- Percent of hiring, firing and promotion that bear no reference to a person's demographic characteristics
- Percent of occupations that have skills exams that are widely used in lieu of educational credentials.

Conclusion

The creation of institutions that make hiring, firing, and promotion decisions based on merit is one of the most important results of progress. Supporters of progress should defend and expand merit-based decision-making because it ensures that those with the skills most relevant to the job are put in the position where they can contribute the most to society. Above all, supporters of progress must roll back government policies that undermine merit.

MAKING COLLEGE AFFORDABLE

The four-year college degree has become the de facto entrance criteria into the American professional class. It is also the way that many young people learn valuable skills related to their future careers. For this reason, society has an interest in ensuring that universities are effective, affordable, and fair.

America's universities have a serious affordability problem. Tuition and other costs associated with getting a college degree have grown far faster than the overall rate of inflation. While college is supposed to be a means of elevating the talented regardless of their background, it often does the opposite.

A big part of the problem is that universities have forgotten that their primary goal is to educate students. To compete against other universities in the Best Colleges rankings that come out every year, they have added more and more amenities, which have driven up the cost of tuition. Moreover, many of these amenities have become so enticing and time-consuming that they distract students from focusing on their studies.

Amenities

Along with competing for rankings on the Best Colleges lists, universities also compete on amenities. Among the most important amenities are the buildings, landscaping, gyms, social activities, sports teams, dorms, and technology. Since all of these amenities can easily be compared visually during visits, universities have the incentive to look their best.

There are only two problems: First, none of these amenities have anything to do with education. Second, they are expensive. Third, they distract students from focusing on their studies.

Ever-increasing spending on amenities is one of the main drivers in the inflation of college tuition fees. In the 2010-11 school year, colleges spent $499 billion. *Less than 30% of that amount goes to instruction.* Almost half of that spending went to non-instructional services, such as student services, public service and academic support. Every year, the percentage of spending that goes to education declines (National Center for Education Statistics).

Universities are becoming more and more like Club Med with books. And unfortunately, the Club Med side keeps growing in terms of both time and money, while the books side keeps shrinking in terms of time devoted (if not money).

If affluent parents want to send their children to a four-year resort with books, and they are willing to pay the entire bill themselves, that is fine. I do not think that it is good for society overall, but parents should be able to spend their money as they choose.

However, when bright working-class or poor students cannot attend college because those amenities have ramped up the cost of tuition to ridiculous levels, you are interfering with the societal good. We want the most academically talented from all classes to be able to go to college even if they happen to be born into families with average or below-average incomes.

It becomes even worse when taxpayers are expected to pick up the tab for those affluent youths to attend a four-year resort with books. Asking working class and poor families to pay the bill for talented youths to go to college is one thing, but when the bulk of the costs go on unnecessary amenities, that seems grossly unfair.

Unfortunately, financial aid only makes the problem worse. Government financial aid to students is much like "affordable housing." It does not lower the cost, it just temporarily shifts the cost and feeds the cost-inflation cycle. Universities know that they can keep raising tuition because students will not pay the final tab. Governments will.

Universities also fear that spending less on amenities will cause them to fall behind other universities in the prestige game.

Less Time In Studies

Not surprisingly, given all the money being devoted to college amenities, full-time students are spending less and less time on their studies. There are simply too many distractions.

Based on data from the Bureau of Labor Statistics Time Use Survey from 2003-2014, the average full-time student devotes only 2.76 hours per day to the classroom, research, and homework. This comes to 19.3 hours per week, basically a part-time job. Ironically, high school students devote 10 hours per week more to their academic work than much older college students (BLS).

In fairness to them, some of this time deficit is made up for in paid employment. Full-time college students work an average of 16.3 hours per week for a total of 35.6 hours on education and work. This number is deceptive, however, as 40% of full-time college students do not have any paid employment. The combined work effort of non-employed college students is much closer to part-time workers than full-time workers (BLS).

Most full-time college students do not take the full course load. They deliberately take a lighter course load and stretch the "college experience" to five or six years. This helps to maximize their free time during the process. The unfortunate result is that only 19% of students graduate from non-flagship universities within four years. And every year they take adds to the tuition cost, the debt load, and the lost wages. (Rosenbaum).

Given that full-time workers routinely work 40 hours per week, it is hard to see why non-employed college students spend less time on their studies than younger and presumably less mature high-school students.

Make Amenities Optional

Because the four-year college degree has become the de facto criteria for entrance into the American professional class, and virtually all of our future leaders will come from that class, society has a strong interest in reducing tuition costs.

We need to shift the incentive structure of universities toward making tuition more affordable. We can do so by allowing students and their parents to decide what level of amenities they are willing to pay for. Public universities and private universities that accept government funding should be required to separate tuition costs from other non-academic costs.

Currently, tuition and all the amenities that the "college experience" has to offer are lumped into one price. Students are forced to pay for the college experience regardless of whether they want to or not. Just as importantly, taxpayers are forced to do so as well. We need to give students and governments the option of paying for education only.

This may seem like a radical change, but it is not. Students already have the option of paying for on-campus housing and meals separately from their tuition bill. No one is forced to pay for the housing or meals of other students. Students and their parents can choose whether they want to pay for housing and meals based on their own personal circumstances. College amenities should be the same.

In practice this would mean that students could choose from a range of four different items on the college menu:
- Tuition (required for all students)
- Housing
- Meals
- Other amenities. Amenities may either be collected as user fees, annual fees per amenity, or as a lump sum covering all activities at the university's discretion.

Tuition costs would only include the costs to pay for the:
- Compensation package for professors, teacher's assistants, and

anyone whose sole job responsibility is teaching students or conducting academic research.

- Construction, maintenance, and repair of buildings devoted exclusively to classrooms and student academic activities.
- Classroom or student lab materials.

Federal and state financial aid or student loans should never pay for amenities, as they are expensive and in no way connected to students learning the valuable skills that societies need to pass on to their children.

State universities are funded partially by tuition fees and partially from direct government subsidies. I believe that direct government subsidies for education makes a great deal of sense. However, direct government subsidies for on-campus amenities has no clear societal good. At the very least, a separate budget for amenities would force state legislatures to discuss the appropriate level of taxpayer subsidies. My guess is that many would then choose education over amenities.

If students are given a choice as to whether they (or more likely their parents) are willing to pay for amenities, many will choose not to do so. The new payment system will also make it painfully clear how much of our current college tuition goes to non-academic amenities. Again, if affluent parents wanted to pay for those amenities out of their own pockets, they would be able to do so. But no one else would be forced to attend college.

Student Loans

As I write, President Biden has just signed an executive order canceling a substantial portion of student debt. Many supporters of this order claim that this is a means of countering the inflation of college tuition.

I believe that this measure will only make the inflation of college tuition worse, as it is telling universities that, no matter how high they raise tuition, the taxpayers will bail them out. When one takes into consideration the fact that a substantial percentage of the money goes to pay for non-academic activities for students from upper-income families, it is a particularly misguided policy.

My proposed payment system will also have a big impact on student loans. Student loans to pay for amenities look very different to both taxpayers and private financial firms than purely academic tuition. If private financial firms want to give what are effectively consumer loans to pay for amenities, they may do so. But the government should never subsidize this system, directly or indirectly.

Student loans to pay exclusively for tuition seem a far more legitimate candidate for taxpayer subsidy. In my next book in this series, *Upward Mobility*, I will go into more detail on how we can enable lower-income students to go to college. Here I will only say that taxpayers should never have to subsidize non-academic college activities.

Cutting Bureaucracy

Another major factor in our rapidly increasing tuition costs is bureaucratization. Over the last 50 years, the number of non-academic administrators per student has grown rapidly.

Between 1993 and 2007, the number of full-time administrators per 100 students increased by 39%, so they now make up double the number of employees dedicated to education. After adjusting for inflation, the cost of these administrators increased by 61%. In most universities, the majority of employees are not directly engaged in education or research. The lion's share of this additional cost is paid for by state and federal governments (Greene).

Unfortunately, this growth in bureaucracy has accelerated over the last decade. The increase of hiring for Diversity, Equity and Inclusion is particularly explosive. Ivy League universities now average a 1:1 ratio of administrators to students. In 2002-03 Yale University employed 3,500 administrators and managers, while it had 5,300 students. By 2021 Yale had more than 5,000 administrators and managers to 4,700 students (Chronicle of Higher Education).

There is absolutely no evidence that this ever-growing bureaucracy improves the quality of the education. In many cases, these administrators increase the quality of the amenities in the college experience, but, as discussed earlier, this is a double-edged sword. The better the amenities, the greater the distraction students have from academic work.

Moreover, these bureaucrats actually do something. They have built a huge administrative apparatus that has undermined the academic freedom of professors and the free speech of students. Far from creating an open learning experience, they are turning campuses into hives of groupthink mentality.

These bureaucrats have also empowered a relatively small proportion of left-wing students and professors to intimidate the entire campus. Because these administrators are well to the left of center in their politics, they often abuse their power by enforcing the rules differently, based on the politics of the perpetrators. Centrists and conservatives are punished far more severely for the same act compared to left-wing activists.

This has created an atmosphere on many campuses where Critical theory is the dominant ideology. Critical theory activists increasingly politicize all campus activities, and campus administrators allow them to intimidate anyone with a different opinion.

Given the huge negative impact on campus culture as well as spiraling tuition fee increases, state legislatures should fight back by mandating that state universities cut back on the total compensation package of non-academic employees. State universities are typically governed by a board of regents, but the state legislature has the power of the purse strings. They need to start using this power to lower the cost of going to college.

A simple mandate to the board of regents to cut the total compensation package of non-academic personal by 10% each year would at the very least stop tuition increases. More likely, it would cause tuition fees to finally start moving downwards.

In return, state legislatures should shift some of the savings towards investments in information technology and automation. This would enable universities to burden their academics with far fewer administrators. State legislatures could also shift some of the savings to increasing the salaries of adjunct professors, who teach the bulk of the classes in many universities.

State university regents and administrators will probably howl in protest that this is impossible to achieve, but they will be wrong. History shows it. If universities could function well in the 1970s with far fewer administrative personnel and virtually no digital technology, there is no reason why the same number of personnel cannot run them today.

Each state legislature and board of regents should look back through their records to the early 1970s, when college bureaucracies were much slimmer. If a person's job title (or something approximating it) did not exist in the early 1970s, they should seriously think about eliminating that position. If the ratio between the number of employees with that job title per student was significantly lower in the early 1970s, they should seriously cut back on the number of personnel with that job title. With those two simple criteria, we could make substantial cuts to administrative costs without lowering academic quality.

In particular, state universities should cut back on the quantity and compensation package of upper- and middle-level bureaucrats. Because of their relatively high salaries, those people will make up a significant percentage of the total compensation package of non-academic employees.

Notice that I am not advocating cutting the compensation package of any job titles that are directly related to education. By radically cutting back on non-academic bureaucrats, we can shift the focus of universities back to education.

More Required Courses

Another reason for increasing tuition has been the dramatic decline in the number of required courses. A relatively short list of required courses has been replaced by a large number of optional courses from which students can choose.

Freedom of choice seems like a great thing, but it has serious cost implications. Each additional course requires a new professor who is capable of teaching it, and it shrinks the overall number of students per class. As the number of students per class shrinks, the cost per student goes up as well.

In the past, universities had a large number of required courses. Many of these courses revolved around the concept of a liberal arts education, while others were more science and mathematics oriented.

Starting in the 1960s, universities began to cut back on the number of required courses. Some required courses have been replaced by breadth requirements, whereby students can choose between many classes within a broad category, such as science, social studies, and foreign languages. Other required courses were simply abolished.

Even within majors, students can typically fulfill many of their requirements by choosing between many different classes. So a history major may no longer be required to take a "History of Western Civilization" course. Instead, that student can choose between courses that focus on Latin America, Africa, East Asia, South Asia, or Central Asia.

Finally, most students can also take a large number of completely optional classes on any topic. In many cases, these optional courses are far less challenging than the previously required courses.

The result has been a dramatic increase in the number of classes. Each requires a professor or teaching assistant, so this increased variety leads to increasing costs, which are then passed on to the tuition bill.

While this may seem like a benefit, the typical college student is often overwhelmed with choices. These choices slow down their progression toward a degree, leading to lower graduation rates and five or six years of tuition payments for those who do graduate.

A Common Curriculum

A very simple reform that would save money, increase graduation rates, and improve the quality of education would be to have more required courses in the freshman and sophomore years. Students should choose between coherent, compatible programs, not hundreds of individual courses. This was widespread before the 1960s, but the pressure to give students greater options has led to their decline.

A typical college experience during that time included required courses filling up the first two years of classes. The second two years were reserved for concentrating on required courses within a specific major that was chosen by the student.

Having a common curriculum for the first two years has many advantages. This lowers the number of courses that a university needs to offer, which limits the number of professors that they need to hire. Or universities could hire more professors to shrink class sizes.

I believe that it also creates a better learning experience for students. I personally went through a one-year Technical Writing program at my local community college.

If memory serves correctly, we took courses every day for three hours straight. Every class had different professors, but the same students. Rather than having different courses at different times and different locations, all of the students had their classes in the same room back-to-back. We got to know each other far better than I ever did when it came to students in more traditional college courses. It was a very enjoyable and intellectually challenging environment.

Each university could establish a core curriculum for the first two years that is in line with their academic orientation. This format might encourage universities to experiment in ways they could not do when students all took different courses.

Some universities might focus the core curriculum on a traditional liberal arts education with many courses in philosophy, history, and language. Others might focus on a science-based or technology-based core curriculum.

Some universities might also break the core curriculum into a handful of meta majors, such as arts, social sciences, science/engineering, health care or business, which students can choose between. Alternatively, the core curriculum might cover a little bit of every track to enable students to make an informed choice on their majors.

By the third year, students would have a solid foundation and then be able to take classes in their declared major. There is no reason why the same general philosophy cannot continue within each major. Rather than having many classes to choose from within each major, each student within the same major would be required to take the same courses.

Having the same classes also makes it possible to schedule those classes back-to-back on the same day. Having experience as both a professor and a student who works full-time, I know how inconvenient schedules are when classes are scattered throughout the week. This is a real inconvenience for professors, students who work, who commute from off-campus housing, or who have parental responsibilities. Clustering all the classes together in time and place makes the college experience much more convenient for everyone.

State Universities Should Specialize

State university systems could also benefit from having different common curriculums. The vast majority of public universities are run by state governments. Typically each state has several universities, state colleges, and community colleges within one overall system.

Universities within the same system almost always have roughly the same curriculum. But what if we change that? What if each university specializes in different fields?

To give one example, the California university system consists of ten university campuses, 23 state campuses, and 115 community college campuses. Rather than have each teach roughly the same courses, each campus could focus on one or a handful of related disciplines.

Each campus might offer the same courses for freshman and sophomore years but specialize in a field for students in their final two years. Students might attend one campus for the first two years, choose a major, and then attend a different campus that offers courses in that subject for their last two years. Or some campuses might specialize in required courses for the first two years.

One big campus in each metro area that focuses on teaching freshmen and sophomores would enable any student to save money by living at home for their first two years. This specialization would reduce costs while enabling students to receive a high-quality education in the field of their interest.

To be clear, I am not arguing that the federal government should force universities to adopt any of these models. I do believe, however, that state legislatures should use the power of the purse strings to force public universities to adopt cost-effective ways to reduce tuition costs, while still maintaining a high-quality learning experience for students. Enabling students to choose between coherent programs rather than hundreds of individual courses will help to do so.

Major-based Tuition

Another very big problem in universities is the number of majors that lead to jobs that pay far below the average income for college graduates. A major reason why governments subsidize universities is that they teach critical skills that are necessary in the workforce. Some skills, however, are far more valuable to society and therefore pay higher wages. Governments and parents pay hefty tuition bills, largely because they believe that it will lead to higher lifetime incomes.

After they graduate from college, however, many youths face underemployment. About 33% of college graduates are underemployed. Particularly among those who do not get a degree in a technical field, a sizable percentage work in relatively low-paying service jobs that do not require a college degree (Federal Reserve Bank of New York).

And this is not always a short-term situation. A sizable percentage of college graduates are still in non-college jobs a decade after graduating (Burning Glass, Strada).

While parents obsess over getting into the right college, in many ways the choice of majors is more important. There is a huge variability in lifetime incomes based on college majors.

The median annual wage of college-educated workers ages 25-59 varied greatly in 2013. It varied between $136,000 for petroleum engineers and $39,000 for early childhood education. By comparison, the average high-school graduate earned $36,000. Not surprisingly, STEM majors did well, as did those who had studied health care and business. Social sciences came out about average (Carnevale).

Universities can potentially play an important role in promoting long-term economic growth by passing on the key skills needed in the economy. The best method of measuring the importance of those skills is to compare the lifetime earnings of their graduates.

Particularly when underemployment is such a widespread problem among college graduates, it will also benefit young people if their chosen major is more focused on viable employment after graduation. Our society tells young people that, in order to be successful, they should "go to college," but the evidence is clear that this is not enough. Just as important is choosing a major that leads to gainful employment.

Taxpayers also have a vested interest in ensuring that money being spent in state universities goes toward the acquisition of critical skills necessary for economic growth. Public universities should not be solely devoted to promoting long-term economic growth, but it should at least be a part of their goal.

State legislatures should seriously consider charging tuition based on the declared major of the student. They could establish a sliding scale where the majors that paid the highest get the most state support in the form of subsidized tuition. Students who choose majors that lead to jobs that pay well below average would receive no state subsidies. This would mean that they paid higher tuition fees.

The market is very good at rewarding those who learn skills that benefit others. Consumers buy products based on what they want or need. Businesses that produce those products broaden their product range and have a strong incentive to hire more skilled workers to make those products. Over time, this increases the salaries of coveted workers, while not doing so for others.

It is no secret that many students and most parents want a college degree leading to a field that pays well. Unfortunately, many students who choose majors that pay relatively poorly still expect to live a comfortable professional-class lifestyle. If parents are willing to pay for those choices, they should be allowed to, but taxpayers should not be forced to do so too.

Departments that repeatedly produce students who earn incomes well below the average for college graduates should not be subsidized by taxpayers. This does not mean that those departments should be shut down. Those departments can still fundraise from philanthropic sources and alumni. And some professors in those departments will be needed to teach required courses. This would effectively mean that those departments function more like private universities.

Setting up a competition between departments to ensure that their students acquire the skills for long-term success should be encouraged. Currently, departments have no institutional incentive to ensure that students get what they need. This should not spell the end of social sciences or humanities, but it will force them to analyze what their students need to learn in the long run and monitor results.

College Drop-Out Rate

While there is often talk about high-school dropout rates, relatively little is said about the problem of college dropout rates. Only about 40% of those who go to college obtain either a 2-year or 4-year degree by their mid-twenties. Only 19% of full-time students who attend four-year schools graduate within four years. Moreover, only 56% graduate within six years.

Most universities do not mind, because longer time periods increase the level of tuition that they harvest from students. And universities get paid regardless of whether or not a student graduates. The worst possible outcome, not receiving a degree while incurring a large debt load, is becoming increasingly common. This wastes taxpayers' and parents' money (Complete College America).

This results in higher levels of college debt and lost wages. Each additional year of four-year college attendance costs $22,826 in higher tuition and living expenses and $45,327 in lost wages. Each additional year for 2-year Associate degrees cost over $50,000 (Complete College America).

Minimum Course Load

One important reason why college students do not graduate is that they are not taking enough courses. Students who take enough courses to graduate within four years have much higher graduation rates than students who take fewer classes (Complete College America).

Universities that require students to take a full course load have much higher graduation rates than universities that do not. In combination with lower spending on amenities and more affordable tuition, this one simple requirement could shift the emphasis of the college experience back to education (Complete College America).

State legislatures should seriously consider mandating all students who enter a four-year public university under the age 25 to enroll in enough courses to graduate within four years. The same requirement should be made for 2-year Associate degrees and 1- to 2-year certificates. In addition, the federal government should mandate that any student who receives tuition subsidies or government-backed loans do the same.

We know that students can do this, because it was a routine schedule in the past. In combination with my previously-discussed reforms, a minimum course load would be possible and effective today.

With lower tuition fees, students will have to work less in gainful employment, giving them more time to focus on their studies. And with fewer on-campus amenities, they will have fewer distractions from their studies. Students who need to work to pay for living expenses will still have plenty of time in the evenings and the summer to work.

Obviously, not all students have the luxury of taking a full course load. Older students, in particular, have family and work obligations. That is why I suggest that, in order to be fair to older students with full-time jobs and family, we should exempt students who first enroll in college at age 25 or higher.

Focus on Results

Key metrics for measuring the success of policies to make college affordable should be (all costs should be indexed for inflation):
- Total cost paid by students (not advertised tuition)
- Tuition paid by students for each university
- Changes in tuition costs compared to inflation
- How much state legislatures spend per student
- Long-term income levels of college graduates
- On-time graduation rates
- Levels of college debt and the monthly cost to former students
- Non-academic costs as a percentage of university spending
- Percent of total compensation spending for non-academic employees.

MAKING ADMISSIONS MERIT-BASED

To promote progress, we need a radical reform of the college admissions process. The four-year degree has become the de facto admission ticket into the American professional class. This class dominates virtually all American institutions, and supplies virtually all of our leaders. We need to ensure that those who get into universities do so based on merit.

Universities benefit financially from being the de facto gatekeeper to the American professional class. Parents in that class will do almost anything to ensure that their children get into the right college. Many will pay almost any level of tuition to ensure the financial future of their children. This gives universities tremendous power to shape the behavior and beliefs of the future leaders of our nation.

Since virtually all of our leaders come from that professional class, society has a real stake in who is accepted into universities. And since state and federal governments pay for a very substantial portion of the higher education budget, they both have a significant amount of influence over the process.

Just as we need corporations to fully embrace skills-based merit, we need universities to fully embrace an admissions process that is solely based on academic merit. In this way, we can build a merit-based pathway into the professional class that is open to all. Unfortunately, discrimination is rampant in the college admissions process.

When most people think about discrimination in the college admissions process, they immediately think about the hot-button issue of affirmative action based on race. Unfortunately, racial discrimination has become a standard part of the college admissions process. Affirmative action started in the 1970s as a temporary step to expand the eligibility pool, but it has become institutionalized racial discrimination. It is a sad fact of life that universities have some of the highest levels of racial discrimination among all institutions in American society.

It is crucial to realize that affirmative action is far from being the only form of anti-academic-merit admissions criteria. Universities, particularly private universities, routinely accept students with far lower academic qualifications because of one or more of the following reasons:

- Their parent's income (i.e. their ability to pay the tuition without financial aid)
- Their parents donated large amounts of money to the college
- Their parents previously attended the same college (leading to them being called legacy students)
- Their parents work for the college.
- Their parents have personal connections to college administrators (i.e. the Dean's list)
- Athletic ability
- The students participate in a large number of extra-curricular activities or volunteer work
- Letters of recommendation from alumni, administrators, guidance counselors, or teachers
- Essays or projects in the entrance exam
- Candidate interviews

All of these non-academic criteria undermine the fairness of the admissions process and give an advantage to the children of White professional-class youths over other more talented youths.

A Legacy of Discrimination

Various combinations of the above admission criteria are currently in use by admissions departments in virtually all private and many public universities. To cover up the goals of the admissions process, universities label the process "holistic" and keep the results and process secret.

This complex and opaque admissions process started in the 1920s at Harvard University. Originally, Harvard and other Ivy League schools admitted applicants who passed fairly easy academic examinations. Because tuition was expensive and the pool of students was local, entrants to Harvard students overwhelmingly came from the Protestant upper-class in the Northeast.

Starting in the 1920s, the sons of Jewish immigrants in New York City began to apply to Harvard. As a result, the percentage of students of Jewish ethnicity began to rapidly increase. By 1925 the percentage of Jewish students at Harvard had jumped from near zero to 27% (SFA).

In an era when anti-semitism was widespread within the upper class, this was considered a scandalous problem that needed to be solved. Harvard President A. Lawrence Howell began a campaign to change the admissions process to get the desired result. This started a long tradition of doing the same in American admissions processes.

Private letters written at the time between President Howell, alumni, and the administrators make it clear that the original purpose of this system was to:

1. Limit the number of Jewish students to a level that was acceptable to its traditional upper-class Protestant students and alumni. Otherwise, those members of the preferred class would enroll in other elite colleges.

2. Create a system so complex and opaque that Harvard could plausibly deny that deliberate discrimination was taking place.

The "reform" worked. Within a year Jewish enrollment was cut in half, and it remained at that level for the next few decades. All of the new requirements – character, photos, essays, letters of recommendation, demographic information, interviews, legacy preferences, and ability to pay tuition – enabled universities to filter out undesirable Jews while claiming not to do so. By the 1960s, Harvard had added a complex docket system that exploited the geographical concentration of Jews to exclude them (SLA).

Thankfully, few universities today are trying to exclude Jews, but now Asians have replaced Jews in the role of "undesirable over-achievers". In addition, universities want to increase the number of Black students to achieve non-merit-based goals of "diversity" and "inclusion."

The overall goal of "holistic" admissions is still to obscure the fact that the process is not based on merit, while enabling administrators to claim that it is. Now, the main goal is to ensure that universities, particularly private ones:

- Don't admit too many Asian students, to make the university look diverse and inclusive.
- Admit a reasonable number of Black students, also to make the university look diverse and inclusive.
- Admit a sizable number of students with lower academic qualifications whose parents are wealthy enough to pay the exorbitant tuition.
- Create a system so complex and opaque that the university can plausibly deny that deliberate discrimination is taking place.

Racial/ethnic discrimination is still at the core of the admissions process. Now we have also added a layer of financial discrimination. Universities systematically set targets for the racial percentage of new students and then rejig the criteria to get the desired result. Any deviations from the targets are made up in the next year. Then they deny that they are doing it (SFA).

Ironically, a system designed to make the university look diverse and inclusive also discriminates in favor of the White professional class. Apart from racial affirmative action, all of the criteria in the holistic admissions process tend to favor students whose parents have four-year college degrees, higher incomes, and connections with the school.

While the actual results of the admissions process are typically kept secret, the recent lawsuit by the Students For Fair Admissions against Harvard University has provided unprecedented insights. Students admitted into Harvard who are recruited as athletes, legacy students, those on the Dean's list and children of faculty and staff (known as

ALDCs) have much lower academic standards than other students admitted into Harvard. According to one study, three-quarters of White ALDC students would have been rejected if admissions had been strictly based on academic merit (Arcidiacono).

Recruited athletes had a 14-times higher rate of admission than non-athletes with comparable academic accomplishments, and they made up 10% of the admitted class. Legacy students had a 5.7-times higher rate of admission, and they made up 14% of the class. Children of faculty and staff have similar rates. All three of these groups were over 68% White, and they had far higher incomes than the average applicant (Arcidiacono).

When the focus shifts to a less prestigious private university, the discrimination shifts more to the ability to pay tuition. With the exception of elite schools, private universities routinely accept below-average students from high-income families (Tough).

In order to make room for those more profitable students, universities must turn away more talented students from lower-income families. High tuition prices have forced most private universities to prioritize the ability to pay over academic merit. Moreover, the Best Colleges algorithms reward colleges for spending lots of money (Tough).

The dirty little secret of private schools is that they give a substantial percentage of financial aid to students from wealthy families. They do so, not because the students need the assistance, but because their research shows that the practice increases the chances that students whose parents can afford to pay their exorbitant tuition fees will choose their school. Unfortunately, this leaves far fewer resources for students who actually need financial aid (Tough).

While each of these admissions criteria has some logic to them, when applied together they lead to a deeply corrupt admissions process. Universities can pretend that they searching for the best young academic minds and only making exceptions for the talented poor, when in fact the entire system achieves the opposite.

Just as Jews were the victim of the admissions process from the 1920s to the 1960s, Asians have been the primary victim since the 1970s. For Asians to get accepted into a university, they must have far higher grades and test scores than other races. By combining the elimination of all the criteria in the holistic admissions process with the elimination of racial discrimination, we can strike a far greater blow against "white privilege" than anything affirmative action can possibly achieve (SFA).

Racial Preferences Cannot Be Made to Work

Racial preferences are based upon many flawed assumptions. One problem is that universities do not admit "a group" into the university. Universities must make a decision for each individual, not for each group. The chosen individual does not represent their racial group, as each individual has unique characteristics.

In addition, all of these preferences appear to be based upon the assumption that Americans come from basically two groups: affluent Whites and poor Blacks. Nothing could be further from the truth.

When a university admits a Black person to satisfy a racial preference, that person is highly unlikely to be poor. The children of poor people are not applying for university in the first place. Racial preferences merely replace a student whose parents are White members of the professional class with a student whose parents are Black members of the professional class. This is only promoting diversity within a system of class privilege.

Nor are there only two races in the United States. Perhaps this biracial system made sense in the 1960s, but it is a gross distortion of America in the 2020s. Depending upon your definitions, the United States currently has five racial groups: Whites, Blacks, Asians, Hispanics, and Native Americans. More to the point, none of these racial groups are monolithic.

The category "Asian" consists of dozens of different cultures. The number approaches the hundreds if we include ethnic minorities within Asian nations. Many of these people share virtually nothing in common, except for the continent where their ancestors once lived.

The category "Hispanic" includes descendants from at least 26 different nations, not to mention religious and ethnic minorities within each nation. Hispanics themselves are largely an amalgamation of Spanish, Portuguese, Black, and a wide range of Native American tribes.

The category of "Black" includes descendants from slaves in the United States, American freemen as well as recent immigrants from Sub-Saharan Africa and the Caribbean. With increased immigration from those nations, the percentage of Blacks who are actually descended from slaves declines every year.

The category of "Native Americans" includes 574 federally recognized tribes, each of which has its own unique cultural traditions. These five racial categories obscure the substantial cultural diversity within them. And even this cultural diversity does not capture the enormous individual diversity within those groups. Universities must admit individuals, not groups.

More to the point, intermarriage across races, religions, and ethnicity is extremely widespread and getting more common with each generation. In total, 10.2% of all married-couple households are interracial and the number is increasing. In 2015, 17% of all newlyweds were married to someone of a different race (Pew, US Census).

The interracial marriage rate for newlyweds is 27% for Hispanics, 29% for Asians, and 18% for Blacks. For native-born Hispanics and Asians, the rate is around 50%. Only a constant stream of new immigrants keeps the original categories from washing away completely. For Native Americans, racial intermarriage rates are even higher (Pew, US Census).

Within each racial category, there are also American citizens and non-citizens in various forms. Our racial categories treat new immigrants from Latin America, Asia, and Africa as if they were in the same category as American citizens whose ancestors come from the same continent.

This is particularly awkward for Blacks, many of whom have ancestors who lived on North American soil for 400 years. A very sizable proportion of Blacks in selective universities are actually recent immigrants from Africa and the Caribbean. To say that a recent immigrant from Africa or the Caribbean somehow represents Black Americans descended from slavery is utterly ridiculous, no matter how you look at it.

Racial preferences play racial minorities off against each other. The primary victim of racial preferences in selective universities is not Whites, but Asians. Asians know they are not competing against other races; they are competing against each other for a deliberately constrained number of slots. The same goes for other racial minorities.

Why Should We Care?

Some may claim that universities, particularly private universities, are independent institutions that should be allowed to set admissions criteria in any way they choose. I am sympathetic to this argument for a few isolated examples, but when the same admissions philosophy pervades the entire university system, it has deeply negative consequences.

A Progress-based reform agenda should require that universities that accept taxpayer money have a simple, transparent, merit-based admissions process. Because acquiring a four-year college degree is a de facto admission requirement for leadership positions in American institutions, society has a vested interest in the admissions process. The more the process is based upon merit, the more contributions our leaders can make to progress.

I also believe that our admissions process has played an important role in the decline of academic rigor. In our current system, with a large percentage of students entering with sub-par academic qualifications, professors are under constant pressure to make grades easier and require less reading and writing from students.

This particularly becomes a problem when identifiable groups, such as racial minorities or athletes know they cannot compete academically, so they put pressure on the university to lower standards for everyone. They effectively create interest groups that support low standards.

Having a student body with a fairly narrow range in academic ability will also make it easier for professors to make their courses more challenging. As a former professor, I have seen first-hand how students who should not have been accepted into a college in the first place force professors to lower their standards.

When all students are fairly homogenous in academic ability, professors can realistically cut grade inflation, and increase the length of paper and reading assignments knowing that they will not leave one-third of the class behind. Declining standards have become so institutionalized that I am not hopeful this change will actually happen, but at least some committed universities and professors could take a stand.

Finally, our public university system is largely based upon taxpayer funding, giving all of society an interest in who gets in and why. Even private schools accept a substantial amount of direct federal research funding and indirect financial aid for students. So our university system has not been truly independent for quite some time.

Merit-Based Admissions

Public universities and private universities that accept government funding should be required by legislation to admit students based purely on clear academic achievement. They should only be allowed to use the following criteria for admission:

1. High-school or post-secondary grade point average.

2. Test scores, such as SAT, SAT Subject, ACT, CLT, AP, TOEFL, or GED.

3. Other academic metrics that are clearly correlated with subsequent college GPA and college graduation rates.

4. These metrics may only be applied if they increase the accuracy of predictions of college success above the first two criteria listed above.

Universities must also require that all their on-site students are American citizens, legal residents, or have valid student visas. Online learners could be exempted from this requirement.

Public universities and private universities who accept government funding should be required by legislation to not use any of the following criteria in the admissions process: race, religion, gender, ethnicity, age, donations from students, donations from parents, attendance or employment in the same school by parents or other family members, opinion's of university deans or administrators, athletic achievements or ability, extra-curricular activities, essays or ability to pay.

The terms of the legislation should make it clear that accepting government funding includes direct government funding as well as indirect funding via financial aid for students. As long as the government is supporting these institutions financially, they should be able to influence the admissions process.

I think that a few reasonable exclusions should be allowed. Universities might want to limit their pool of students either partially or entirely to their own city, metro area, state, or region. This would enable some schools to offer a unique educational experience based on their local geography and history. Universities should not, however, be allowed to establish a complex docket system that sets limits for many different regions across the United States. This system is too open to cheating.

To ensure a fully transparent system, public universities and private universities that accept government funding should be required to display the cut-offs used for GPAs and test scores for each year on the internet. The website should include a simple calculator that enables anyone to enter a combination of GPA and test scores to see what the results should be. That will ensure that everyone knows the rules, and can see that the rules are being applied fairly to everyone.

Public universities and private universities that accept government funding should be required to make all admission applications completely anonymous before any college employees view their record.

This will ensure that admissions make their admission decisions exclusively based on legal characteristics.

Public universities and private universities that accept government funding should be required to publish anonymous online databases listing all students who applied, their GPA, test scores, and demographic characteristics along with their admission results. Then anyone who is treated unfairly has the data to back their discrimination claim.

Because private schools rely on students with below-average academic qualifications from wealthy families to pay tuition fees, they will be faced with a choice. They can either maintain their current admissions process and drop government funding or overhaul their admissions process.

Any private school that wants to continue receiving government funding directly or indirectly via student financial aid or loans may be forced to radically cut the cost of their tuition fees. Without being able to cherry-pick students whose parents can pay the tuition, nor being able to pass the bill on to the government, they may have no other choice.

The Ivy League and other most prestigious private schools have large enough endowments that they might be able to do as they choose. These large endowments will enable them to maintain current practices without government subsidies. My guess, however, is that, if the rest of the university system changes to a more merit-based system, the Ivy League schools will have a difficult time justifying their current practices to students and alumni.

I believe that certain types of educational institutions should be exempted from some of these requirements. Historically black colleges may require that some or all of their students are black. Historically religious colleges may require that some or all of their students are members of a certain religious faith. Historically women's colleges may require that some or all of their students are women. As long as the practices are not too widespread, I see no problem with allowing such practices to continue.

College Sports

College sports are a uniquely American institution. To the best of my knowledge, no other nation or culture has anything quite like it. Universities in other nations have few highly-competitive sports teams that function as feeders to professional leagues.

In some ways, college sports are the most merit-oriented of all university activities. All athletes must relentlessly compete and the results on the field or court are obvious to all.

Unfortunately, that merit is based on athletic ability, not academic ability. Those two abilities are so far apart from each other that it will be impossible to mesh them together.

I know that my Progress-based reform agenda will face serious resistance if it leads to the abolition of college sports. And I must confess that I am a huge college football fan. Since college sports are such a major part of American culture and the campus lifestyle, certain athletic exemptions should be put in place for major college sports.

If we combine an exemption with an acknowledgment that college athletes are athletes first and students second, this seems justified. In particular, we should acknowledge that big-time college sports are highly profitable industries that exploit young unpaid labor. Just as the Olympics finally gave up on the charade that amateurism is a necessary ideal, so should college sports.

Realistically this means football and basketball. These are the only college sports that are revenue-making. All other sports programs, with very few exceptions, lose revenue.

As a special exemption, college football and basketball athletes could be accepted into college based exclusively on their athletic ability in that sport. In exchange, universities should pay their athletes. During the season of that sport, the student would be considered a full-time athlete who is paid at least minimum wage and not required to attend classes. Outside the sports season, the student would be considered to be a full-time student who takes classes full-time.

Athletes in all other sports would have to meet the same academic requirements as all other students, and their academic ability would not be allowed to play a role in their admission. Since the vast majority of those athletes come from the White professional class, this in no way undermines concerns about diversity or racial equity (Tough).

If a university does not wish to pay its football and basketball athletes or the programs do not earn enough revenue to pay their salaries, then the athletes should be admitted by the same criteria as non-athletes.

Focus on Results

Key metrics for measuring the success of policies to make college admissions merit-based should be percent of universities that:
- Allow only GPA and test scores as part of their admission process.
- Publish their admission cut-offs online each year.
- Make all applications anonymous before any employees view their record.
- Publish anonymous databases of students who applied and their characteristic (as described earlier).

Conclusion

Because the four-year college degree has become the de facto admission ticket into the American professional class, and a portion of that class will provide the future leaders of our society, American society has a strong interest in ensuring that college admissions are entirely merit-based.

SKILLS-BASED IMMIGRATION

I n the first book in this series, *From Poverty to Progress*, I made the case that we seriously underestimate the importance of skills in using and making technologies. Technological innovation plays a substantial role in promoting progress, but technologies cannot exist without related human skills.

While biological organisms can survive and reproduce without human intervention (except for some domesticated plants and animals), technologies cannot exist without human intervention. For it to survive and reproduce (by getting widely used by humans), technology requires humans to possess highly specialized skills.

Even the simplest technology needs some amount of skill to use. In addition, conceiving of the technology, designing it, building it, and repairing it are important related skills. Until people possess these skills, a specific piece of technology cannot come into being, or if it does, it will not last very long. It will certainly never spread far enough to become an important part of a society's technological suite.

For this reason, the acquisition and transmission of new skills is a key bottleneck in the ability of technological innovation to deliver real progress for the masses. In future books in this series, I will propose reforms to our educational and job training systems to improve the skills required in the workforce, particularly for youths. In this book, I want to talk about the role that our immigration policy can play in boosting American skills.

Immigration is one of the most controversial domains of public policy. This should not be surprising, as nothing has a bigger impact on the future of a society than its people. By allowing certain types of people into a nation rather than others, you are shaping the future of your nation. Citizens want to take part in the discussion as to how we do so.

Skilled Immigration In the Past

Ever since the city states of medieval Northern Italy founded the first Commercial societies, the immigration of skilled workers has played an important role in sustaining progress. Skilled immigration enables talented people to relocate to societies where they can put their talents to the best use. When the most talented are given a chance to excel, everyone wins; the person wins, their families win, their community wins, and their nation wins.

Merchants, bankers, and artisans in Commercial societies were particularly mobile. Often starting their professions in small market towns, the most talented had the incentive to move to bigger cities with more opportunities.

The medieval apprenticeship system often created more artisans than could profitably work in cities. Masters recruited apprenticeships as workers for their workshops. The masters returned the favor by promising to train them and give them room and board. Once the apprentice had proven their talents, they became journeymen. Journeymen typically had the skills to run their own workshop, but they lacked the experience and the capital to do so.

Many journeymen chose to immigrate to other cities on the European continent. They had a strong incentive to go to cities where their particular skills were in greater demand than the local labor force could supply. In this way, skills in a particular technology naturally diffused from city to city throughout the continent.

Political instability and the oppression of minorities accelerated the migration of skilled workers. In the 16th Century, Antwerp was a highly innovative and competitive city with thriving export industries. When Spanish troops sacked the city in 1576 and massacred much of the population, a huge number of the skilled individuals who survived migrated as refugees to Dutch cities. These skilled immigrants laid the foundation for the Dutch Golden era. During the 17th Century, Dutch cities were the most economically competitive in the entire world, partly due to skilled immigrants from Flanders.

The repression of Protestants in France led to a massive flow of skilled refugees to England and the Netherlands. Each migrant brought valuable skills that enabled entirely new industries to spring up in those two nations. Skilled immigrants from Britain and what is now Germany played a substantial role in promoting the development of American industry.

Today, many of America's largest and most innovative businesses were founded by immigrants or the children of immigrants. Apple was co-founded by Steve Jobs, the son of a Syrian immigrant. AT&T was founded by Alexander Graham Bell, who immigrated from Scotland and Canada. EBay was founded by Pierre Omidyar, who was born to Iranian parents in France. Google was co-founded by Sergey Brin, who is an immigrant from Russia. Tesla was founded by Elon Musk, an immigrant from South Africa. And this is just a partial list of the stunning contributions that highly-skilled immigrants have made to the American economy.

Skills-based Immigration Today

The United States is the nation where the most talented have the greatest chance of achieving personal success. That success not only benefits themselves and their families, but, if given a chance, it will also benefit their cities and the nation as a whole. Unfortunately, encouraging skilled immigration is only a very small part of current American immigration policy.

A Progress-based reform agenda should put promoting skilled immigrants to the United States to be at the core of our immigration policy.

Family Reunification

Currently, U.S. immigration law is based on the following principles: the reunification of families, admitting skilled immigrants, and admitting refugees while promoting diversity. In many cases, these goals conflict with each other.

Since the Immigration and Nationality Act of 1965, family reunification has been at the core of U.S. immigration law. Potential legal immigrants who have family members with American citizenship are strongly preferred.

While the total number of immigrants is capped at 675,000 as of 2019, family members are completely uncapped. This is not a trivial exclusion as, in the same year, more than 480,000 immigrants were allowed in for the purposes of family reunification.

Typically what this means is that an immigrant comes to the United States, whether illegally or legally, and then acquires American citizenship. Sometimes this is through the standard immigration process, while other times it is through periodic amnesties granted by Congress. The first immigrant can sponsor immediate family members, and then those family members can sponsor additional family members at a later date.

Implementing family reunification in this way has created the phenomenon of chain migration. All it takes is for one immigrant, illegal or legal, to eventually acquire American citizenship, for an entire extended family to do so in the following decades.

Most American citizens whose family members were not recent immigrants have very few relatives who live overseas. This is for the simple reason that American citizens tend to marry other American citizens. This seemingly mundane fact means that our immigration policy is unintentionally biased toward favoring the family members of recent immigrants over other American citizens.

Since immigration from 1965 until about 2007 was dominated by relatively unskilled Mexican immigrants, rules designed to promote family reunification have unintentionally promoted the legal migration of unskilled Mexican workers.

The Impact of Immigration

The impact of immigration on American society is one of the most controversial issues in American politics. Multiculturalists and libertarians assert that virtually all immigration is good for the nation, and that restricting immigration violates basic human rights. Nativists claim that virtually all immigration is bad for the nation as it undermines American culture and creates competition that lowers wages.

Though I cannot possibly present evidence that would convince the true believers on either side, I believe the following:

1.   Immigrants with high skills benefit American society, because they generate more economic growth, pay more in taxes, and consume far fewer government benefits.

2.   Immigrants with low skills provide, at best, mixed benefits for American society as they pay much less in taxes, receive higher levels of government benefits, and depress per capita GDP. In addition, there is some evidence that they compete for jobs with low-skilled American jobs, making it more difficult for the existing working class candidates to earn a living wage.

Skills-based Immigration

A new American immigration policy should shift the emphasis of legal immigration from family reunification to skills and economic benefit to the nation. A complete overhaul of American immigration policy is far beyond the scope of this book. Such a proposal would have to deal with border enforcement, amnesties, and many other issues that are not directly related to the concept of progress. In this book, I want to focus on policies that directly focus on promoting progress.

One possible way to promote progress via skilled immigration would be to copy Canada and Australia. Both nations have a point-based system that is largely designed to acquire as many skilled workers as possible. Some have proposed that we copy such a system. Such a proposal might eliminate all the special categories of immigrants, such as family-based immigrants, the diversity lottery, and separate quotas for refugees and asylum seekers. All immigrants would be placed into one points-based system.

I would be in favor of such a reform, but I do not see the need to overhaul immigration policy when we can offer more targeted reforms. Points-based systems are always highly complicated, as they try to balance many competing goals.

The goal of a Progress-based reform agenda should be to promote skill immigration as much as possible, without getting bogged down in all the implementation details that a comprehensive overhaul of immigration policy would require.

I believe that a Progress-based reform agenda should be based upon a few simple changes that would have sweeping effects. All legal immigrants must fulfill the following criteria:

• Mastery of the English language (speaking, verbal comprehension, reading, and writing), and

• One or more of the following:

• A four-year college degree from an accredited university in a field that pays above the average wage for college graduates in the United States.

• Demonstrated work experience in such a field.

• The ability to pass skill-based tests that are necessary to be hired in such a field in the United States (discussed earlier).

• Being the owner of a business that can realistically be relocated to the United States and employ at least one additional US worker each year for five years.

• Be willing to invest at least $500,000 in establishing a new job-creating enterprise that employs at least 10 full-time unrelated US workers. Ideally, the amount should go towards manufacturing or physical infrastructure. Real estate should not count towards this amount.

In other words, everyone admitted must communicate well in English and be highly skilled or willing to invest capital. Family members of American citizens could still be admitted under this new system as long as they fulfill these requirements. Refugees and asylum seekers could still be admitted, as long as they fulfilled these requirements. In theory, every new immigrant could be a refugee or a family member, so this reform does not necessarily cut their numbers. It just sets two additional criteria.

Temporary Pause to Immigration

One of the big concerns opponents of immigration express is that immigrants will be in competition for jobs with American citizens, and too many citizens will lose their jobs or have their wages pushed down. While the economy is growing rapidly, I do not think that this is a major concern, but the situation does change during times of recession when unemployment rates increase.

This is also a difficult situation for legal immigrants. During times of economic growth, immigrants can typically find a job relatively quickly. During a recession, however, this is far from the case. While immigrants who arrived a few years earlier may already have established career paths, immigrants who just arrived have no jobs, and no work experience in their new country.

To protect both American citizens and legal immigrants from temporary economic hardship, there should be a temporary pause to immigration when the unemployment rate is 50% higher than its average over the previous ten years. This would stop new immigrants from entering the United States during recessions and give the economy a few years to recover to more typical unemployment rates. This would make it much easier for new immigrants to find jobs.

I believe that this would also have a positive effect when it comes to calming concerns about excessive immigration. People are much more likely to be concerned about economic competition from immigrants during times of sluggish economic growth. In general, during times of economic growth, such concerns are much lower as American citizens have much less trouble finding jobs.

Recruiting Overseas Talent

A major goal of every American embassy and consulate should be recruiting skilled workers to immigrate to the United States. The new immigration criteria would give them a simple framework for the type of worker that should be courted.

Paying for targeted advertising campaigns to increase awareness of the new rules would help those who can most benefit the United States to start thinking about the possibilities. Highly targeted speaking tours with professional and business associations should get out the word to the right people with relatively little expense.

In particular, we should recruit entrepreneurs of small businesses that have a real opportunity to grow if they are relocated to the United States. I personally know of a number of entrepreneurs who struggled to expand their businesses in Europe, immigrated to the United States, and then reestablished their businesses on our soil. Using the power of the internet, online supply chains, consignment, and domestic labor, they grew their small businesses into profitable enterprises that employed many American citizens. In doing so, they benefitted themselves, their family, their community, the American economy, and its tax base. This practice should be far more widespread.

There is no reason why large enterprises could not be courted as well. With abundant, affordable energy and housing, lower regulations and taxes and many skilled workers, large enterprises in Europe, Canada and Japan would have excellent reasons for relocating operations to the United States.

As labor costs rise, production in China is becoming increasingly expensive, so many corporations are seriously thinking about relocating. Lower value-added manufacturing that requires low-skilled and low-paid workers will probably relocate to Southeast Asia, but higher value-added sectors may seriously consider the United States. This is particularly true in energy-intensive fields that require skilled labor, for which there would be a strong incentive to relocate production facilities.

Recruiting skilled workers should be a particular focus in repressive regimes that are hostile to the United States. Embassies in Russia, China, Iran, Venezuela, Cuba, Belarus, and Nicaragua could simultaneously help to undermine the economic prospects of those regimes, provide safe harbor for refugees, and promote American economic development. We can thus simultaneously hurt our enemies and help ourselves.

Recruiting skilled workers should also be a priority in affluent nations that give fewer opportunities to the talented. Here the primary problem is high taxes and regulations that make it hard to start up and scale a business.

In the past, talented Canadians and Europeans flocked to the United States searching for better opportunities, but our current immigration policy makes it much harder for them to do so. A combination of a skills-based immigration policy and active recruitment could bring a new wave of talented Europeans and Canadians to the United States.

Archipelago of Talent

With the exception of Sub-Saharan Africa, world populations are expected to start shrinking within the next few decades. The primary driving force of this change is fertility rates that are substantially below the replacement rate of 2.1. Europe and East Asia are particularly likely to see massively declining population levels over the next century. In the long run, even African populations will start declining.

The world's progress over the last 200 years has been undergirded by expanding populations. Expanding populations have become such an ever-present phenomenon that we do not know what types of impact a declining population will have on society overall. They will likely be profound. Some will be good, and some will be bad.

One thing that is clear is that the overall balance of power will be disrupted by declining populations. China and Russia, in particular, are likely to see a drastic drop in their influence in the world over the course of this century due to declining populations.

Public policy to increase fertility rates seems unlikely to work. Many nations have tried paying women to have more children, but these policies have not been very successful. Nor is it clear that pro-natal policies are desirable.

If nothing else, the declining human population will be a boon to the natural environment. Declining population combined with urbanization and highly productive agriculture will drastically reduce the land footprint of humanity on the natural environment.

The only method for fighting population decline that seems to have a reasonable chance of success is immigration. I believe that relatively high levels of immigration combined with a skills-based immigration policy will cement American power and influence over the next century.

Let's assume that the following trends occur over the next few centuries:

1. Low fertility rates cause population declines almost everywhere in the world.

2. The most talented migrate to the United States for greater opportunities.

3. This migration causes the American population and the American economy to keep growing, perhaps the only nation that will experience such growth.

4. Because of ever-increasing levels of talent compared to the rest of the world, the American economy keeps booming. This then creates additional incentives for American policymakers to continue skilled immigration and incentives for the most talented to choose to move to the United States.

For the last 200 years, people have migrated from rural areas to cities for greater opportunities. The vast majority of this trend has been within nations. But what if we expand this trend internationally? What if the combination of the above forces makes the United States the top immigration destination for skilled workers?

What is going to disrupt this positive feedback loop? Well, bad politics, of course, but aside from that, I think that is a stable long-term trend.

In the distant future, let's say the year 2120, I can foresee a world with a declining population, and the United States making up a higher and higher percentage of the world population. People may complain about American "hyper-power" today, but if this trend occurs, American influence will go far beyond even that. The United States might effectively become the metropolis for the entire world. Obviously, this is not a prediction of the future, but the scenario is not so implausible as it first might seem.

As populations in the rest of the world decline, this will lead to a "rewilding" of the rest of the world. Agriculture and rural areas will gradually decline in land use, and wild habitats will take their place. Tropical nations might see vast regrowth of forests.

What if the world population in the 2100s keeps declining (as it is projected to), while only one nation keeps growing and keeps getting more skilled? These two factors will probably become a self-sustaining feedback loop. A higher and higher percentage of the world's population will live in the United States, while more and more land in other nations gets transformed back into wild habitat.

Of course, there are limits to the number of immigrants that the United States can support. But assuming that we can build houses fast enough and create enough jobs, the limit is actually quite high. The Mountain West and Great Plains are still almost devoid of population, with the exception of a few isolated cities. There are no fundamental geographical reasons why dozens of additional cities cannot grow in those regions.

This should be a long-term goal that both Greens and those who favor progress can get behind. Obviously, this will take centuries to accomplish, but it is a worthy long-term goal.

Focus on Results

Key metrics for measuring the success of policies to make immigration merit-based should be:

- Percent of new legal residents with full-time employment.
- Percent of new legal residents with full-time employment in household.
- Percent of new legal residents with full-time employment by national origin
- Average income of new legal residents
- Average income of new legal residents by national origin
- Percent of new legal residents that are unemployed.
- Percent of new legal residents that are unemployed by national origin
- Number of US citizens employed by company established by new legal residents
- Number of companies established by new legal residents
- Percent of legal residents convicted of a felony
- Percent of legal residents convicted of a felony by national origin
- Percent of recent immigrants who entered the country legally
- Percent of temporary residents who overstay their visa▉

Conclusion

In order to promote the acquisition of the critical skills that are necessary for long-term economic growth, American immigration policy should exclusively admit skilled workers. This will power economic growth, reduce controversies over immigration policy and enable the American population to keep growing.

In this part of the book, I made many proposals that can help wealthy nations that are already experiencing progress to sustain it in the future. All of these proposals are closely linked to the concept of the Five Keys to Progress and How Progress Works. Some of these proposals seek to eliminate government policies that currently undermine progress, while others are new programs that seek to accelerate progress.

I believe that it is essential to build policy proposals on the concept of the Five Keys to Progress because they are the critical preconditions that enable societies to make a better world for their citizens. They are the critical preconditions for creating and sustaining the vast, decentralized problem-solving network that is a modern society.

I do not claim that these policy reforms are the only possible means to promote progress. I do claim that, since each is tied to the key factors which promote progress, they stand a far greater chance of having a real impact on people's lives than other proposals.

In particular, I claim that the Progress-based reform agenda will be far more beneficial to the American people and mankind than either of the policy platforms of liberal Democrats or conservative Republicans.

These proposals are not meant to be an exhaustive list of all possible proposals that can be derived from the Five Keys to Progress. Indeed, I am confident that I can derive many more, and others who buy into the concept can do even better. I hope this book helps them to do so.

Even more so, I hope this book inspires large organizations, such as governments and corporations, to test these proposals with small experiments and scale them up rapidly if they prove useful.

PART THREE: WHAT WEALTHY NATIONS CAN DO TO HELP

S o far this book has mainly focused on wealthy nations that industrialized centuries ago. In the following two parts of this book, I will shift the focus to developing nations. These developing nations have often experienced at least some level of progress, but they would benefit from increasing the rate of progress.

This part focuses on what wealthy nations can do to help developing nations experience greater progress via long-term economic growth.

KEEP PROGRESS GOING

The single most important thing that wealthy nations can do to help developing nations is to keep their own progress going. By that, I mean that wealthy nations need to first and foremost keep their long-term economic growth going.

Developing nations desperately need to scale up their export industries (the fourth Key to Progress). The easiest way to do so is to export to wealthy nations, for the simple reason that this is where the money is. The most viable means for developing nations to promote local progress is to gradually work their way up the value-added chain of export industries. Since wealthy nations are by far their biggest export markets, developing nations desperately need economic growth in wealthy nations to continue.

In addition to providing export markets, the technological innovations, skills, and organizations created in wealthy nations can be highly beneficial to developing nations. Slower economic growth in wealthy nations would undermine the investment in technological innovation that indirectly benefits developing nations.

Most new innovations start out being too expensive for developing nations to afford to purchase. But sometimes this changes very fast.

For example, the invention of mobile phones has made it possible for developing nations to completely skip constructing what would otherwise be expensive hard-line phone networks. Better yet, they now have much cheaper and more useful mobile devices than the richest Westerners had in the 1980s. Medical and scientific advances also quickly diffuse from the wealthy nations that invent them to developing nations.

Another example is the internet. The internet has drastically lowered the barriers to information and skills that wealthy nations have and developing nations need. A poor person who cannot afford to buy a book can stop by an internet café and have access to an amazing amount of information. In fact, the total amount of information that is accessible on the internet now dwarfs anything that the richest person had in 1990.

Electric cars and batteries are being rapidly improved and getting more affordable in wealthy nations. It seems likely that, as they get cheaper, those transportation devices will diffuse through the developing world as well.

Some people think that economic growth in wealthy nations comes at the expense of poor people in the developing world, but nothing could be further from the truth. If wealthy nations want to help developing nations, then they must maintain their current progress above all else.

MAINTAINING THE GLOBAL TRADE SYSTEM

The second essential method for assisting developing nations is to maintain the current global trade system. This system rests upon economic, diplomatic, and military foundations that only the United States can provide.

While many who claim to speak for developing nations are hostile to this global trade system, it is this system that enabled all the current progress in developing nations over the last three decades. This global trade system lowered the barriers for developing nations to acquire the Five Keys to Progress.

The global trade system enabled any nation in the world to leverage the energy, transportation, and agricultural technologies invented by Industrial societies in the West. Now, even poor countries enjoy the benefits of automobiles, container ships and ports, the internet, skyscrapers, mobile devices, trains, airports, jet airplanes, trucks, highways, synthetic fertilizer, and dozens of other industrial technologies.

This global trade system transformed a world dominated by *geopolitical competition between the Great Powers* into a world dominated by *economic efficiency and global supply chains*. Before 1945, the primary focus of rulers was defending themselves against military threats from predatory empires. This meant focusing limited food and energy resources on building military power.

Before 1945, only the United States had the necessary geographic isolation, large population size, and the energy and food resources to make economic efficiency the prime goal for its society. In some ways, the current global trade system is an export of the unique conditions that the United States enjoyed throughout its history. Without Allied victories in World War I and World War II, this system would not have been possible, as European and Asian powers had no interest in participating.

Our current global trade system was established by the United States immediately after World War II. During the Cold War, it was largely restricted to Western nations and Japan. With the collapse of the Soviet Union in 1991, the global trade system expanded to encompass the entire world.

During the Cold War, this global trade system was seriously constrained by the military and ideological power of the Soviet Union. After the Soviet collapse, the security threat from predatory empires was drastically reduced.

Now leaders all over the world can focus on economic efficiency. Food (the first Key to Progress) and energy resources (the fifth Key to Progress) can be focused on building trade-based cities (the second Key to Progress) and world-class export industries (the fourth Key to Progress). Supply chains have expanded to include virtually every country in the world.

The cornerstone of this global trade system has been the unchallenged dominance of the United States Navy on the high seas. The last major naval battle was at Leyte Gulf in 1944 when the U.S. Navy destroyed the last remnants of the Imperial Japanese Navy. That battle inaugurated the current era of Pax Americana on the high seas.

Almost no other power in world history has achieved such a long period of naval dominance over the world's oceans. Many navies have tried, but except for the British Royal Navy in the 19th Century, they all failed.

Just as importantly, the U.S. Navy choose to use that power to promote peaceful trade on the high seas rather than destroying rival trade. So much has been written about the downside of this global trade system that we have forgotten how bad the alternatives were. Geostrategic competition between the Great Powers with smaller polities as their pawns has dominated much of human history.

This global trade system is based on a few key foundations:

1. A system of sovereign nation states facing a much lower military threat from predatory empires. Before 1945, developing nations were dominated by European empires. Then the Soviet Union took their place. Only since 1991 have we had a system of sovereign nation states and relative global peace.

2. Military alliances of the democratic powers to keep potential predatory empires, such as Russia and China, in check. With a lower level of military threat, nations could decentralize their political and economic system (the third Key to Progress).

3. Secure access to commercial shipping on the high seas given by the protection of the United States Navy, which gives:

4. Access to American consumer markets, the largest economic market on the globe. This relatively free trade enables nations to specialize in certain sectors of the economy. While tariffs have not been eliminated, they are far lower than in previous eras.

5. Access to agricultural inputs, such as nitrogen, phosphate and potassium fertilizers, from anywhere in the world. This makes productive agriculture (the first Key to Progress) far easier to achieve.

6. Access to food imports from anywhere in the world. This lowers the threshold for how productive domestic food production systems need to be.

7. Access to energy imports from anywhere in the world. This enables nations without domestic fossil fuel resources to adopt widespread use of this critical energy source (the fifth Key to Progress).

8. Access to other raw material imports from anywhere in the world, and the ability to export value-added manufacturing products to anywhere in the world (the fourth Key to Progress).

9. The English language as the de facto language of global finance, trade and economics.

10. The American dollar as a de facto world currency. About 70 percent of global currencies are in some way tied to the dollar.

The Russian invasion of Ukraine in 2022 and the potential Chinese invasion of Taiwan show that the world of geopolitics has not magically gone away. There are still plenty of authoritarian regimes willing to fill the void if the global trade system collapses.

In this global trade system, the United States plays an indispensable role. No other nation can match its economic and military power. That power is enhanced by NATO and military alliances with Asian nations that fear China. While retreating to within its borders might benefit the United States in the short term, it would cause many of the global foundations of progress to collapse.

This collapse would cause widespread political and economic disorder that is likely to lead to another war. It might even lead to an entire series of wars as lesser powers struggle to fill the void. They will only be able to do so by diverting energy, food, and manufacturing resources away from making their people richer towards building powerful military machines.

Inevitably, Russia, China, Iran, Saudi Arabia, Turkey, and perhaps other powers will step in with military force to take advantage of the disorder of an American retreat. Eventually, one of them will seek to dominate a region that Americans perceive as vital to their national interest.

Just as in World War I, World War II, and the Cold War, the United States will inevitably be dragged into another global military conflict. Then, assuming that the US wins that conflict, which is certainly not guaranteed, we will need to construct a new global trade system out of the ashes of the first. It will be far better to maintain the one we currently have.

Contrary to what the Left claims, the true alternative to global capitalism is not a world based on social justice. It is a world of greater poverty, brutal authoritarian regimes, and warring powers that seek to dominate lesser nations. It is a world where governments divert economic resources to military and domestic repression rather than promoting long-term economic growth, education, health care, and pensions.

In the end, however, there is only so much wealthy nations can do to assist developing nations to experience the progress that Western nations take for granted. Maintaining economic growth and the global trade system is necessary, but not sufficient. Developing nations must find a way to copy wealthy nations and acquire the Five Keys to Progress.

Elite Incentives

If we survey human history, we can see that elite incentives have radically changed.

Phase 1: Political elites oppose innovation: Between the invention of agriculture and the Industrial Revolution, elites largely opposed innovations that were necessary to create economic growth. They did so because they feared innovations would create economic wealth for those who might challenge political elites in the future. Elites in agricultural regimes preferred to live in a poor nation with them in total control compared to a richer nation that they did not control. Life was zero-sum.

Phase 2: Political elites promote the copying of innovations to promote economic growth, but only when it enhances their military power: Then political elites gradually realized that technological innovation and economic growth would help them to build powerful military machines. A powerful military would enable political elites to win in the zero-sum military struggle against other political elites. Leaders in less developed nations realized that they had to copy the innovations made in wealthier nations, to avoid falling behind their militaries.

From about 1200 to well into the early 20th Century, European political leaders gradually lost their aversion to innovation because they knew that they had no choice. They were still afraid of the future political consequences (and rightly so), but they knew that they had to keep up with other nations. In general, political leaders in Northwest

Europe learned this lesson faster than political leaders in Eastern Europe. Not surprisingly, those leaders won most wars.

This view carried over into the totalitarian regimes of the 20th Century, including Fascist Italy, Nazi Germany, Imperial Japan, the Soviet Union, and Communist China. They all promoted economic growth, but only as long as it translated into military power.

Phase 3: Political elites promote the copying of innovations to promote economic growth to enhance their popular support: As political freedom and democratic governance spread within Northwest Europe and North America, elites were forced to take into account mass opinion. Copying innovations in wealthier nations and economic growth were critical for doing so.

With the radical reduction of security threats at the end of the Cold War, political elites shifted from zero-sum military competition to positive-sum economic growth. Even authoritarian leaders realized that they needed to give their people positive reasons to support them. Political leaders are still concerned that economic growth will lead to rival power sources, and they are still concerned about falling behind militarily, but these are now secondary to economics.

The global trade system is a powerful incentive for political elites remaining in phase 3. If that global trade system were to fall or be seriously disrupted, political elites would shift back into phases 1 and 2.

Let's not let that happen.

PRODUCTIVE AGRICULTURE

The First Key to Progress: A highly efficient food production and distribution system. This enables societies to overcome geographical constraints to food production so that large numbers of people can focus on solving problems other than getting enough food to eat.

F ood has been the critical constraint on innovation and progress throughout the vast bulk of human history. Over the last 10,000 years increasing food production per unit of human labor has been a key driving force in progress.

I know that this fact is very hard for modern readers to relate to, but it is true. Today when we are hungry, we go to the refrigerator or pantry. When the refrigerator or pantry is empty, we go to the grocery store. Easy, right?

Well, no. Not for our ancestors.

While getting enough food to survive is easy in modern societies, it was an epic task for our ancestors. For the overwhelming majority of our ancestors, the quest to acquire enough food to survive took up the majority of their waking hours. It was an obsession, and all of society was organized around the most effective means to do so within the local environment.

Before one can innovate, one must first survive. To survive, one must eat large amounts of food. If one has to spend the vast majority of one's time focused on acquiring food, one cannot devote much time to innovating non-agricultural skills, technologies, and organizations. Our ancestors effectively traded time for food.

The vast majority of mankind devoted the bulk of their waking hours to the quest to produce enough food to eat. Very gradually over time, they innovated new technologies, skills, and processes that enabled more effective means of producing and distributing food. This quest for food production was so all-encompassing that we can categorize entire societies by how they did so.

This quest for food greatly affected where we lived. Until the last few centuries, humans had to disperse geographically to acquire food, because the subsistence technology of the day was not productive enough for one family to grow enough of a food surplus to support urban populations. The endless drudgery of acquiring food has stifled the human potential for innovation and progress for millennia.

There is only so much food that can be acquired from any one acre of land with simple technology. With technological innovation, we have been able to radically increase this amount, but for any given natural environment and a suite of technologies, there is a fixed amount of food that can be produced per acre.

So humanity dispersed to survive. They had no choice. Survival comes first.

But this dispersal undermined the ability of large numbers of people to interact regularly. Dispersal made it harder to copy technologies, skills, and organizations. With far fewer models to copy, innovation and diffusion were far slower than they could have been.

To make things worse, the type of food that can be produced in any specific area is highly constrained. In some regions, fishing or hunting marine mammals is possible, but not in most areas. In other regions, hunting big game is possible, but not in most areas. In some areas, cultivating rice is possible, but not wheat or corn. In other areas, cultivating wheat is possible, but not other staple crops.

Since food production and distribution is not something that one individual can do, the entire society had to be sculpted around the type of food that could be produced. Technologies, skills, organizations, and values of societies were all greatly affected by what type of food could be produced in their geographical environment.

What is more, each one of these food types had very different amounts of energy and nutrients relative to the human work effort. This meant that some societies had huge advantages over others, simply because they lived in regions with the most cost-effective food sources.

Some geographical regions simply could not support much food production, so they doomed their residents to be trapped in poverty. Fortunately, there was one important exception to this rule: Northwest Europe and the regions settled by Northwest Europeans. While other agricultural systems hardly changed for thousands of years, these regions have undergone many transformations. Each of these transformations resulted in a significantly increased food surplus per family of farmers.

As I document in my book, *From Poverty to Progress*, those regions repeatedly transformed their agricultural systems by innovating new technologies, skills, processes and institutions. The achievements laid the foundations for the growth of Commercial societies in Northern Italy, Flanders, Netherlands, and Southeast England. The result was the first widely-shared progress on planet Earth.

Later agricultural transformations laid a strong foundation for the Industrial Revolution in Britain. The Industrial Revolution included the invention of agricultural, food processing, food storage, and transportation technologies that spread those benefits even wider. Agricultural productivity accelerated rapidly in Britain, Northwest Europe, the United States, Australia, and New Zealand. In particular, the United States was able to turn the prairies of the Midwest into massive export industries that enabled other nations to specialize in crops other than grain. While it took centuries for the benefits to spread beyond a few regions, today we have an astoundingly productive world agricultural system.

The Green Revolution

The Green Revolution of the 1950s, 60s, and 70s accelerated the trend even further and spread the benefits to Latin America and Asia. The Green Revolution consisted of new agricultural technologies such as bioengineering of high-yield varieties of cereals, animal breeding, chemical fertilizers, pesticides, herbicides, fungicides, and irrigation. These technologies enabled much greater mechanization of agriculture in Asia, which enabled peasants to generate a food surplus that enabled their children to migrate to cities and get jobs in emerging manufacturing industries.

The Green Revolution laid the foundation for the industrialization of South Korea, Taiwan, Hong Kong, Singapore, China, India, and parts of Southeast Asia. The Green Revolution had a mixed impact on Latin America because that region was unable to develop competitive export industries (the Fourth Key to Progress).

Global Food Distribution System

Today's modern food surpluses are based on the following:

1. The application of modern agricultural technology, most of which is based upon fossil fuels, fossil fuel byproducts, and genetic research.

2. Regional specialization in food production

3. The global trade system (which I described in detail in another chapter).

The combination of these three factors has effectively overcome the greatest constraint to progress in virtually every society in history: geographical constraints on food production and distribution. All of these factors were created by Western nations that first experienced progress, particularly the United States. Developing nations enjoy the benefits of that progress to the extent that they can copy modern agricultural technologies.

The Limits of the Green Revolution

Unfortunately, the Green Revolution had relatively little impact on Sub-Saharan Africa. This is the primary reason why that region has experienced the least progress over the last century. A key factor is that agricultural innovation is heavily constrained by local geography.

Africa's geography is particularly challenging. Africa consists mainly of Desert, Tropical Forests, and Tropical Grasslands (or Savanna). The non-Forest ecoregions in Africa experience extremes in precipitation. Rain is almost entirely concentrated in the rainy season, while the dry season is close to Desert conditions. Many regions also have relatively unproductive soil.

Previous agricultural researchers deliberately targeted Asia and Latin America because the regions had geography better suited for plow-based cereal agriculture. Africa's agricultural system, which was largely based on hand-tilled root vegetables presented different and in some ways more difficult challenges.

In addition to geographical differences between Sub-Saharan Africa and the rest of the world, the region also suffers from great geographical variability *within* the region. Geographical heterogeneity is far greater in Sub-Saharan Africa than in any other region in the world. Among the differences are soil, acidity, moisture, and temperature, all of which are critical to agriculture. There are even substantial differences in these characteristics within small plots of land. These geographical variations mean that one big solution or set of solutions (i.e. the Green Revolution) does not work for the entire continent (Suri and Udry).

Opposition to Green Revolution

Another reason that the Green Revolution failed to impact Sub-Saharan Africa was due to intense opposition from Green activists. Ironically, the Greens strongly opposed, and still oppose the Green Revolution.

Today political activists, NGOs, and multilateral aid institutions attack the foundations of agricultural productivity in the name of "sustainability." Research and use of fertilizers, genetically modified organisms, pesticides, irrigation, and other agricultural technologies have been brought to an almost complete halt in the poorest countries. Nor do wealthy nations do much to take up the slack.

Greens have demonized wide swaths of agricultural research that are desperately needed by developing nations and can create better products in rich nations. Some have even stooped to physically destroying experiments to create new crops, such as Golden rice, that can save millions of children from malnutrition and death. Governments are afraid to fund many studies in the field for fear of backlash from the Greens.

The major successes of the Green Revolution in Asia and Latin America occurred in the 1950s, 60s, and 70s before the Green movement became politically influential among international NGOs. For this reason, Greens failed to stop the Green Revolution in Asia and Latin America in the earlier phase, but they succeeded in doing so in the later phases of the revolution.

Agricultural productivity in Sub-Saharan Africa (except for South Africa) since 1960 has lagged far behind trends in the rest of the world. These yield gaps are largely due to differing levels of technologies. In particular, the usage of fertilizer and irrigation in Sub-Saharan Africa lags far behind the rest of the world (Suri and Udry).

Some researchers have claimed that impoverished African farmers do not have the capital to invest in the latest technology, but limits in their ability to finance investments using credit explain only a small part of the problem. Nor is the problem with crop insurance or a lack of information (Suri and Udry).

A Second Green Revolution

We need a Second Green Revolution that dramatically increases agricultural productivity in Sub-Saharan Africa and other poor developing nations. A Second Green Revolution would enable local farmers to grow more crops, enabling rural people to migrate to more productive cities and increase the amount of wild habitat by reducing farm acreage.

Public agricultural universities played a key role in making American agriculture the most productive in the world. In addition, that funding played a key role in promoting the Green Revolution that drastically increased agricultural productivity in Latin America and Asia.

Without these critical increases in agricultural productivity, most developing nations would still be rural, as their people would have had to remain dispersed to grow crops. Just as increased agricultural productivity promoted the growth of Commercial societies in Europe and their later industrialization, so did it promote today's transformational economic growth in Asia.

In a previous chapter, I argued that innovation prizes are the most cost-effective means to trigger breakthrough innovation. Obviously, governments in Sub-Saharan Africa do not have the financial resources to sponsor innovation prizes. But governments in wealthy nations and NGOs that raise money from the same nations do have the financial resources.

We should create innovation prizes that enable developing nations, particularly in Sub-Saharan Africa, to radically increase the productivity of local agriculture. This will not only greatly increase the standard of living in those regions, but also reduce the human footprint on natural habitats. Low-productivity agriculture promotes poverty and habitat degradation, while high-productivity agriculture promotes wealth and reduces farm acreage.

A Second Green Revolution targeting Sub-Saharan Africa, preferably funded via prizes, could have a profound positive effect on the region. Latin America, Asia, and wealthy nations in North America and Europe would also benefit. Given the current political climate, the United States seems to be the only country with the potential to initiate another Green Revolution, and they have not done so yet because of ideology.

Agricultural research funded by the American government and American corporations was critical to making progress on farm productivity. American agricultural universities and the USDA have played a leading role in this for well over a century. We need more of this, not less. It is probably the single most effective way to expand wild habitat, so it is disturbing that environmentalists are so strongly against it.

Admittedly the intense geographical variations within Sub-Saharan Africa will make it difficult to design effective innovation prizes. We will most likely need an entire constellation of innovation prizes that focus on specific crops and specific sub-regions within the continent.

The best solution is not clear to me at this point, but I have confidence that if Western governments, agricultural corporations, and agricultural research stations come together with local African agricultural research stations and farmers, they can come up with effective prize designs that can enable a few carefully chosen pilot projects. If those first innovation prizes yield results, then the concept can be expanded to many more innovation prizes that span the continent.

Agricultural Tariffs

In addition to supporting agricultural research and development, wealthy nations must also repeal long-standing policies which undermine agricultural productivity and global agricultural trade. Many wealthy Western nations have government policies that undermine farm productivity and drive up food costs. Agriculture is one of the few sectors where high tariffs and subsidies are still common. This is particularly true in Europe.

Tariffs make food exports from developing nations more expensive, hurting their economies. While politicians in Europe and the United States may see this as a good trade-off to protect their farming constituents, it raises food prices and undermines agricultural productivity and export opportunities for developing nations.

We should lower these tariffs on food as much as possible. They will lower the cost of food in wealthy nations as well as give farmers in developing nations greater export opportunities.

Agricultural Subsidies

The American and European governments have also been subsidizing farm production since 1930. Originally designed to protect farmers from low prices, it has become a massive transfer of wealth from consumers to farmers. And little of that wealth goes to small family farmers. Most of these subsidies go to large landowners, many of whom are absentee owners.

Every attempt to eliminate these farm subsidies fails because rural Congresspersons want to give away money to their constituents. These subsidies undermine farm productivity, raise food prices, and make it difficult for farmers in developing nations to compete.

Ethanol Fuel Mandates

The American government also heavily subsidizes converting corn into ethanol with fuel mandates. At one time, it was reasonable to believe that this lowered carbon emissions, but now it is pretty clear from detailed environmental studies that this is not true. These mandates lower the amount of corn used for food and animal feed, driving up prices. This hurts the poor and developing nations that import large amounts of American corn.

Organic Foods

Another factor that drives up food prices is organic foods. Currently, in many Western nations, affluent consumers have a strong preference for organic foods without "synthetic" fertilizers, pesticides, or herbicides. Typically, organic foods substitute petroleum-based fertilizers, pesticides, and herbicides for "organic" versions.

As long as this does not become a dominant trend, it is probably fairly harmless. Unfortunately, the trend is moving past that point.

Like many products in the modern world, synthetic fertilizers, pesticides, and herbicides are petroleum byproducts.

Ironically, *petroleum and coal are organic*. Petroleum is composed of the organic matter left over from prehistoric organisms that have been compressed by the weight of the rock over millions of years. Coal is formed from prehistoric plants under similar conditions.

At a chemical level, petroleum and coal are composed of carbon, hydrogen, nitrogen, oxygen, and sulfur, all of which are organic elements. That is why petroleum and coal are often called organic hydrocarbons.

In reality, "organic" foods substitute organic materials that are sourced from above ground with organic materials that are sourced from below ground. Neither type of organics are any more organic or synthetic. The primary difference is how long ago the organism died.

And organic foods only are different for one step in the agricultural supply chain. Petroleum is still essential in all the other steps, including planting, harvesting, collecting, storing, transporting, packaging, distributing, retailing, and storing in consumers' homes. Organic foods are just as dependent on the widespread usage of fossil fuels as other foods.

Organic foods are a clear example of a status product. Affluent people are always looking to purchase products that differentiate themselves from the masses visually and morally. Now that industrial farming techniques have made food so inexpensive that the poor and working class can easily afford it, status-seeking affluent people looked for the most costly alternatives.

By purchasing organic foods, shoppers who are repelled by the idea of conspicuous consumption can effectively consume conspicuously and feel good about it. Ironically, few organic lovers realize that these products contain pesticides, just different ones that are no safer nor better for the environment (Applied Methodology).

Nor do they think through the consequences of more expensive food on the poor. Because organic farming is inherently less productive than modern alternatives, organic food is always more expensive. This may not be a problem for affluent shoppers who want to make a moral statement with their purchases, but it does matter for poor people who desperately need affordable food. If the current consumer preferences of the affluent become the entire market, this will raise food prices and hurt the poor.

Organic foods are almost always more expensive than non-organic foods because the growing process is less productive. Organic foods simply require more land per unit of food than non-organic foods. While it varies greatly by the food type, organic foods typically range from 10% to 50% less productive. This results in higher food prices (Applied Methodology).

Higher food prices may not matter very much to rich Westerners, but they can be devastating to the poor in developing nations. Those people typically spend a far higher percentage of their total income on grains.

Perhaps the most effective measurement of the standard of living of a person or nation is the percentage of annual spending that is devoted to grains, such as wheat, rice, and corn. Very poor people have historically devoted upwards of 50% of their spending to grains. As very poor people in developing nations increase in wealth, they spend more on other types of foods that are less energy dense, more expensive, but tastier. People in wealthy nations spend a very small portion of their total spending on grains or any other type of food for that matter.

Organic farming also precludes one of the most environmentally beneficial farming techniques: no-till farming. No-till farming is where the soil is not churned up by tractors, meaning that there is far less nitrogen run-off into streams, rivers, lakes, and oceans. Because no-till soil requires herbicides, and there are currently no effective organic herbicides, organic no-till farming requires large amounts of hand labor. This undermines productivity, drives up the cost, and increases farm acreage. No-till farming is particularly beneficial in sandy and dry soils on sloping terrain, where nitrogen run-off is a serious problem.

Since organic foods are more land-intensive, this means that they are less Green. Land that could otherwise be devoted to other crops or wild habitat is consumed by organic foods. So environmentally conscious consumers should be against organic foods, but they are not.

High-Tech Ag Is Green

And these shoppers delude themselves if they think that they are helping the environment. The biggest threat to the environment is not urban sprawl, pesticides, or GMOs; it is farm acreage. Farms destroy land that could otherwise be devoted to natural habitat. Farm acreage is essential to our survival and prosperity, but we should try to limit the impact of farm acreage on natural habitats. Increasing agricultural productivity is the key to doing so.

Environmentalists should be in favor of increased farming productivity above all else. Nothing else humans do has a more negative effect on the natural environment than agriculture. As farms have become more productive in wealthy nations, farmers have effectively abandoned the least productive soil allowing it to turn back into natural habitat. This is good. This is what environmentalists and eco-friendly shoppers should want, but the consequences of their misguided views create the opposite.

Natural Is Bad For the Environment

Affluent Westerners have convinced themselves that "natural" is good for the environment, and "man-made" is bad for the environment. In fact, it is exactly the opposite. Natural products come from critical habitat that could otherwise be used by nature. Products made from synthetic materials that come from underground do not. So Greens should be in favor of synthetic materials that do not take away resources from wild plants and animals. Unfortunately, they favor the opposite.

One can see this reverse logic again and again. Wild-caught fish are deemed better than aquaculture, even though commercial fishing has caused many fish populations to crash. Organic farms preclude no-till methods that could radically decrease the run-off of nitrogen fertilizer. Products made from wood are deemed better than products made from steel and concrete. DDT was banned, even though it is a very effective weapon against malaria, one of the leading killers in developing countries.

Green Opposition to Agricultural R&D

All of these attitudes of affluent Western consumers are fairly harmless if kept to a minor fashion trend. But when it gets to agricultural research and GMOs, it can get dangerous. Governments and corporations in wealthy nations should increase funding for agricultural research and development.

Public agricultural universities played a key role in making American agriculture the most productive in the world. In addition, that funding played a key role in promoting the Green Revolution that drastically increased agricultural productivity in Latin America and Asia.

Without these critical increases in agricultural productivity, most developing nations would still be rural, as their people would have had to remain dispersed to grow crops. Just as increased agricultural productivity promoted the growth of Commercial societies in Europe and their later Industrialization, so did it promote today's transformational economic growth in Asia.

In listing out ways that government programs and consumer preferences are undermining farm productivity, I do not mean to suggest that the first key is in grave danger. American farm productivity and to a lesser extent in other wealthy nations is extremely high. Increasing productivity would help, but it would be an incremental improvement.

Ironically, its biggest impact would be helping the environment and the poorest nations, but the environmentalists who are so skeptical of progress are against these reforms.

Focus on Results

Key metrics for measuring agricultural productivity should be:
- Grilli-Yang global agricultural price index
- Global net cereal production
- Cereal net production in Sub-Saharan Africa

- Cereal net production in low-income nations
- Daily supply of calories in Sub-Saharan Africa
- Daily supply of calories in low-income nations
- Global per capita deaths due to famine

Conclusion

Some of the best methods for wealthy nations to help developing nations experience progress would be to establish innovation prizes to trigger a Second Green Revolution in Sub-Saharan Africa and to roll back agricultural tariffs, subsidies, and ethanol fuel mandates. More public education on the negative consequences of organic foods on the environment, developing nations, and the poor in the wealthy nations would also be useful.

PART FOUR: WHAT DEVELOPING NATIONS CAN DO

Part Four of this book focuses on actionable policies that developing nations can implement to create and sustain domestic material progress. As was true of the previous parts of this book, each of these policies are derived from the Five Keys to Progress. The goal of these policies is to assist developing nations to either:

- Create the conditions for future progress, or
- Enable existing progress to accelerate

Which goal is more important depends upon the current level of development of the individual nations being discussed. Some wealthier developing nations, such as China, need to focus on sustaining their current progress, while poorer developing nations, such as Congo, need to create better conditions so their current slow progress can accelerate greatly.

In some ways, I hesitate to use the term "developing nations." While the term meant something in the 1990s, there has been so much economic growth in so many different nations over the last 30 years that their paths have diverged greatly. I use the term developing nations only because the term seems to have stuck and everyone knows what it means (or at least they think they do).

In fact, the United States, Europe and Japan are developing just as much as the rest of the world. As I see it, "developing" is just another word for "experiencing progress." Applying that term only to poorer nations is somewhat patronizing and confusing because it implies that what wealthy nations and developing nations need to do are completely unrelated. The term also implies that wealthy nations have reached a final state.

Both wealthy nations and developing nations need to keep their focus on their relative levels of the Five Keys to Progress. Think of the keys as a scorecard that enables nations to see what is most important to focus on while in their current state.

As conditions change, the scorecard changes. As the scorecard changes, the necessary strategy and policies change as well. But the focus should always be on the Five Keys to Progress.

It is important to keep in mind, however, that there are vast differences between developing nations. Some export massive amounts of petroleum and natural gas, while others export none. Some have very large populations, while some are tiny islands with few inhabitants. Some border wealthy nations, while others are far away and have no ocean ports. Some have tropical climates, while a few have temperate climates.

Some have a history of European colonialism, while others were never conquered. Some have a recent history of Communism, while most do not. Some are democracies, while others are authoritarian or totalitarian regimes. Developing nations also diverge greatly by language, religion, ethnicity and history.

Most importantly, developing nations diverge greatly by current levels of per capita GDP (PPP). Some nations, such as Taiwan and South Korea, are as rich as many European nations and have highly diverse export-based economies. Other nations such as Brazil, China, India, Indonesia, Mexico and Turkey are much poorer but have experienced significant economic growth over the last 30 years. Then there are nations such as Afghanistan, Liberia, Congo and Haiti who are still living in serious poverty (although, as I show in my book, *From Poverty to Progress*, the 20 poorest nations in 1990 have improved faster than the rest of the world).

Is it possible to give relevant and actionable advice to a group that contains such diversity? Let's give it a try.

PROMOTING PROGRESS

CURRENT EXPERT ADVICE

Economic development in developing nations (formerly known as "Third World nations") is a controversial domain of academic inquiry. I believe that most advice given to developing nations by Western experts is misguided, albeit well-intentioned. Before outlining my proposals, I will briefly overview the currently proposed alternatives.

Economic School

Currently, there are four schools of thought among Western experts who advise developing nations. Economists who believe in free-market economies dominate the first school of thought. These economists believe that good institutions build the foundations that enable self-interested individuals to solve problems that benefit all of society.

They believe that, if developing nations implement free trade, reduce corruption, establish the rule of law and property rights, eliminate counter-productive government interventions in the economy, and build legal and law enforcement institutions to enforce those principles, free markets will naturally emerge. Those free markets will then usher their nations into prosperity. This school of thought is sometimes called the "Washington Consensus."

Foreign Aid School

The second school of thought is dominated by development experts and non-governmental organizations (NGOs). Jeffrey Sachs is the key thinker in this school.

The "foreign aid" school, as I will call it, believe that wealthy nations and individuals should spend more on foreign aid to assist developing nations to get out of "poverty traps". They believe that poor nations are trapped in poverty that only can be overcome with foreign aid. In general, they argue for increased foreign aid that is targeted at improving education, sanitation, and health care. Once this foreign aid overcomes the poverty traps, these people believe that developing nations can grow into wealthier nations.

Rights School

The third school of thought focuses on individual rights. William Easterly is the key thinker in this school. This school of thought believes that developing nations are run by authoritarian regimes that will not reform their institutions because it is against their self-interest. They also believe that these regimes channel foreign aid into strengthening those authoritarian power structures rather than helping the poor.

This school believes that the poor in all nations need the same political freedoms that wealthy nations enjoy. They believe that democracy is one of those freedoms. Once the people have those rights, their nations can grow their way out of their poverty.

Sustainable Development School

The fourth school of thought focuses on what they call "sustainable development." Exactly what this term means is a little unclear, but it focuses quite heavily on renewable energy and less resource-intensive agriculture, transportation, and manufacturing.

The sustainable development school believes that a greener version of the Industrial Revolution is possible and will lead to better outcomes for the natural environment and poor people in developing nations. They believe that more traditional paths to prosperity will seriously hurt the natural environment, so developing nations need to find a different path.

The Wrong Keys

For the most part, I do not oppose much of what is said by any of these schools. I just think that they all miss the point because they do not understand the importance of the Five Keys to Progress. And, because of that, their proposals have not achieved the desired results.

Moreover, it is not clear that any of these schools have produced positive results for developing nations. In fact, the current progress in developing nations has come largely from developing nations ignoring Western experts and following very different paths.

When viewed from a very high level, one can see that all four schools have a perspective somewhat similar to mine. I believe that once a society establishes the Five Keys to Progress, societies will naturally experience progress and individuals will work to solve their own problems without help from outside.

The difference is that **we all believe in different keys to progress**. Economists believe that good institutions and free markets are the keys to progress. Development experts believe that foreign aid in the areas of education, sanitation, and health is the key to progress. The rights school believes that individual rights and democracy are the keys to progress. The sustainable development school believes that green energy and agricultural technologies are the keys to progress while protecting the environment.

We all agree that there are a few keys to progress, but we all disagree as to which they are. So who is correct?

I believe that all four of the competing schools of thought are talking about factors that matter. But I also believe that none of the current schools give very helpful advice to developing nations. So let's go through them one by one so that I can explain why.

Why Economists Are Wrong

The economists are correct in that lowering corruption, establishing the rule of law, free trade and property rights, eliminating counter-productive government interventions in the economy, and building legal and law enforcement institutions to enforce those principles are all good things. But I disagree that these are essential factors in triggering long-term economic growth. I see all those factors as many of the benefits of what takes place *after* a nation initiates progress.

To the best of my knowledge, no nation has established all of the supposed keys proposed by economists *before* triggering economic growth. Every previous nation that experienced long-term economic growth lacked many or all of these factors before the growth period started.

I would suggest that economists are experts at keeping economic growth going, but they do not have a useful model for getting it started in the first place. This "problem of origins" and confusing cause and effect are endemic to the study of progress.

In response, many economic historians who focus on the origins of the Industrial Revolution and who believe in the important role of institutions point to Britain and the United States as models. They claim that those two nations are examples that illustrate their point.

Their argument implies that they believe that Britain and the United States effectively implemented what Western economists advise developing nations to implement today, and the result was the Industrial Revolution. While there is some truth to these claims, this school of thought seriously misrepresents the reality of Britain and the United States in the 19th Century.

Both Britain and the United States in the 19th Century had serious problems with corruption, counter-productive economic policies, tariffs, and legal systems that worked to the benefit of the rich and powerful. Britain and the United States also often went to war to promote trade. Britain built an entire empire. Both nations also had a serious problem of traditional Agrarian elites biasing economic policy to support their self-interest.

It was only well into the 20th Century that one can find a model of what modern economists would consider good government in both Britain and the United States. So the supposed causes came long after decades or even centuries of economic growth. And later in the 20th Century, both nations built expansive welfare states that the school believes undermine, or at least do not contribute to, economic growth.

So there is no period in either British or American history that this economic school can use as a model. Moreover, most of the policies that this school advocates came after both nations industrialized.

And Britain and the United States are the best cases for these theories. All other nations' histories depart widely from the predictions of this economic school of thought.

There is an implicit assumption that, if developing nations overhaul their institutions and policies to match those of 20th Century Britain and the United States while not building an expansive welfare state as those two nations did, then developing nations can transition to economic growth without doing anything else. Given that the school cannot point to any nation that fits the pure model, it is hard to get away from the fact that economists seem to be giving advice based on economic theory, not what has actually worked in the past.

As I mentioned in the first book in this series, *From Poverty to Progress*, Britain and the United States were unusual because they were Commercial societies long before they industrialized. This was also true of Northern Italy, Belgium, and the Netherlands. While they were Commercial societies and had not yet industrialized, they all made some progress in building what we now call good government, but they were far from what experts recommend developing nations should do today.

If the institutions and policies of Britain and the United States were not good enough to fit the model and it took centuries of evolution as

Commercial societies to get where they did, what are open-minded reformers in developing nations supposed to do? It is just not realistic to expect developing nations to overhaul all their political, legal, and economic institutions and wait for decades or centuries for economic benefits.

And many of the nations that have tried to follow the recommendations of Western economists, particularly in Latin America, have not had impressive results. Given that some of the counter-productive government interventions that the school wants to cut benefit important political constituencies and poor people, it seems like political suicide to follow this advice in the face of evidence that it often (and perhaps always) does not work.

I think that most of the advice given by institutional economists is very helpful for a nation that has already experienced significant periods of economic growth and wants to use some of the political capital that it gains from that growth to implement a reform agenda. But that is very different from what the economists say they propose. The economic school wants to reform institutions first. In politics, the sequencing of policy actions is critical.

But even if the economics school is correct, it is not clear what a dedicated reformer should do. The proposed institutional reform agenda is actually a very long and unprioritized list.

Which reform do you implement first? What is the exact sequence that works best? How soon will they show results? What reforms have been implemented by developing nations that are best practices to follow? It is easy to see why developing nations are increasingly skeptical of advice from this school. And this school is the dominant school of development advice in the West.

Why Foreign Aid Advocates Are Wrong

The advice of foreign aid experts has even bigger problems. Their advice is heavily dependent upon the willingness of wealthy nations to spend lots of money on foreign aid. It is even more heavily dependent upon them doing so wisely, and local officials in developing nations not stealing the money to use for their own purposes.

A bigger problem is that they have no evidence that significant gains in health care, sanitation, and education cause long-term economic growth. To the best of my knowledge, no evidence supports their case in this area.

Nor do they have much evidence that the people living in developing nations live in poverty traps in all these domains. As we see more Asian nations transform themselves without significant amounts of foreign aid, it looks like an increasingly unreasonable assumption.

And if a poor nation does not experience long-term economic growth, how will they pay for these programs in the long run? It is naïve to believe that wealthy nations will keep foreign aid flowing forever. At some point in time, developing nations need to take the lead. Without economic growth, I do not see any way out of this conundrum.

Just like economists, foreign aid development experts point to very good things that are the result of progress, not the cause of it.

Health care, sanitation, and education are all good things, but they do not create progress or economic growth. And just like economists give unrealistic advice to overhaul institutions, building a health care, sanitation, and education system is very expensive and time-consuming.

If done correctly, it will lead to benefits that voters will notice, and perhaps it will create a self-sustaining feedback loop for increased funding. But then that leads back to the problem of where the money comes from in the first place, and what you spend it on when you get it.

While well-intentioned, I do not see how foreign aid or domestic government spending in health care, sanitation, and education will lead to long-term sustained economic growth. It might make a difference in the quality of poor people's lives, but that should not be the goal.

A nation trapped in poverty with a sophisticated and expensive health care, sanitation, and education infrastructure is simply not sustainable. The economic system will not have a broad enough tax base to fund that infrastructure. Nor is it clear that the infrastructure can be achieved, even with massive amounts of foreign aid.

Ironically, while this school of thought focuses on "poverty traps," they are advising developing nations to create a different type of poverty trap. Developing nations need to create economic growth, and building vast social infrastructures wastes valuable resources that would be far more effective if used for other purposes.

Why Rights Are Not Enough

William Easterly's more skeptical advice on the actual results of foreign aid is based upon an incisive analysis of how authoritarian regimes function, but it is not clear that his advice is actionable. He is correct to say that Britain, the United States, Northern Italy, and the Netherlands had significant political rights and at least somewhat democratic governance. Those rights and their democracy took centuries to grow and did so within unique geographical and political environments.

But what is a reformer living within an authoritarian regime to do? They cannot change geography, nor can they wait for centuries.

They could become political activists opposing the regime and build a non-violent mass movement against that regime. They might also be willing to use violence in the name of freedom. Since all nations that are currently democracies with freedom initially established those freedoms through mass movements and at least some political violence, this may be unavoidable.

So let's just assume that the reformers win. They overthrow the authoritarian regime with some mixture of violence and non-violence. Then what? Perhaps Easterly would say that you can follow the advice of the economists to build good institutions, or maybe he has another plan. I am not clear on this point.

Such a fledgling democratic regime desperately needs economic growth to provide some stability. Otherwise, opponents will take advantage of the inevitable instability that follows the revolution. Maybe the opponents will be better, and maybe they will be worse. But all reformers are left in basically the same situation.

What should they do now?

Just like the other three schools of thought, there is no evidence that Easterly's proposals will lead to a transition to progress. The freedom and democratic governance that he argues for are great things. I wish all nations had them, but they do not cause progress by themselves. Like all the other supposed causes, they are one of the many results of progress.

Sustainable Development Isn't

So now we go on to the school of sustainable development. Of all the four, this is the one that I have the most problems with. While the school has some good ideas, their proposals are potentially quite dangerous.

The fundamental problem is that sustainable development is not sustainable economically, nor will it lead to development. Nor will it even lead to much improvement for the natural environment.

First of all, what does "sustainable" actually mean? How do we figure out whether a policy or practice is sustainable or not? Presumably, it requires some form of numeric calculation; but what is the formula to calculate sustainability? And what are we trying to sustain? Sustained for what timeframe?

In practice, the word "sustainable" has no meaning other than "what Greens think is a good idea." It feels like international development agencies have cobbled together a concept that connects what economists want with what environmentalists want. It is more a political compromise between two Western schools of thought than a real reform agenda.

International development agencies promote this agenda, not because they have any evidence that the policies work, but because it creates a stronger political alliance within wealthy nations to support aid and reform abroad. But what is good politics in wealthy nations is not necessarily good in triggering progress in developing nations.

There is no evidence, for example, that those who support sustainable development have done any of the mathematical calculations to determine if a specific policy or practice actually is sustainable.

In practice, how sustainable a specific technology is far more dependent upon economics, not on its effect on the environment. Most technologies or new organizations collapse long before they butt up against any limits created by nature. And when they do so, all of society has a very strong incentive to create a better solution. That is exactly how the vast, decentralized problem-solving network works.

So the word "sustainable" appears to be nothing but a feel-good political buzzword. It may make activists feel good to say it, but it is not actionable, because no one is quite sure how to evaluate the long-term impact on the environment before technology has been implemented.

More to the point, why should poor nations care about whether the current practice can be sustained for 50 years? They have far more immediate problems, and they will be much more equipped to deal with those future problems if they are far wealthier. Within 50 years, practices are guaranteed to be very different regardless of their environmental consequences.

If we leave aside where sustainable development overlaps the institutional reforms that economists want, we are left with two policies that seriously undermine two of the Five Keys to Progress.

Those who promote sustainable development are hostile to essential agricultural technologies: tractors, herbicides, nitrogen fertilizer, new GMO crops, irrigation, and many others. The school is correct that, for some regions and individuals, these practices are not "appropriate." But those practices should not be deemed inappropriate because they conflict with Green ideology or harm the environment. They should be deemed inappropriate when they do not lead to more productive agriculture.

Far too often, those who promote sustainable development romanticize traditional agricultural practices and show photos of happy farmers hand-tilling the soil. But let's look at the reality of these practices: thousands of years of poverty at a level which we have difficulty imagining in modern Western societies.

More to the point, farmers in developing nations want the latest technologies. They are not always able to figure out how to pay for them, but that should be dealt with directly by helping them do so. I myself loan monthly to farmers in poor nations via Kiva.org. I suggest that you do the same.

It is not modern agricultural technologies that are "inappropriate." It is the advice that environmentalists in the West who have never been farmers in their lives give to farmers in developing nations.

And deliberately trying to stop agricultural research by wealthy governments and corporations is just as bad. Of course, we should be concerned about the possible negative effects of modern agricultural technologies.

The single best way to help preserve the environment is to *increase* agricultural productivity. This will reduce the amount of land needed to grow food, and some of it can thus transition back into wild habitat.

This is not a utopian idea. The United States reached "peak farm acreage" around 1950. Farm acreage in the United States and other wealthy nations has been declining since that time. Globally we appear to have reached peak farm acreage sometime after 2000 (Our World in Data).

The key reason for this trend is the improving agricultural productivity caused by technological innovation. There is every reason to believe that further innovation can do the same in developing nations.

And the advice that those that promote sustainable development give in the field of energy is far more dangerous. They oppose energy sources such as petroleum, coal, natural gas, nuclear and hydroelectric. Instead, they push solar, wind, and other renewable energy sources. (By the way "renewable" is another buzzword that actually means "what Greens think is a good idea").

Developing nations desperately need to rapidly increase their energy usage and build modern electrical grids. Thinking that solar and wind can do it by themselves is both naïve and dangerous.

Both energy sources vary greatly by geography. Most developing nations have few regions where the wind is strong enough to be a cost-effective source of energy. Very few regions outside of the oceans, the Great Plains in the United State, the North Sea, Argentina, and interior China have wide-spread wind resources.

And while tropical nations have plenty of sun and lower latitudes, they also have humid atmospheres that undermine solar efficiency. And what are nations with tropical forests to do? Do environmentalists propose that these trees be cut down to make way for acres of solar panels?

Don't laugh; it is happening in wealthy nations, and it is terrible for the environment. Worse is biomass, which effectively burns forests in the name of helping the environment.

The fact that no wealthy nation has come even close to an electrical grid based 100% on solar and wind makes it seems extremely unlikely that developing nations can do so. And electricity accounts for only 18% of global carbon emissions, so even 100% success within the electrical grid does not get you very far.

The reality is that developing nations need fossil fuels, hydroelectric dams, and nuclear power just as much and even more than wealthy nations do. That is why those energy sources make up well over 80% of all energy use. And that is why the widespread usage of fossil fuels is one of the Five Keys to Progress.

Given that not one single nation has made the transition from poverty to progress based on the principles of sustainable development, I find this advice very dangerous for developing nations. Moreover, I am skeptical that following their policies will help the environment much either.

That is why all developing nations choose some blend of petroleum, coal, natural gas, nuclear and hydroelectric to power their energy systems. None use solar or wind in sufficient abundance to come even close to a majority of their energy production. That should tell you something.

Telling wealthy nations that they should slow down economic growth in favor of saving the natural environment by eliminating fossil fuels is terrible advice. Telling developing nations that they should do so is a moral outrage.

Rich people might as well tell poor people to just accept poverty and learn to enjoy it. Fortunately, developing nations are having none of it.

ASSESSING THE FIVE KEYS

S o we are left with none of the four schools giving very useful advice. It should not be surprising that developing nations are getting increasingly skeptical of Western advice and finding their own path.

So should we just give up and insist that nothing works? No, and if you doubt me, take a look at my first book, *From Poverty to Progress*. Despite poor advice from Western experts, progress is happening all over the globe. Better yet, that progress is particularly strong in the poorest nations.

So if we take the advice of most experts, nothing works in theory, but a great deal of it works in practice!

We must do better. We must focus on the Five Keys to Progress.

Key #1: Productive Agriculture

The first key (agriculture) is largely a solved problem. By that, I mean that we know what works, and the vast majority of developing nations are moving in the right direction.

Agriculture is far more productive than it was two centuries ago, and it is likely to keep getting more productive. We also have a global distribution system that moves the food surplus from wealthy nations to poor nations. Famine has been virtually eliminated and undernourishment is also rapidly declining.

I have already outlined the benefits of the Second Green Revolution in Sub-Saharan Africa and the dangers of opposition to modern agricultural technologies. This is probably more of a problem with the politics in wealthy nations than anything that developing nations can deal with themselves. So, unless a nation has a particularly unproductive agricultural system, it is probably wise to focus efforts elsewhere.

Just don't completely ignore farmers; they are a foundation of progress.

Key #2: Cities

The second key (cities) is also already a solved problem. More than half of humanity now lives in cities, and virtually every developing nation has either high rates of urbanization or rates that are rapidly increasing. It is difficult to see how this can be reversed. As I showed in my first book, the massive slums that haunted our imagination in the late 20th Century are disappearing rapidly.

Of course, governments can do more in this area. They need to ensure that housing stays affordable by not restricting home construction, particularly on the outskirts of metro areas.

Governments can also make cities more livable and functional by building a foundation upon which the vast decentralized problem-solving network of people living in cities can solve problems. Governments should ensure that energy, transportation, and communication for their cities' infrastructures get constructed and well maintained. This might be by direct government services or by the government giving private companies incentives to do so.

In addition, low-cost investment in education to promote literacy, numeracy, and advanced technical knowledge, such as engineering, can increase the level and diversity of skills in cities. Finally, basic investments in vaccinations, sanitation, water filtration, and public health can have a significant positive impact on the quality of life in urban areas.

All of this makes sense to most people and to a large extent, it is already happening. Governments in developing nations are doing so by copying the infrastructure, institutions, and policies that are already working in wealthy nations.

So all of this is a solved problem in the sense that we know what works, and developing nations are moving in the right direction. Sure, they can do more, but I doubt that doing so will be the most effective use of scarce revenues.

And most importantly, where does the money to pay for all of this investment come from? Most developing nations are already realistically doing all they can in this area.

In this domain, I agree with William Easterly. Foreign aid has a very bad track record of accomplishing these tasks. Authoritarian leaders and corrupt officials use the money for their self-interest, so much of that money only reinforces the problem. And wealthy nations do not have infinite resources of goodwill to spend the trillions of dollars necessary to make it happen.

Developing nations must find a solution that is not dependent upon generous foreign aid or large increases in government revenue. More on this later…

Highly cost-effective investments, such as those that I mentioned above seem reasonable, but they do not get to the heart of the problem.

Key #3: Decentralization of Power

The third key (decentralization of political, economic, religious, and ideological power) is a difficult problem to solve. From the fall of the Soviet Union to about 2005, non-Western nations across the world made an incredible shift to democracy and freedom.

But then, around 2005, progress in this domain slowed down and even reversed somewhat. Fortunately, this did not slow down economic growth because the political reforms between 1991 and 2005 were enough to initiate real progress and the regression in these rights has not been enough to choke off that progress.

In this area again, I agree with William Easterly. Convincing political and economic elites that they should undermine their own power is not realistic. Just like monarchies in 18th Century Europe, many of those elites fear progress because of what it might do to their power base. They do not want to create economic wealth in people who might use that wealth to threaten their political power. But like elected politicians in rich nations, they know that promoting long-term economic growth is critical to maintaining the legitimacy of their regime.

Like the 19th Century monarchies of Germany, Austria-Hungary, Italy, Russia, and Japan, modern-day dictators are desperately trying to get the benefits of progress without that same progress undermining their regime. As the post-World War I collapse of those empires shows, this is a difficult balancing act that can lead to very bad results.

Fortunately, there is no evidence that nations need democracy in order to *start* progress. Very few nations have been democratic before they transitioned to a state of progress. And many authoritarian regimes in Europe and East Asia have been able to initiate progress before it inevitably undermined their power and their nation transitioned to democracy.

I believe strongly in democracy and political rights. I think that they have worked in so many different cultures that they can function in any nation. Polls clearly show that the vast majority of people on Planet Earth want them (Pew).

But I am not sure that promoting democracy and political rights in developing nations will by itself lead to progress. Except for a few hardline totalitarian nations, such as North Korea, there is already enough non-violent competition between institutions to get the ball of progress rolling if all the other conditions apply. The other conditions are the four other Five Keys to Progress.

Proposals That Might Actually Work

Unlike the other four schools that we already discussed, I am hesitant to offer advice to developing nations. They have rightly grown skeptical of such advice and have largely followed their own path.

In addition, there are enormous variations between them. It is difficult to offer useful advice to China, Congo, Argentina, Honduras, Bhutan, Moldova, Iraq, and Palestine because they all live in very different circumstances. To cover so many different nations with so many different circumstances, one has to keep the advice very general, and this interferes with the advice being actionable. It is hard to find the right balance, but here goes.

My advice to leaders in developing nations would be:

1. Do not try to do everything. You have few resources, so you must focus on what matters most. With proper prioritization and solving the most important problems first, you can unlock solutions to all the other problems.

2. Do not follow the advice of current Western experts. Their advice is based on theory and ideology, not what has worked in the past.

3. Stay positive. Despite the bad advice coming from Western experts, many other developing nations have improved the lives of their citizens greatly over the last few decades.

4. Look to the actual history of how societies transformed from poverty to progress, not theory or ideology.

5. Focus intensely on the Five Keys to Progress.

6. In particular, look at the fourth key: a society must have at least one high-value-added industry that exports to the rest of the world.

7. And do not listen to those who are trying to undermine the fifth key: widespread usage of fossil fuels.

All Five Keys to Progress matter, but I believe that the fourth and fifth keys are the most relevant to developing nations today. I will go into much more detail on each in the following chapters.

PROMOTING PROGRESS

THRIVING EXPORT INDUSTRIES

The Fourth Key to Progress: At least one high-value-added industry that exports to the rest of the world. This injects wealth into the city or region, accelerates economic growth and creates markets for smaller local industries and services.

R egardless of how productive agriculture, energy systems, or innovative cities are, for progress to take place, a society must have at least one high-value-added industry that exports to the rest of the world. These industries inject wealth into the region and accelerate economic growth. Other than expanding energy usage, I believe this is by far the most effective strategy that developing nations can implement to initiate progress and keep it going.

For current developing nations, I would reword the general principle a bit to "having as many export industries as possible, and each of those industries should be as high-value-added as possible given the current state." The wealth created by high-value-added export industries can then be spent locally by its employees, generating demand for a gaggle of smaller local businesses. This wealth also creates a steady revenue stream for governments to invest in education, health, transportation, sanitation, and energy infrastructure.

By exporting to the rest of the world, an industry radically increases the potential demand for its goods. Except for the United States and perhaps China, no nation has the domestic demand necessary for large-scale industry without exporting to the rest of the world.

If a farm or city is restricted to customers within its borders, its economy has far less growth potential. And the more value the industry generates, the higher the potential profits. That is why high-value-added industries that are competitive enough to export to the rest of the world are so critical to promoting progress within a region.

The nature of the industry that is needed varies greatly over time. In the distant past, a mineral or crop might have been sufficient. More typically today, it requires some form of manufacturing. Textiles, steel, and consumer electronics are all industries that played critical roles in various nations during their initial industrialization.

To successfully export, a city needs the necessary technology, skills, organizations, and capital. These factors are typically acquired by copying them from richer regions that already have them, modifying them for the local environment, and then slowly learning by doing. Skilled immigrants from richer nations often play a critical training role in the learning of new skills.

The emerging discipline of Economic Complexity gives us the best understanding of how this process works. Cesar Hidalgo and Ricardo Hausmann have played pioneering roles in this field. Hidalgo and Hausmann argue that modern societies acquire productive knowledge by distributing that knowledge among many specialized workers. Organizations and markets then combine that knowledge to make useful products. This fits in nicely with my observations about How Progress Works.

The skills needed for industries can only be taught face-to-face. Typically, people learn through face-to-face guidance from people who have already mastered the skills. This makes knowledge transfer across long distances very difficult.

And transferring some of the necessary skills for an export industry is not enough. An export industry needs all the necessary skills. If an industry is missing only one key skill, it cannot be competitive.

This places poorer nations in a Catch-22 situation. They cannot create high-value-added industries until they acquire the necessary skills, but they cannot acquire the necessary skills until they already have a functioning industry. This creates a fundamental gap that developing nations have difficulty bridging.

On the face of it, this appears to make economic growth impossible. Fortunately, we know from history that economic growth is possible.

The theory of economic complexity gives us the key intellectual breakthrough that industries are related to each other because they share common skills. For example, manufacturing shoes is closely related to manufacturing hats, because they share common production skills. Those same industries are far less related to manufacturing tractors or pharmaceuticals because those industries require very different skills.

And skills are not the only factor. Related industries also require similar technologies and organizational needs. This makes it theoretically possible for poor nations to leverage the limited knowledge that they have from current sectors of the economy to other related sectors that offer higher value.

Voyage of the Monkey

Hidalgo and Hausmann use the analogy of a monkey traveling through a forest in search of food. The monkey is on one side of the forest with few bananas (limited export options) and wants to get to the other side of the forest with many bananas (many profitable high-value-added export industries). The monkey can only travel one branch at-a-time, and it must survive each step by consuming bananas (i.e. acquiring the energy to survive).

So what does the monkey do? He gradually moves to the nearest branch with more bananas than the one he is currently on. He then uses the energy gained from the bananas (i.e. the technologies, skills, organizations, and capital) to go to the next branch. It is a long, slow process, but eventually, the monkey reaches the part of the forest with many bananas. This assumes, of course, that there are branches that are sufficiently close to each other along the way. Hidalgo and Hausmann's breakthrough is that they show through sophisticated statistical techniques that there is a pathway of branches from one side of the forest to the other.

This viewpoint gives us a clear understanding of how economies developed both in the past and the present. Commercial societies in northern Italy, Flanders, Netherlands, and England pioneered the innovations that created high-value-added industries. This was a long, slow process because they had no one to copy at first. There was a huge amount of learning by doing, with many mistakes along the way. As long as four of the Five Keys to Progress created the necessary preconditions for progress, they could keep experimenting and innovating for centuries.

Eventually, this led to the critical breakthrough of the Industrial Revolution in Britain. This largely involved the application of fossil fuels to the critical transportation, communication, agricultural, and materials sectors. Industrial technologies overcame some, but not all, of the geographical constraints on progress.

Today, developing nations face a different problem. All of the necessary technologies, skills, and organizations have already been invented, so they only need to copy them rather than creating them from scratch. However, because skills typically require a face-to-face transfer, it is hard for people in developing nations to learn everything they need to know. Worse, they face highly competitive industries in the richer nations that are vastly more productive. The one important advantage that developing nations have is cheaper labor.

The logic of this viewpoint leads to a clear economic learning strategy for developing nations:

1. Identify all your existing domestic industries.

2. Identify other industries that are closely related to existing industries and which also produce equal or higher added value.

3. Leverage the necessary technologies, skills, organizations, and capital from existing industries to learn the skills needed for the new industry and use the advantage of cheaper labor to outcompete richer nations. This will often involve selling an existing product at a cheaper price than richer nations can produce it for. It also involves focusing on

the low end of the market, where price is more important than quality, while leaving richer nations to focus on the higher end of the market.

4. Keep repeating the process for decades.

It is a nice theory, but does it work? Hidalgo, Hausmann, and others give compelling evidence that economic complexity is a useful concept, but it is not yet clear whether it can be put into practice.

By statistical analysis, Hidalgo and Hausmann show that complexity explains 73% of the variation in income across 128 countries. They also show that the difference between national income and level of complexity is the single best predictor of future economic growth. In other words, poor countries that have established a beachhead in higher-value-added products experience much higher growth rates in the immediate future than those that do not.

Free Trade or Fair Trade?

For centuries there have been bitter economic debates between free traders who abhor industrial policy and economic nationalists who see tariffs as crucial for promoting national economic growth. Overall, I am convinced by the arguments of free traders that industrial policies often lead to bad economic outcomes by subsidizing failing companies and those with insider connections.

I believe, however, that the theory of economic complexity creates a compelling middle ground. Instead of government bureaucrats "picking winners" based on political pressures, let the economic data do so. If government bureaucrats are forced by law to only pick industries that comply with the above algorithm, this might greatly reduce corruption and incorrect guesses.

As I mentioned before, it is still very unclear what specific policies a government should implement once they have identified an industry. I do think further research and inexpensive experimentation are warranted in this area. The theory just makes too much sense to be completely wrong.

A Viable Export Strategy

Developing nations should learn to implement Hidalgo and Haussmann's analogy: think like a monkey who wants to move from one side of the forest with a few bananas to the other side of the forest with many bananas, while not going hungry along the way. I particularly recommend that government officials, entrepreneurs, engineers, and venture capitalists in developing nations learn to think that way.

I recommend that anyone who lives in a developing nation read their book: The *Atlas of Economic Complexity* and study the companion website. The section for each nation that is currently labeled "Country Profiles" reveals economic statistics that are more actionable, timely, and specific than I have seen anywhere else.

The most relevant section for each nation is currently entitled "New Product Opportunities." This section lists all of the industries that their theory predicts that the selected nation should invest resources in promoting. The site does not explain exactly how to do so, but I hope that as their theory attracts more attention from developing nations, they can gradually learn how to do so by trial and error.

A reasonable starting point for a long-term development strategy via exports would include:

1. Select a few industries recommended by the website to focus on.

2. Collate all information that is currently available on the internet about the knowledge and skills that are needed within the target industries.

3. If necessary, translate that information into the native language.

4. Publish that information onto one website, so citizens of their nation can easily find them.

5. Organize conferences and networks of managers, entrepreneurs, engineers, skilled workers, and venture capitalists who have a detailed knowledge of the existing adjacent industries within their nations.

6. Focus the discussion on what those actors already know about

the current industry, and how they might leverage that knowledge and skills to apply in the new target industry.

7. Identify "missing skills" that the nations do not have but need to grow the new target industry.

8. Pay foreign industry experts to give lectures, write articles and create videos that specifically address the needs of both the target industry and the nation in question. A particular focus should be on the missing skills.

9. Provide venture capital to entrepreneurs who are willing to found new companies in the target industry.

10. Provide seed money to establish local venture capital companies, so that funding sources can shift from the government to private equity in the long run.

11. Continue that funding for a few years, but then make further funding based upon clear, transparent export metrics. If other citizens of other nations are willing to buy a company's product, that company must be doing something right. This gives evidence for a further round of funding. If not, funding should be cut off.

12. Pay foreign industry experts to provide on-the-job training to new employees. In the past, this required them to relocate to foreign countries, but short visits and digital conferencing may now be an adequate substitute. These meetings should "train the trainer" so that, after a local employee gains the necessary expertise, they could then do face-to-face training with other employees on site.

13. Establish departments within public universities and secondary education that are specifically designed to teach critical skills to future entrepreneurs, engineers, skilled workers, and venture capitalists. Most likely, foreign experts will be needed for instruction, at least at the start. As the economy changes, this curriculum should be constantly updated to reflect those changes.

14. Keep experimenting. It will take time to learn what works.

15. Compare notes with other developing nations who are trying similar strategies, to learn what they learned.

According to the other schools of thought that I discussed earlier, none of this is necessary because these efforts are not focused on what matters. But I do not believe that free trade, fighting corruption, or establishing property rights will help developing nations build profitable export industries. Nor do I believe that foreign aid for education, sanitation, and health care will do so; nor will democracy, political rights, or sustainable development. None of the other proposed strategies are focused enough to make a difference in what matters: higher value-added export industries.

My proposed strategy also has many important advantages over the competing proposals coming from the other schools:

- It leverages the money, knowledge, and skills of wealthy nations without requiring consent from their governments or multilateral organizations.
- It does not require massive reform of institutions or constitutions.
- It does not require foreign aid or large amounts of domestic funding.
- It does not require a massive transition to democracy and freedom.
- It does not require many different departments to cooperate.
- It does not threaten authoritarian leaders who run the nation (more on this later).
- It is the only strategy that focuses on the Five Keys to Progress.

Whereas the other proposals require some sort of agreement from domestic political leadership, multilateral organizations, or foreign governments, one small department with a relatively small budget can implement my proposal. This gives it a huge advantage over the other proposals.

It is quite conceivable that one particularly energetic Minister of the Economy or lower-level official within the same department might be able to start the process without much budget or approval from above.

Most of my proposal involves figuring out what needs to be learned, learning those skills, and then getting the right people together to coordinate their actions. Depending upon the industry at hand, initial seed money may not need to be extravagant.

High-level leaders may prefer not to know too many of the details of what is going on so that they can rely on plausible deniability if it all fails.

I believe that developing nations should focus on perfecting this strategy to gradually build higher-value-added export industries that are competitive on the world market. This strategy will enable developing nations to gradually leverage all the existing technology, skills, organizations, and capital to build new industries.

Over decades, this process can build a thriving economy that experiences progress. So many nations have transformed themselves within one generation that I refuse to believe that it is impossible.

There are two important problems with my proposal: the most important is that, because it has never been tried before, it might well fail. Failure is the most likely outcome of all new experiments, but that does not mean that one should not try.

We know that nations have made the transition from poverty to progress, so something works. And by thinking through how previous nations did do (as opposed to listening to the theories and ideologies of other schools), developing nations might be able to radically speed up the process.

With the proper knowledge and the right people, evolutionary processes can be accelerated. That is exactly why understanding the real causes of modern progress in wealthy nations is so critical.

So, have other nations used my proposed strategy? No, not if you focus on the details. But I think that if you look at strategies that Commercial societies in Northwest Europe used, what European nations used to industrialize in the 19th Century, and what Asian nations did at a later date, I believe that there are strong resemblances.

Because historical societies did not have the benefits of the theory of economic complexity, nor its associated books and websites, they were forced to rely on the idea of ratcheting up export industries via "learning by doing". I have every confidence that current developing nations can get even better results with the help of those critical resources.

Moreover, based upon a study of history, it is plausible that previous nations followed a similar strategy without necessarily being clear in their minds as to what they were doing. They may have just solved one problem at a time, copied others, and gradually worked their way through my proposed list without realizing it.

Because they did not do this regularly within a relatively short period, there was no reason for national governments to develop a formal methodology. And each of these nations, feeling that they were in competition with all the others, had a strong reason not to enlighten the rest of the world, let alone publish it in a book as I do.

What Does the Great Leader Think?

The other problem with my proposal is that some authoritarian leaders and all totalitarian leaders would never accept it. Lower-level officials might try it on their own initiative thinking that "this is what the Great Leader would want if only I could talk with him." But once their superiors found out about these attempts, they would squash the effort.

High-value export industries create wealth. Authoritarian leaders want to monopolize as much wealth as they can and then redistribute most of it to supporters with a particular focus on security services. This is how authoritarian regimes maintain their power. As strange as it may sound to rich Westerners, many leaders do not want productive wealth in the parts of the economy that they do not control.

Ultimately it comes down to the individual preferences of the leader and their highest-level supporters. They might feel threatened by my proposal, and they might not. Remember, they are trying to balance a desire to not let rival power bases emerge with the need to promote economic growth to maintain their legitimacy. Individual leaders will have different preferences, and those preferences will vary over time.

While I am sure that many authoritarian and all totalitarian leaders would ruthlessly suppress any hints of implementing my proposal, I believe that most leaders in developing nations would not. And some leaders might enthusiastically support it. So while my proposal may not work for every developing nation at all times, I am confident that it can be put into practice by more than a few nations.

The beautiful thing about my proposal is that it is flexible enough to apply to all developing nations (and probably wealthy ones too), and it is self-sustaining. If a nation gets real results by establishing one new export industry, this builds political support for trying the methodology out on another industry.

Success in building one industry also leads to learning, so hopefully, nations will get better at it with each try. With each victory, the department that oversees the effort will get more and more political legitimacy and bigger budgets (assuming the highest leaders like the effort, of course).

Better yet is the effect on the rest of the economy. Employees in high-value export industries will probably earn higher than average incomes. Those employees will spend money in the local economy and provide markets for small local businesses.

The tax base would also be broadened. Some of the revenue will undoubtedly be stolen by corrupt officials or wasted on useless programs, but some of it might be used for investing in infrastructure, sanitation, health care, and education. Either way, the money coming in will get support from at least some actors, corrupt or not.

Most importantly, the nation will learn valuable skills, implement new technology, start up new institutions and get new sources of working capital. All of this can then be used for starting the next industry. If properly implemented and maintained, it could create many competitive exporting industries in a relatively short period.

Focus on Results

Key metrics for measuring the success of policies to create thriving export industries in developing nations should be:

- Change in economic complexity for each nation
- Export revenue
- Decadal average growth in GDP
- For new businesses established in targeted industries:
- Number of businesses started
- Time to acquire licenses
- Domestic venture capital raised
- Export revenue generated
- Employment created
- Total compensation for new employees

Conclusion

Because most developing nations have a reasonable level of four of the Five Keys to Progress and they have access to the global trade system, they have a very real chance to increase their level of prosperity by building thriving export industries. Doing so will not be easy, but so many Asian nations have done so that we know that it is possible. I believe that the principles in this chapter give developing nations a far better chance of doing so than any other development theories advocated by Western experts.

ENERGY FOR DEVELOPING NATIONS

The Fifth Key to Progress: Widespread use of fossil fuels.
The incredible energy density of fossil fuels injects vast amounts of useful energy into society, enabling it to solve a wide variety of problems. Without this energy, life would return to the daily struggle for survival that dominated most of human history.

Since I have three other chapters that discuss energy policy, I will not go into as much detail on desirable energy policies for developing nations here. The Progress-based energy policy for developing nations is very similar to what I previously proposed for wealthy nations.

When developing nations innovate new export industries, they should invest a significant proportion of the proceeds into building an abundant, affordable and secure energy system. In particular, a robust electrical grid will allow consumers to reliably power many of the electrical devices that wealthy nations take for granted.

Among these electrical devices are pumps for indoor plumbing, lights, computers, mobile devices, the internet, air conditioning, fans, refrigerators, freezers, microwaves, ovens, clothes washers, and clothes dryers. In the long run, it will also include electric cars and trucks.

These electrical devices may seem like trivial items for consumers in wealthy nations, but they greatly improve the quality of life of people living in developing nations. They also drastically reduce the number of hours that women need to devote to household choirs. This gives women more time for child-rearing and employment. Many of these items are fairly inexpensive to purchase, but they are heavily dependent on a reliable electrical grid, which many developing nations do not have.

Just as abundant, affordable, and secure energy is essential for economic growth in wealthy nations, it is equally important in developing nations. An abundant, affordable, and secure energy system will enable developing nations to power farms, sanitation, hospitals, health clinics, schools, government buildings, factories, housing construction, transportation, and other vital systems. Affordable electricity makes everything else more affordable.

The most dangerous threat to abundant, affordable, and secure energy are Green energy policies that are hostile to fossil fuels. Greens have pushed an idea of "sustainable development" based upon promoting wind, solar and organic farming in developing nations. As I already mentioned, "sustainable development" is not sustainable economically, nor will it lead to development. We need a Progress-based development model that promotes long-term economic development while gradually transitioning developing nations onto lower carbon energy sources.

To the best of my knowledge, there is not a single example of a nation experiencing rapid economic growth without the widespread usage of fossil fuels. Any developing nation that refuses to use fossil fuels is guaranteeing that it will not transition to progress. Moreover, if they already have progress going, it would be one of the fastest ways to kill that progress.

Just don't do it.

To experience long-term economic growth, developing nations need to:

1. Construct an abundant, affordable, and secure electrical grid based on natural gas, nuclear, hydroelectric, and coal. Wherever possible, prefer the first three sources over coal.

2. Where geography and economics allow, these power sources can be supplemented by solar, wind, and geothermal, but natural gas,

nuclear, hydroelectric, and coal will produce the vast majority of the electricity.

3. Encourage shale gas companies to explore, drill, and distribute shale oil and gas within your national borders. This will lower the cost of domestically-produced natural gas, making it cost-competitive with coal.

4. When the Grand Bargain that I propose in a later chapter is agreed to, gradually phase out coal in favor of the other energy sources listed above.

5. Construct a rail, road, and shipping transportation system based on internal combustion engines and petroleum.

6. When wealthy nations make electric cars and their batteries affordable, electrify your transportation system.

7. As wealthy nations invent new energy sources (with incentives from innovation prizes) shift towards them as the economics allow you to. In the meantime rely on proven energy sources.

8. Do not make any global commitments to lower carbon emissions. Focus on promoting long-term widely-shared economic growth.

Maybe sometime in the future, we will have nuclear fusion or wind/solar/geothermal power that can be easily purchased by developing nations, but not now. Developing nations should focus on what works and then deal with any negative environmental consequences later, when they are much richer.

While I disagree strongly with the Green goal of eliminating fossil fuels, I do believe that we should limit the growth of global carbon emissions in a way that does not undermine long-term economic growth. Unfortunately, in many developing nations, by far the most cost-effective means to generate electricity and power industrial processes is by burning coal. Particularly in East Asia, South Asia, and Southeast Asia, solar and wind are simply not an option due to geographical constraints. This region is critical because half the human population lives there and the bulk of the developing nations are experiencing long-term economic growth.

Fortunately, there are other options if wealthy nations implement the Progress-based energy policy that I introduced in the earlier *Energy Abundance* chapter. Conventional natural gas and shale gas fields are widespread enough in Asia that energy companies can extract vast amounts of low-carbon energy. This, combined with the incentives of a coal tax will encourage Asia to shift from coal to natural gas, nuclear and hydroelectric power.

China has the largest technically recoverable shale gas resources in the world. India has a very large shale field underneath the Ganges river basin, where the majority of its residents live. Indonesia, Bangladesh, Pakistan, Argentina, Algeria, Mexico, and South Africa also have substantial shale gas fields.

Many developing nations have shale gas resources, but what they are missing the technology, skills, organizations and capital to exploit those critical energy resources. Unlike conventional gas fields, every shale gas field has very different geological properties that make extracting the gas a unique challenge.

Currently, the United States is the only nation that possesses the necessary technology, skills, and organizations. By cooperating, American shale companies and Asian nations can greatly increase natural gas production, enabling coal to gradually be phased out.

In the more distant future, the innovation prizes that I explained earlier will lead to a radical new energy source that is far better than any current one. Until my proposed Progress-based energy policy is implemented, Asian nations will continue to construct coal-burning power plants, whether Greens like it or not.

Focus on Results

The key metrics would be identical the metrics listed at the end of the *Energy Abundance* chapter.

Conclusion

In this part of the book, I made some proposals that can help developing nations move further up the transition to progress. All of these proposals are closely linked to the concept of the Five Keys to Progress.

I believe that it is essential to build policy proposals on that concept because the Five Keys to Progress are the critical preconditions that enable societies to make a better world for their citizens. The Five Keys are also the critical preconditions for creating and sustaining the vast, decentralized problem-solving network that is a modern society.

Developing nations today are in similar circumstances to earlier Commercial societies in pre-Industrial Europe. They have enough of four of the five keys to generate some progress for their citizens, but not enough for a jump to truly transformative progress.

Commercial societies in pre-Industrial Europe lacked fossil fuels. When Britain industrialized, it added the fifth key. The result was an economic transformation that spread across the world.

Most developing nations today lack a different key: a critical mass of high-value-added export industries. I believe that the methodology that I suggested earlier can help to overcome this problem and create transformative progress in developing nations. Since the vast majority of developing nations have made at least some improvements on each of the other Five Keys to Progress, acquiring the fifth can have a transformative effect on their society.

These proposals are not meant to be an exhaustive list of all possible proposals that can be derived from the concept of the Five Keys to Progress. I hope this book inspires developing nations to test these proposals with small experiments and scale them up rapidly if they prove useful. I also hope that it causes Western experts to seriously rethink their assumptions of what works and change their advice to developing nations.

PART FIVE: MITIGATING SIDE EFFECTS OF PROGRESS

Ill good things in life have bad things associated with them. Nothing in life is completely good, nor is there anything in life that is completely bad.

The same is true for progress. While material progress has created huge benefits for mankind, it has done so at some cost.

Many ideologues on both the Left and Right win credibility for their claims that progress is bad by focusing on those negative consequences. Among the most commonly mentioned negative consequences of material progress are inequality, climate change, air pollution, water pollution, destruction of wild habitat, job disruptions, business bankruptcy, death/injuries due to technology, and a feeling of "too much change." All of the above are very real and should not be ignored, but neither should they be obsessed over while the benefits of progress are ignored.

It would be far too time-consuming to go through each of these topics in detail, but I will focus on the one that is most often mentioned: climate change. Using this example, I claim that the goal should not be rolling back or constraining progress. I believe that the goal should be **mitigating the negative side effects of progress while keeping**

progress going. In particular, we need to maintain the Five Keys to Progress plus the factors for How Progress works. Ideally, we should keep improving all of them, while mitigating the negative side-effects in a cost-effective way.

Ideologues on both the Left and Right ignore how extraordinarily successful modern Industrial societies have become at solving problems. Once a society achieves the Five Keys to Progress, it becomes a vast decentralized problem-solving network. Rather than slowing down that network, we should find ways for it to focus on solving new problems.

While technology cannot solve all problems, if a problem can be solved, it is very likely to include an application of technology. More often than not, innovative new technologies enable us to break the link between a side effect of progress and it having a negative effect on society.

An example of the way technology can help to solve the negative side effects of progress is the automobile. There can be no doubt that this technology has created negative side effects related to air pollution and traffic deaths. Some activists on the Left have tried to establish policies that reduce or eliminate the driving of cars. These policies have had limited success, as automobiles (and trucks) are by far the most commonly used transportation device.

Despite the rapid increase in car use, air pollution is declining rapidly. The technological innovation of the catalytic converter has dramatically reduced levels of carbon monoxide, nitrous oxides, and other pollutants. Government regulation of exhaust emissions undoubtedly helped to spread their adoption in the 1970s, but without private industries inventing the catalytic converter, none of this would have been possible.

The same goes for traffic deaths. Traffic fatalities are one of the leading causes of death. Over the last few generations, a large number of automotive safety technologies have drastically lowered traffic deaths per mile driven. These include padded dashboards, padded steering wheels, lap seatbelts, shoulder seatbelts, rack-and-pinion steering, anti-lock braking systems, electronic stability control, airbags, tires with better traction, and driving-assist technologies.

In some cases, government regulations forced car companies to use these technologies, but car companies competing based on safety ratings also played an important role. More to the point, with the technological innovations made by engineers, none of this decline in deaths per mile would have been possible.

The cost-effectiveness of a specific regulation is highly dependent on the technologies that private industry is able to innovate. Where private industry can innovate highly cost-effective technologies, government regulations mandating their adoption can be beneficial.

Where technical barriers prevent private industry from innovating cost-effective technologies, government regulations will generally have a negative effect on progress. This may cause the government to modify or roll back the regulation, but more often than not, they will proceed regardless of results.

Government regulators need to (but rarely do) carefully balance the benefits of mitigating a negative side effect of progress with the cost of designing, testing and manufacturing the technology. They also need to be aware of any unanticipated negative costs that the new technology introduces.

In all these cases, there is a trade-off between the cost of paying for these new technologies and the benefits of mitigating the negative side effects of progress. In the domain of automotive safety, these new technologies appear to be worth the minor negative impact on economic growth. In the case of Green policies to lower carbon emissions, the trade-off is very different.

CUTTING GLOBAL CARBON EMISSIONS

To promote long-term economic growth, developing nations desperately need abundant, affordable, and secure energy systems. In particular, they need advanced electrical grids that enable every home, industry, and commercial building to harness the awesome power of electricity.

Western nations take for granted the ability to plug in lights, kitchen appliances, computers, air conditioning, and other electric-powered products. They also take for granted battery-powered products that recharge via those same wall outlets. Most electric and battery-powered products are far cheaper than the alternative, but they need a robust electrical grid to function.

Few investments would do more to promote long-term widely-shared economic growth in developing nations than a robust electrical grid. Unfortunately, this is diametrically opposed to Green ideology because this goal cannot be accomplished without fossil fuels, nuclear or hydroelectric power. And Greens oppose all of them.

Concern for increasing global carbon emissions is legitimate, but we cannot implement policies that undermine progress in wealthy nations and throw out the possibility of progress in developing nations. We must first promote progress and secondly, we must mitigate the negative side-effects of that progress on the natural environment. One of those negative side effects is climate change. Another is air and water pollution.

Fortunately, there is a way to do so, but such a policy would be very different from current Green policies.

The Failure of Green Energy Policies

Despite investing trillions of dollars in renewable energy sources, governments implementing Green energy policies have not been able to substantially lower global carbon emissions. While the increase in global carbon emissions has slowed a bit, the trend is still upward. So *by their own criteria, Green energy policies have failed.*

Renewable energy sources have not *substituted* for fossil fuels (as is the declared goal). Renewable energy sources have been *in addition to* fossil fuels. That is why Green energy policies will inevitably fail to lower global carbon emissions.

Since 1990, annual global carbon emissions have increased from 22.76 to 37.12 billion tons. The percentage of fossil fuels in global energy production has dropped only slightly from 85% to about 83%. In the United States, fossil fuels make up 79% of energy use, and it is not much different in Europe. If you believe that it is essential to radically reduce the global usage of fossil fuels to avoid a global catastrophe, then current Green policies must be regarded as a huge policy failure (Our World In Data).

Rather than admit that their energy policy is failing, Greens want to double down on failure by spending even more money. A lack of funding, however, is clearly not the problem. The amount of money invested in renewable energy over the last three decades probably makes it the single largest peacetime government program in world history. There is no reason to believe that additional resources will fundamentally change the outcome.

Green Policies Do Not Lower Temperatures

The fundamental problem with Green energy policies is that *radical changes in energy usage lead to very small changes in future temperatures.* This means that even if the West is successful at eliminating fossil fuels rapidly, which I argue is virtually impossible, doing so will have very little impact on future temperatures. Remember that the goal of Green energy policy is not to build renewable energy. It is to reduce the future increase in global temperatures by drastically reducing global carbon emissions.

According to the US EPA's MAGICC climate model, if the United States completely eliminated fossil fuel consumption today, it would only lead to 0.33 degrees F lower temperature by the end of the century. If you made the same computation for all wealthy nations, it would only lead to 0.8 degrees F cooler. This is such a small change in temperature that most thermometers cannot even measure the difference. It is just not credible to believe that such a small decline in average temperature would avert a climate disaster (Lomborg).

This is partly because much of the carbon dioxide that will affect future temperatures are already in the atmosphere. The IPCC assumes that carbon dioxide remains in the atmosphere for 100 years or more, though many peer-reviewed estimates come to much shorter durations (Andrews). Under current technology, we have no cost-effective method to remove carbon dioxide from the atmosphere, so we have no choice but to adapt to future temperature increases.

So Green energy policies are not reducing global carbon emissions, and, even if they did succeed, those reductions would not matter. Proposing radical policies with huge negative consequences and tiny long-term benefits is the height of folly.

We need a better energy policy, one that promotes abundant, affordable, and secure energy while mitigating the damage to the natural environment. To do so, we must throw out all the Green assumptions on what works.

Which Is More Important?

One of the key reasons why Greens have been able to dominate our discourse on energy policy is that no one has come up with a credible alternative policy. But there are alternative policies. In the earlier *Energy*

Abundance chapter, I outlined a Progress-based energy policy to create abundant, affordable and secure energy systems in the wealthy nations. In this chapter, I will show how it can be extended to reduce global carbon emissions at a far more rapid rate than current Green policies.

Before determining future policy choices, one must first make a moral decision as to what one is trying to optimize: human progress or minimizing human impacts on the natural environment. I know that this is not an easy choice, but we must make a decision. Humans naturally want to have it all, and we have a difficult time choosing between two important values.

While it is not a zero-sum conflict between the two, as more radical environmentalists believe, there are some very real trade-offs between economic growth and eliminating carbon emissions. Since the widespread use of fossil fuels is one of the key foundations of human progress, we should not easily dismiss it.

Radically lowering the standard of living of Westerners would hurt the working class and the poor the most. Worse, it would make economic development in the rest of the world all but impossible. To anyone who believes in human material progress, this outcome should be unacceptable.

I believe that we should put human progress first.

Greens Have the Wrong Goal

Supporters of progress should not agree to the Green goal of eliminating (or even radically lowering) carbon emissions. **Our goal should be mitigating the damage of carbon emissions and other pollutants while maintaining the foundations of human progress**. The latter goal is compatible with human progress. Unfortunately, Greens have adopted a goal that is incompatible with it.

We cannot assume that only one problem (carbon emissions) matters to the exclusion of all other problems. The vast, decentralized problem-solving network that is a modern society solves thousands of problems, and it needs vast amounts of dense and controllable energy to function properly. With current technology, only a combination of fossil fuels, nuclear and hydroelectric power make this progress possible.

The positive impact that fossil fuels have made over the last two centuries is incalculable. The potential useful energy from human power, animal power, wind, sun, and water is far too diffuse to have sustained recent material progress. Quite simply, without coal, petroleum, and natural gas, the world would be much worse than it is today. And that is even when we take into account their very real damage to the environment.

It is not just the climate that needs to be sustained. **We must also sustain progress**.

In reality, climate change is not the only problem we face; it is one of hundreds or even thousands of problems. Like all problems, we partly mitigate them with new technology and partly adapt to them.

We must also be aware that proposed solutions to big problems are often worse than the original problem that they were trying to solve. This is particularly true if they undermine one of the Five Keys to Progress, which I argue are the necessary preconditions that allow progress to exist.

Climate activists seem to believe that, just because they are convinced climate change is the biggest problem, we should be willing to undermine the very thing that helps us solve all other problems: the vast, decentralized problem-solving network. Without vast amounts of dense, secure, controllable energy, this network cannot function.

Nor do climate activists acknowledge the possibility that fossil fuels are more beneficial to society, even if a climate disaster occurs. Climate change may be bad, but the benefits of fossil fuels might also be so great, that eliminating their use at this stage would make the world a worse place. Climate activists act as if this is not even a possibility. But it is more than a possibility; it is very likely to be true.

All good things have bad side effects, even renewable energy. The solution to one problem can never be destroying all good things, which abolishing fossil fuels risks.

It is far better to use the vast, decentralized problem-solving network to develop solutions that lower the negative side effects of progress or adapt to those side effects. And sweeping government edicts and global agreements are not effective in doing so.

As for future man-made climate change, humanity has no prior experience in dealing with this. It is hubris to expect that we know what works, and we should therefore just ram through what the loudest voices propose.

Climate Change Is A Risk

It is probably better to view climate change as a risk, not a threat. Climate change is one of thousands of risks. Those risks all vary in severity and probability of occurring. All of them have a great deal of uncertainty attached to them.

As for climate change, there is some unknown possibility of very bad outcomes. I believe that there is a dramatically higher chance of far less extreme outcomes that are better dealt with by adapting to them in the future. It seems reasonable to take steps to lower the risk, **as long as doing so does not undermine progress**.

Climate activists' solutions to climate change would be like seeing the problem of obesity and calling on the world to abolish food within 1-3 decades. Obesity is a very serious problem. It is perhaps the most serious health problem in the United States. We know that it is caused by consuming too much food relative to the number of calories burnt in daily life. Phasing out food would solve the problem.

Obviously, no one would propose abolishing food because they know that, despite the problem of obesity, food is essential for survival. So too, by the way, is carbon dioxide, which is essential for plant growth. And fossil fuels are essential to widely-shared economic growth.

To seek to abolish fossil fuels is almost as misguided as seeking to abolish food.

Energy Transitions Take Time

In the earlier *Energy Abundance* chapter, I discussed energy transitions. So far mankind has gone through three fundamental energy transitions. The Third Energy Transition is still underway. My Progress-based energy policy is about accelerating the Third Energy Transition.

But here is the thing. Energy transitions take long periods of time. Energy transitions are measured in generations, not years.

As Vaclav Smil has documented in his outstanding books on energy, energy transitions take place over many decades, and they shift from relatively diffuse energy sources to denser sources (i.e. they shift from materials that yield more energy per unit of mass). Shifting quickly from a dense energy source (fossil fuels) to a less dense energy source (renewables) is unprecedented and goes against the flow of human history. My guess is that, assuming that we want to maintain world progress while doing so, it is also impossible.

It is a Question of Time Scale

There is another way of looking at the problem. It is all a question of timescale, something that is completely ignored by both sides on the climate debate.

The fundamental problem with the Green energy agenda is not so much that they want to abolish fossil fuels. *It is that they want to do it quickly.* If we shift the timeframe from phasing out fossil fuels within 30 years to doing so within 100 years, that completely transforms the scale of the problem.

Fossil fuels are an extraordinarily useful energy technology, but like all technologies they will someday become obsolete. It seems quite likely that within 100 years, we will invent a new energy source that is far denser and cost-effective than fossil fuels.

My guess is that 100 years from now, fossil fuels will make up a far smaller percentage of total energy usage, regardless of any policy that we implement today. In 100 years, fossil fuel usage might even be zero.

In 2120, fossil fuels will probably seem as quaint as wood-burning stoves do today.

Such an extended timeframe will probably require far fewer government interventions or disruptions to the economy. Such a timescale will allow the vast, decentralized problem-solving network to find much better solutions than governments and activists can.

Phasing out fossil fuels slowly (i.e. over the next 100 years) will probably be easy and inevitable given current trends of technological innovation and decarbonization. The attempt to phase out fossil fuels in only 10-30 years, however, will lead to devastating economic consequences that make the goal of maintaining human progress impossible.

I believe that eliminating fossil fuels within one to three decades would be catastrophic to human progress. We simply do not have the technology to support such a rapid transition. The economic consequences would be devastating to wealthy nations, and condemn developing nations to eternal poverty.

Democratic societies simply will not allow the rapid decline in energy usage once these consequences become more obvious. Once the results become clear, voters will rebel. They will demand a more reasonable plan to reduce carbon emissions while maintaining human progress.

Nor will developing nations play along. Even authoritarian regimes know that their political legitimacy is largely based upon their ability to promote long-term economic growth. This, by the way, is enormous progress from times when authoritarian regimes did not care about economic growth or were actively opposed to it because it might destabilize their regime.

If Greens set a goal of gradually diminishing fossil fuel usage over the next century as well as fund innovation for replacement technologies, I could be in strong agreement within them.

Fundamental innovations in energy technologies have been one of the driving forces in world progress. The invention of windmills, watermills, and sailing ships were tremendously important in generating early pre-Industrial progress. The invention of nuclear energy and hydroelectric dams also helped to push modern progress forward.

A new energy source that is far better than fossil fuels is not just possible; it is close to inevitable (given enough time). But that goal is very different from trying to force an energy transition through before better technology becomes available due to an imagined climate emergency. Such a goal endangers world progress and hurts the working class in rich nations as well as all citizens in developing nations.

It Is Not About the West

For the past 40 years, Green energy policies have focused on wealthy Western nations. The current consensus among climate activists as to how to fight climate change emerged in the 1980s: the West should decarbonize by rapidly replacing fossil fuels with solar, wind, and other renewables. The argument went that this would give room for developing countries to grow economically using fossil fuels and later transition to renewables when they become rich enough to do so.

Back in the 1980s and early 1990s, this idea made some sense. Global carbon emissions in 1990 were 22.75 trillion tons. In that year the United States, Canada, Europe, and Japan emitted the majority of carbon emissions. In such a world, an exclusive focus on wealthy nations made some sense (Global Carbon Project 2021).

The United Nations Framework Convention on Climate Change in 1992 and the subsequent Kyoto Protocol of 1997 were built on this political consensus. By the time of the Copenhagen Accord of 2009, however, the assumptions behind this political consensus had collapsed. No one, least of all the climate activists, foresaw what was to come in the three decades after 1990.

Transition from Coal, Not Fossil Fuels

Once you cut through all the ideology and all the doomsday rhetoric, we can identify practical solutions that lower global carbon emissions faster than Green proposals without endangering world economic growth.

The big problem with air pollution and carbon emissions is not fossil fuels in general, but more specifically coal. One area where I agree with environmentalists is the dangers of coal. Wherever there are no huge cost disparities between coal and petroleum, natural gas, nuclear or hydroelectric, I would avoid coal if possible.

Coal is the worst carbon emitter (apart from wood) and by far the worst air and water polluter. Ending the use of coal is a very realistic goal in many nations, as long as they do not try to do so exclusively with solar and wind.

Unfortunately, coal is currently the cheapest form of energy in many regions. This is exactly why developing nations have built so many coal plants. Wealthy nations need a better alternative to coal than pushing solar and wind.

Since we are on the topic of coal use, I should mention China, India, and Indonesia. China alone consumes more than half of all coal burned in the world. India and Indonesia are second and third on the list. Together these three nations consume two-thirds of all coal used in the world. Unfortunately, environmentalists ignore this crucial fact (Global Energy Monitor).

If the goal is to reduce *global* carbon emissions as fast as possible without endangering economic growth in developing nations, it is far more cost-effective to transition those three nations from coal to a blend of natural gas, nuclear and hydroelectric power than for the West to install solar and wind. If those three nations can make the transition, then it will be easier for all the other developing nations to do so as well.

Gas or Coal

The choice we have today is not between fossil fuels and renewables. It is between American natural gas and Asian coal. The combination of the Shale Revolution and combined-cycle gas turbines (CCGT) make for a cost-effective and easily scalable "Coal Killer" in the United States. We should be doing everything possible to export those technologies to the rest of the world. This would drastically reduce global use of coal, particularly in Asia, without hurting economic growth.

Unfortunately, Green energy policies encourage increased use of Asian coal rather than American natural gas technologies. Current Green policies also undermine the ability of American natural gas companies to spread the technologies, skills, and organization that led to the Shale Revolution to the rest of the world.

The United States is the largest single economic market in the world. Over the last few decades, American industry has relocated to Asia in search of cheaper labor. Many of the goods produced in Asian nations are then transported back to the American market. The unintended outcome of this Asia-Pacific supply chain has been a radical increase in the consumption of coal.

Industries desperately need affordable energy to be competitive in the global trading system. If they cannot purchase affordable natural gas in the United States or Europe, then they will relocate to Asia. If they do not, then they will be replaced by Chinese companies and the result will be the same. Every Green policy that makes natural gas expensive (or illegal) only increases the use of Asian coal. This leads to increased carbon emissions.

Coal Tax

An important part of my Progress-based energy policy should be an international coal tax. The coal tax would work if it is exclusively implemented in the United States, but ideally it would be implemented in all wealthy nations. A coal tax implemented in the United States, Europe, and Japan could have a dramatic effect on global carbon emissions without disrupting global economic growth and maintaining affordable energy.

I briefly mentioned a coal tax earlier, but since the effects would be global, I reserved a full discussion for here. A coal tax would be levied on all products that are mined, refined, or manufactured anywhere on the planet using coal power. Most importantly, the tax would be levied on all goods, regardless of their point of origin: domestic or imported.

Nations that implement the coal tax would estimate the amount of total coal burned to create that product in the specific nation that produced it. Getting an exact amount would be very difficult, but all that is really needed is a rough estimate that is consistently applied to each nation and product. Since much coal usage comes from electricity, the overall percentage of electricity generated from coal would be a key part of the equation.

The amount should be equivalent to a carbon tax of $100 per ton of carbon dioxide. The coal tax should only be imposed once Congress agrees to pay for the rapid replacement of coal-burning power plants with the most energy-efficient combined-cycle natural gas power plant (CCGT). This would immediately reduce carbon emissions from those power plants by about two-thirds and even more radically reduce pollutants.

Because CCGT plants are very inexpensive and fast to install, the process could take place very quickly in the United States. It would cost only $148 billion to replace every American coal plant with CCGT. This is less than 30% of the cost of the recent Inflation Reduction Act of 2022. These new plants would reduce their carbon emissions by two-thirds (US EIA 2018, Frank).

The biggest delays would be caused by companies like General Electric having to ramp up production of CCGT quickly as well as construct additional gas pipelines to the new plants. Because CCGT plants are much smaller than coal plants, they could be placed on the same site, so there will be no permitting delays.

The coal tax would give American industries that currently use coal in their manufacturing processes a strong incentive to switch to natural gas. For most manufacturing processes, natural gas can substitute for coal (and crude oil) where it is economically feasible. As long as gas pipelines are in their general area, this should be a fairly smooth transition. All of this means that the United States could quickly phase out coal in favor of natural gas in 10 years and accomplish most of this transition in 5 years or less.

Best of all, this will cause no disruption for American consumers. They will probably notice no change at all, except for far less haze in the sky and cleaner air. The Shale Revolution has made natural gas so cheap that their electrical bills will probably get cheaper.

With a highly dependable domestic market, natural gas producers in the shale fields would have a strong incentive to ramp up production and keep prices relatively constant. Given that shale sites require only a few weeks to ramp up production, keeping prices low and stable should not be too much of a problem.

In theory, the coal tax might also stimulate construction of nuclear and hydroelectric power plants, but given their very high construction costs and long construction periods, it seems unlikely in the short term. Natural gas drill pads can ramp up production so fast that coal will probably be almost completely phased out before the first new nuclear or hydroelectric plant comes online.

Once coal is fully phased out in the United States, then our energy system can make decisions based on cost and dependability, just as it did before Green energy policies were implemented. With coal completely phased out, there is no reason for the government to choose between low-carbon natural gas and zero-carbon solar, wind, nuclear and hydroelectric.

Better Than a Carbon Tax

The purpose of my proposed coal tax is to give companies and nations a strong economic incentive to move beyond coal power. In some ways, this tax is similar to a carbon tax, often favored by more moderate climate activists, but it is levied exclusively on coal.

Carbon taxes are designed to give companies an incentive to shift to carbon-free energy sources. The problem is that carbon taxes disincentivize natural gas and crude oil, which currently have no viable alternatives. In particular, since natural gas is the most cost-effective means in the United States to reduce carbon emissions while maintaining a stable and affordable energy system, carbon taxes create very bad incentives.

Carbon taxes increase the cost of energy without creating any direct benefits. Companies or consumers will have to pay the taxes and then, on top of that, pay for the construction of the infrastructure required to lower carbon emissions. With the coal tax that I am proposing, the revenue generated from the coal tax would go directly into building up the Third Energy Transition energy infrastructure.

Right now, we should not be trying to get off fossil fuels. We should be trying to get off coal. A modern combined-cycle natural gas plant (CCGT) generates only one-third of the carbon emissions of an older coal-burning power plant. Because CCGT plants are very inexpensive to construct, they are the most cost-effective replacements for coal plants.

Carbon taxes also tax crude oil, which currently does not have a viable alternative for transportation. Electric cars are still in their infancy, and they will remain so if the electrical grid is powered largely by solar and wind. Once the electrical grid of wealthy nations is powered largely by natural gas, nuclear power, and hydroelectric dams, then and only then is the electrification of transportation at scale viable.

A coal tax should be combined with a widespread rollback of regulations that undermine the exploration, drilling, and transportation of natural gas. The United States has the expertise to exploit conventional gas fields and shale gas fields in Europe and Asia, but they are restricted from doing so by government regulations.

Funding Energy Infrastructure

The money raised from the coal tax would be exclusively used for the following purposes:

1. Installation of domestic natural gas, nuclear and hydroelectric power plants. The exact blend of the three will largely be determined by geography and cost. In the United States, this would be almost

exclusively natural gas because of its clear cost advantage.

2.   Financing loans for the construction of any additional pipelines or electrical power lines necessary for the above.

3.   Financing loans for the construction of pipelines and electrical power lines connecting Canada and Mexico to create a true NAFTA-wide energy market.

4.   Financing loans for the construction of liquefied natural gas (LNG) conversion sites, so the United States can export natural gas to Asia, Europe, and South America.

5.   Paying for refundable tax credits for the purchase of electric cars, buses, trucks, and other transportation devices. Many of these are already in place.

6.   Assisting developing nations that agree to the Grand Bargain (which I discuss later) to make the transition away from coal to a blend of natural gas, nuclear and hydroelectric.

In the short run, a coal tax would give American companies a strong incentive to reshore their industries back to American soil. Given how easy it will be to transition from coal to natural gas in the United States, that nation will reap the largest initial benefits.

Europe will also enjoy the benefits of a coal tax, but the transition will take longer. With assistance from American energy companies, particularly those skilled in horizontal drilling and hydraulic fracturing, Europe can rapidly increase its domestic natural gas production and lower its energy costs. This will make the transition from Russian natural gas far easier. By reinvigorating energy production and stopping the forced expansion of renewable energy, European manufacturing will be far more competitive in the long run.

Electrifying Transportation

An affordable and abundant electrical grid gives the United States a stable platform for a transition toward electric cars, buses, and delivery vans. Because electric cars are more energy efficient as internal combustion engines (ICE), this will enable the United States to export a higher percentage of its domestic petroleum production overseas.

One of the many positive side-effects of progress is enhanced personal mobility. Currently, that enhanced mobility is almost entirely fueled by gasoline and diesel, both of which are derivatives of crude oil.

There are compelling reasons for electrifying transportation. Electric motors are three to four times more energy-efficient than internal combustion engines (ICE). Electric vehicles routinely achieve well over the equivalent of 100 mpg.

Even when one factors in the cost, weight and emissions of batteries, this is a big win for energy efficiency. Assuming that the electrical grid is affordable and stable, this efficiency gives a strong economic incentive to convert to electric. This conversion will result in a much bigger decline in carbon emissions than renewable electricity can possibly offer.

Let's use some numbers from the U.S. Office of Energy Efficiency and Renewable Energy. They have created a handy online calculator that enables you to calculate greenhouse emissions by car type and zip code. The calculator factors in tailpipe emissions as well as upstream emissions for getting oil and electricity from the ground into your car. Unfortunately, the calculator does not include emissions from the initial production of the car.

Since every region in the United States has a different blend of energy sources, I will use New England as a model. If we were to fully implement my Progress-based energy proposal (i.e. replace coal with natural gas), then the entire national electrical grid would closely resemble New England's current grid.

In 2022 New England's electrical grid consists of 53.2% natural gas, 26.4% nuclear, 6.5% hydro, 13.3% wind/solar/biomass and 0.2% coal. The national numbers are 19.3% coal and 11.7% wind/solar/biomass. The New England grid is not a perfect analogy for my proposal, but it is close.

A Tesla Model 3, currently the bestselling electric car, emits 70g/mile of greenhouse gases in New England, while an average new internal combustion engine (ICE) vehicle emits 410g/mile. Going electric leads to a more than an 80% reduction in carbon emissions. Vehicles powered by electricity generated by natural gas also emit far less carbon monoxide and other pollutants, and they move those pollutants out of the cities (because the power stations are typically located on the outskirts of the metro area).

Note that a Tesla Model 3 would emit 110g/mile using the average US electricity mix. The Tesla still only emits 190 g/mile in coal-crazy Missouri, which generates 61.5% of its electricity from coal. Though the calculator does not include overseas data, it seems likely that electric cars beat ICE cars even in coal-dominant China.

Limitations of EVs

Electric cars clearly have limitations. My wife and I own a 2015 Nissan Leaf. It was essentially the first practical and affordable electrical car ever mass-produced. Back in 2015 the Tesla was still a very expensive luxury car that was unaffordable for most people.

Our Nissan Leaf had an EPA estimated range of 81 miles. This range, while accurate, does not include use of the heater, air conditioning, window defrosters, and hills, all of which degrades that range. So does driving in sub-freezing temperatures. Our car is great when you stay within one metro region, but forget about using it for long road trips.

The big advantage that our car has (in common with all other electric cars) is far lower operating costs. Electricity is typically far cheaper than gasoline, there is no need for oil changes and the pads on regenerative brakes last far longer than on traditional brakes. Replacing and aligning tires are the major repair costs for electric cars, neither of which are costly.

The problem with electric cars is their big, heavy and expensive battery. Nissan has not released actual numbers, but the battery in our Nissan likely makes up one quarter to one third of the price of the car. The same can be said for the weight. And the range of the battery gradually degrades over time, so it will eventually need to be replaced.

Fortunately, since 2015, the price of batteries has declined substantially and ranges over 200 miles are becoming standard. Electric cars are rapidly becoming credible as replacements for ICE cars for transportation within metro regions. Electric delivery vans, pickups and buses are also becoming increasingly viable.

40 miles Is the Magic Number

To accelerate the electrification of transportation, we should mandate that all cars, vans and light trucks sold 5 years from now have a 40-mile electric-only range. Five years is the typical design cycle for new cars, so that time period will give automotive designers plenty of time to redesign their cars with the new mandate in mind. Car manufacturers and consumers could then decide whether they want to go full electric or plug-in hybrid.

While potential buyers of electric cars focus on getting 300+ miles of range, the shorter 40-mile range has many advantages:

1. It requires a much smaller battery, which is far cheaper. Since the battery is the single most expensive part in an electric car, this is a significant cost savings.

2. Smaller batteries produce far fewer carbon emissions during production than full-size electric batteries.

3. Smaller batteries can be recharged much faster. This makes the standard 120-volt ports, that almost all homeowners have in or near their garage, enough for typical overnight charging. Smaller batteries make expensive fast chargers less necessary.

4. A 40-mile range covers about 80% of daily trips. The average daily commute is about 29 miles. This means that a plug-in hybrid with a 40-mile range will function as an electric vehicle for the vast majority of daily trips (US DOT).

5. A smaller range leaves open the possibilities of plug-in hybrids which are a much better choice for most consumers in the near future.

A minimum 40-mile electric-only range is not a fanciful flight of imagination (as many Green proposals are). It is achievable using current technology.

The 2022 Toyota RAV4 Prime has a 42-mile electric-only range, as well as getting 38 mpg overall. Except for the power train, the Prime is identical to a typical crossover SUV. For all but the largest family, it can cover electric-only daily commuting and errands, while still carrying the entire family on a 1000-mile road trip. With a 5-year lead to redesign their cars, I see no reason why other car manufacturers cannot achieve similar results.

Using the US Department of Energy online calculator, we can compute that a Toyota RAV4 Prime would emit only 160 CO_2 g/mile in New England versus 410 CO_2 g/mile for the average new gasoline vehicle. This is a 61% reduction in carbon emissions per vehicle. This is not as good as the fully-electric Tesla, but it is a big step in the right direction. For the record, the Prime would emit only 270 CO_2 g/mile in coal-heavy Missouri, still significantly better than the average new gasoline vehicle today.

Much of the range anxiety that potential EV buyers feel is due to the fact that 20% of the trips are much longer than 40 miles, and most consumers do not want to give up on family road trips or rent a separate car. For those drivers, a plug-in hybrid makes a great choice. A plug-in hybrid introduces drivers to the advantages of recharging their cars in their garage, while giving them the flexibility to periodically make long road trips.

Fleet Transitions Take a Long Time

Even with a highly aggressive transition to electrified transportation, it will still take far longer than climate activists demand. As of 2022, electric cars make up about 4% of the new car market in the United States. This is a huge jump from essentially zero only 10 years ago. And this increase is with substantial federal and state subsidies and mandates to encourage manufacturers to produce electric cars, as well as consumers to buy them.

What slows down the transition is the fact that the typical car lasts about 15 years on the road. So if the new car market sticks at 4% electric, 96% of the cars on the road in 2037 will still be powered by internal combustion engines.

Another way of looking at it, is that, even if 100% of all new car sales are electric starting in 2022, we cannot hope to get near 100% electric cars on the road until 2037. And this is assuming that no one prefers to hold onto their ICE car, which seems extremely unlikely.

And it only gets more difficult. Cars are the easiest large transportation device to electrify. Long-haul trucking, tractors, ships, airplanes and military vehicles are going to be much, much harder. A fully electric transportation sector will take generations to achieve, and it can only really start after the electrical grid has largely transitioned to natural gas, nuclear and hydroelectric.

So, no matter how we look at it, the electrification of transportation will take generations, even under the most optimistic assumption. And *Green policies will actually slow down the transition, not speed it up*. I believe that the Third Energy Transition is likely to conclude within the lifetime of someone being born today, but the timescale is far beyond what climate activists claim is essential to avoid a catastrophe.

A Grand Bargain That Might Actually Work

Rather than take part in toothless global agreements where nations pretend to promise to cut carbon emissions, we should focus on leveraging the coal tax into a Grand Bargain to transition the world from burning coal and wood. I suggest that the wealthy nations (United States, Europe, and Japan) and the biggest coal-burning developing nations (China, India, and Indonesia) come to a Grand Bargain to implement a global Third Energy Transition.

This Grand Bargain should be based on the following principles:

1. The United States, Europe and Japan agree to implement the

coal tax that I outlined earlier.

2. All nations that sign up agree to stop all further construction of coal and wood-burning plants.

3. The United States, Europe, and Japan agree to phase out all existing coal and wood-burning electrical plants and the use of coal in industry in favor of a blend of natural gas, nuclear and hydroelectric as fast as economically feasible. This would be paid for by revenues from the coal tax.

4. The United States agrees to export liquefied natural gas (LNG) only to nations that sign the Grand Bargain and abide by its terms. This would create a strong incentive to sign.

5. All nations that sign agree to allow American shale gas companies to explore and drill within potential conventional and shale gas fields on their territory.

6. As this expanded exploration and drilling increases natural gas production, the United States, Europe, and Japan agree to fund the construction of natural gas, nuclear and hydroelectric power plants, pipelines and electrical power lines in China, India, and Indonesia. The revenue to do so would come out of the coal tax.

7. As these new power plants come online in their nation, China, India, and Indonesia deactivate an equivalent mega wattage of coal plants.

8. The United States, Europe, and Japan promise to pay for a $100 billion innovation prize for new energy sources (discussed earlier).

9. The United States, Europe, and Japan promise to provide financial and technical assistance for funding installations of this new energy source, once it becomes practical and cost-effective.

Similar agreements could also be made with other coal-consuming and coal-producing nations such as Australia, Russia, and South Africa. International trade organizations, such as the WTO may need to get involved as well. There is no fundamental reason why this Grand Bargain cannot be applied globally.

In the long run, this Grand Bargain would be a win-win for all nations. Developing nations would get assistance with their energy needs, they would receive the economic benefits of abundant and affordable energy, and they would get cleaner air from eliminating coal. Wealthy nations get to continue their economic growth, while radically reducing global carbon emissions far beyond anything possible using renewable energy.

A Global Bargain With Teeth

My proposed global agreement has both strong incentives and enforcement mechanisms. All nations will feel the negative incentives of the coal tax whether they agree to the bargain or not. They will only get the benefits of American LNG imports if they agree to phase out coal and allow natural gas exploration, drilling and distribution on their soil.

The nation most unlikely to accept this Grand Bargain is China, because it has far more coal plants than any other nation. China also has export industries that are heavily dependent upon their energy production.

This is where the coal tax is far better than current Green policies. Green energy policies have been pushed overseas primarily by periodic global climate agreements that consist mainly of empty promises. Any nation that chooses not to follow through on those promises suffers no negative consequences. And because those promises to limit carbon emissions seriously undermine long-term economic growth, developing nations are smart enough to not promise anything. The result has been global climate agreements that are increasingly just farcical political theater.

Unlike current global carbon reduction treaties, the coal tax gives other nations a method for forcing compliance. The United States, Europe, and Japan could establish a coal tax on all domestic and imported goods *regardless of whether other nations agree to it.*

The coal tax on imports would function as a de facto tariff as long as the exporting nations continue the widespread use of coal. So any nation that refuses to go along with the Grand Bargain receives all the pain from the coal tax without any of the benefits of help implementing the Third Energy Transition.

In the short run, if China refuses to go along with this, then export industries might shift from China to American soil. They would do so not because of concern for climate change, but because they want to avoid paying coal taxes.

A coal tax would have a devastating effect on the Chinese economy, unless it is combined with a shift from coal to natural gas, nuclear and hydroelectric power plants. Entering the Grand Bargain would make the transition easier.

Without such an agreement the increased costs due to the coal tax would undermine the cost advantage of Chinese industries and turn it into a cost disadvantage. Unable to profitably export to the United States, Europe, and Japan, Chinese export industries would collapse just when they are undergoing economic and demographic strains.

The largest barriers to this Grand Bargain are Green ideology and the institutions that support it. It is time for environmentalists to seriously question their current strategy. They must acknowledge that solar and wind will not come close to replacing fossil fuels, nuclear power, or hydroelectric dams within the next few generations. Fortunately, there is a much easier transition to a dynamic global economy and declining global carbon emissions.

It is not too late to change, and if you truly believe that we are facing a crisis, you cannot reject my proposed alternative out of hand.

Until such a Grand Bargain is reached, however, all developing nations must choose between fossil fuels and poverty with cooler temperatures. They should choose fossil fuels.

Waging the Cold War 2.0

A more selective Grand Bargain that includes only American national security allies would also be a highly effective means of waging economic warfare against China and Russia. A coal tax would seriously undermine Chinese manufacturing exports, a key part of their economy. American LNG and crude oil exports would seriously undermine Russian energy exports, also a key part of their economy. The combined effect would radically undercut the global influence of those two increasingly hostile nations.

Europe, Japan, South Korea and Taiwan would greatly benefit from American energy exports. Europe, in particular, would benefit from American assistance to rebuild their domestic gas industries. Energy security would solidify military alliances.

India and Indonesia, two potential allies against China, may not be terribly excited about this bargain because of their heavy coal usage. They may be skeptical that Western nations will follow through on their part of the bargain. But both nations are far less dependent upon coal to fund export industries than China is. And both nations will want access to American crude oil and LNG exports.

Western assistance in constructing an abundant, affordable, and secure energy sector in India and Indonesia would greatly help their domestic economic growth and help them to see benefits of cooperating with the United States on security issues.

An aggressive China, Western military power, energy abundance and economic growth all give India and Indonesia reasons to side with the West in the emerging Cold War 2.0. Reduced carbon emissions and pollution would be the icing on the cake.

ABC... It Is All Bout China (and the rest of Asia)

Rather than focusing on wealthy Western nations, those who want to reduce carbon emissions need to think globally. Climate emissions are no longer a Western problem. Now carbon emissions are mainly an Asian problem.

Between 1990 and 2020 the geographical distribution of carbon emissions changed radically. **Now China alone emits more carbon than North America, the European Union, and Japan combined.** In those 30 years, China increased its annual carbon emissions by 381%, while India increased its emissions by 302.7% (Global Carbon Project 2021).

In 2020, China alone emitted 30% of world carbon emissions, by far the highest of any nation. India is now the third leading carbon emitter. Even worse, for future emissions, a bevy of Asian nations are rapidly increasing their emissions as well. In 2020, Asia made up a full 53% of all global carbon emissions, and there is every reason to expect this share to grow in the future (Global Carbon Project 2021).

Greens and the Left in general have not integrated this fundamental geographical change into their worldview. They still behave as if carbon emissions are concentrated in rich Western nations, and so they assume that is where the biggest reductions are needed.

Quite frankly, if you do not have a climate change solution that involves China and the rest of Asia, then you do not have a workable solution at all. And the Greens do not have a solution that involves China and the rest of Asia. China and the rest of Asia have essentially ignored climate change while pretending to care.

We have reached a point where the future trend of Western emissions does not matter very much. Their carbon emissions will decline regardless of public policy. Going forward, it is all about China and the rest of Asia.

ABC… It Is All Bout Coal (in China)

What caused this enormous increase in carbon emissions in China and the rest of Asia? It was overwhelmingly the construction of coal-burning power plants. While it is clear that this trend is bad for the natural environment, it is important to understand why so many Asian nations are turning to coal for their primary energy needs.

Why did so many Asian nations construct coal-burning power plants? There are four reasons:

1. Abundant, affordable, and secure energy is essential for long-term economic growth.

2. The leaders of Asian nations want their economies to grow

to maintain public support and national security, and increase their influence in the world.

3. Most Asian nations have substantial domestic coal fields. This coal can be burned to create abundant, affordable, and secure electricity. Coal can also be combusted directly in their economically critical export industries.

4. Most Asian nations have no other energy source that can offer all the benefits of coal.

As long as these four factors remain in effect, Asian nations will continue to construct coal-burning power plants. The effects of this trend dwarf any countervailing trends in rich Western nations.

With a few exceptions, developing nations have chosen coal as their primary energy source. China is the premier example of this trend. Between 2000 and 2021 China built 1,011 GW (gigawatts) of coal power plants. **This made up 81.6% of all new power plants constructed in the entire world!**

For comparison, a very large coal plant puts out about 1 GW of electricity, and all coal plants in the United States together put out 217.8 GW. This is barely 20% of the capacity that China constructed in just 20 years. So, in 20 years, China constructed five times the amount of coal plants that currently exist in the United States (Global Power Plant Tracker by End Coal)!

While China has been the global leader in the construction of coal-burning power plants, it was not alone. Other Asia countries also constructed a large number of coal power plants. Between 2000 and 2021, India added 188.6 GW, while Indonesia added 34 GW. Other Asian countries such as Japan (26.3 GW), South Korea (28.2 GW), and Vietnam (22.8 GW) also built substantial numbers of coal plants. In total, over 90% of all new power plants constructed over the last thirty years were in Asia (Global Power Plant Tracker by End Coal).

And there is no sign that this trend will stop. As of July 2022, China has officially announced, pre-permitted, permitted, or is in the middle of construction of coal plants that will emit an estimated 44,000 million tons of carbon dioxide over their lifetime. When one adds in similar plants in the rest of the world, the estimate comes to 74,000 tons of total future carbon emissions (Global Power Plant Tracker by End Coal).

Meanwhile, carbon emissions in the United States and European emissions declined by almost 20%. Europe started reducing carbon emissions in the 1980s when they started decommissioning older coal plants in favor of nuclear and natural gas. The United States did the same starting around 2006 with the Shale Revolution. These reductions of carbon emissions are largely due to Third Energy Transition involving natural gas, nuclear and hydroelectric power.

One might think that climate activists would rapidly update their rhetoric and proposed policies to shift from the western nations to Asia, particularly China. Nothing of the sort happened. Virtually all the political focus of climate activists has been on the United States (15% of global emissions) and the EU (10% of global emissions). So, while Asia emits more than double the amount of carbon of the USA and EU combined, Asia get very little political attention.

At best, climate change activists claim that solar and wind are cheaper than coal, so it is short-sighted of Asia to continue building coal plants. As we shall see, this is a very dubious assumption.

Regardless of whether I am right, China, India, Indonesia, and the rest of Asia apparently agree with me as they are rapidly building coal-burning power plants. Though this trend has slowed substantially, there is no widespread move to decommission coal plants in favor of wind/solar in Asia.

Given that China alone has carbon emissions greater than the United States, Canada, and the European Union combined, attempts to lower global carbon emissions with renewable energy in the West are like Don Quixote tilting at windmills. They are not even focused on the location of the real problem, which is in Asia.

Advantages of Coal

Asian governments are not stupid or short-sighted in their use of coal. It has been a rational choice focused on the long-term benefits of economic growth.

Coal has many advantages, particularly for developing nations:

1.   Except for wood, coal is the most widely available energy source by geography. Most nations have little or no cost-effective reserves of petroleum, solar, wind, or geothermal power. The vast majority of nations have at least some coal reserves.

2.   Coal is a far denser energy source than wood, solar, wind, or geothermal (density is essentially the amount of energy per unit of mass).

3.   Coal is relatively easy and cost-effective to extract, transport, store and combust.

4.   Coal-burning power plants are relatively cheap to construct, depending upon their size.

5.   Coal provides reliable base-load power for the electrical grid as well as having many industrial applications.

6.   Coal can be converted to a liquid or gas, if necessary. Coal-burning power plants can also be used to charge electric cars and buses. This reduces the need to import petroleum.

China and the rest of Asia are clearly going through the First Energy Transition (from wood to coal) for exactly the same reason that Europe, North American and Japan did so in the past. Coal is far more affordable, abundant and secure than renewable energy either in the form of wood, wind or solar.

Disadvantages of Coal

While coal has many advantages, particularly to developing nations, coal has very serious negative side effects on the natural environment and human health. Greens have very good reasons for being against coal, but they fail to acknowledge how much worse coal is compared to other energy sources that they equally despise.

1. Except for wood, coal emits more carbon dioxide per unit of energy than any other source (Climate Registry).

2. Pollution from coal plants causes approximately one million deaths each year around the world. This is a far higher death rate than any other energy source (WHO).

3. Coal mining is a notoriously dangerous occupation.

4. Open-pit mining devastates large areas of land, and it takes decades for vegetation to regrow after the mine closes.

5. Tailings, overburden and chemicals from mines clog up and poison downstream rivers and lakes.

6. Coal power plants must be run almost 24-7 to function economically. Cycling coal plants off and on seriously undermines their efficiency and life expectancy.

Beyond Coal

Climate activists and Greens in general must recognize that **the enemy is not fossil fuels, nor is it nuclear or hydro-electric. The enemy is coal.** Coal emits far more carbon dioxide, carbon monoxide, nitrogen oxide, sulfur dioxides, particulates and mercury than either natural gas or petroleum. In particular, natural gas is remarkably low in pollution and carbon emissions.

A goal of phasing out coal-burning power plants in favor of natural gas as quickly as possible would unite a wide swath of the political spectrum in the United States. We should start doing so first in the United States, which has abundant and affordable natural gas. Then we should accelerate the Third Energy Transition in other wealthy countries in Europe and East Asia. For anyone concerned about carbon emissions, this should be a no-brainer.

First of all, transitioning from coal to natural gas in wealthy nations would be remarkably inexpensive. Coal-burning power plants in the United States currently generate just under 218 GW of electricity. The most energy-efficient form of natural-gas-burning CCGT power plant costs about \$680/kW to construct. As I mentioned, this means that we could replace every single coal plant in the United States for \$148 billion.

There is also no reason to believe that American manufacturing firms will have a problem rapidly scaling up the production of CCGT plants. In 2002 and 2003 the United States installed almost 40 GW of CCGT plants annually. At that rate we could replace every coal plant with energy-efficient CCGT plants in just over 5 years.

The same goes for the European Union. Coal-burning power plants in the EU currently generate just under 107 GW of electricity. This means that we could replace every single coal plant in the EU for only \$73 billion. This is a tiny fraction of what has been spent thus far on Green energy in Germany alone. American LNG exports could make this transition much easier, but Europe also needs to start exploring and drilling in its conventional gas and shale gas fields.

Now apply this cost to the entire world. Globally, coal-burning power plants currently generate about 2067 GW of electricity. Replacing them with CCGT plants would cost just over \$1.4 trillion.

Obviously, this is a very substantial amount of money, but it is somewhere in the ballpark of what has already been spent globally on Green energy sources, with far less impact on carbon emissions.

Particularly in the United States, there would be very little Republican resistance against switching from coal to natural gas. The primary opposition to such a policy comes from the left-wing of the Democratic party, the supposed stewards of the environment. Democrats must abandon their current Green energy policies, in favor of a Progress-based energy policy.

Once the Democrats can overcome their ideological resistance to these policies, change could happen quickly. Political support for coal in the United States is mainly restricted to a handful of few coal-mining states: Wyoming, West Virginia and Tennessee.

The list of states with natural gas fields is much larger, including: Texas, Louisiana, North Dakota, South Dakota, Pennsylvania, Ohio, and Michigan. These natural-gas-producing states would benefit with thousands of jobs, while lowering carbon emissions.

Ironically, it is political resistance from the Left that is making reducing global carbon emissions difficult to accomplish. Because of the clear disadvantages of coal, particularly due to negative impacts on the natural environment, Greens should favor phasing it out. They should also favor natural gas, nuclear and hydroelectric power as alternatives to coal.

Unfortunately, they do not.

Green Opposition to Natural Gas

In the 1980s and early 1990s, the environmental movement was largely in favor of natural gas. Natural gas was correctly viewed as the only reasonable alternative to coal and nuclear power. As climate change became their all-consuming focus, environmentalists began to lump natural gas together with coal as a fossil fuel that needs to be eliminated as rapidly as possible.

Now climate activists are overwhelmingly opposed to natural gas. Climate activists work hard to ban fracking and new pipeline construction. They even oppose pipelines that will capture flaring natural gas that is being released directly into the atmosphere (essentially free natural gas that would reduce methane emissions). At this point, it seems impossible to change their minds, regardless of the facts.

This is a shame, as the Green prejudice against natural gas is the single biggest barrier to creating a workable energy policy that promotes human progress while mitigating damage to the environment.

Green Opposition to Nuclear Power

This would not be the first time that Green energy policy has led to the opposite of their desired intentions. The massive expansion of coal usage in Asia did not have to happen.

Asian nations essentially adopted coal because it was the cheapest and most widely available energy source in their region. But it is not difficult to imagine a different world where nuclear energy is cost-competitive with coal.

Wealthy Western nations as well as Communist nations widely adopted nuclear power in the 1960s and 70s. The United States, Canada, the Soviet Union, France, Belgium, Finland, Sweden, Switzerland, Czechoslovakia and other nations mounted serious nuclear programs.

During that period, nuclear power seemed to be the energy source of the future. As is typical in new industries, as designs and construction techniques improved, costs dropped substantially. Lower costs built political support for further expansion, and the industry triggered a major energy transition. The nuclear industry bragged that electricity would soon become "too cheap to meter."

The energy crises of the 1970s appeared to give nuclear power a major boost. Up until that time, oil-fired power plants were widespread, so dramatic increases in oil prices caused nations to look for alternatives. As natural gas was still in its infancy, the choice was clear: coal or nuclear.

Unfortunately, coal was the big winner. The single biggest reason why coal won was the mobilization of the environmental movement against nuclear power. Opposition started in the late 1990s, but then ramped up quickly in the 1970s. The incidents at Three Mile Island (no injuries or deaths) and Chernobyl (an obsolete design that was far less safe than Western designs) caused a wave of fear regarding nuclear power.

Public opinion turned from strongly supportive towards nuclear power to strongly opposed. In response, government regulations radically increased in their complexity, and construction costs performed a U-Turn. Whereas construction costs of nuclear plants in the United States had been dropping rapidly, they suddenly increased, so the energy source was no longer competitive with coal (Lane).

If the trend of declining cost of nuclear power had continued to the present day, nuclear power would be around 10% of its current cost. At such costs, every nation would have favored construction of nuclear-powered plants over coal. World carbon emissions would be 11Gt lower (Lane).

If nuclear plant construction costs had been much cheaper than coal over the last 30 years, Asia probably would have built nuclear plants rather than coal plants. We might have had radically lower global carbon emissions right now. But to my knowledge, no climate change activists have acknowledged the movement's responsibility for vast amounts of carbon emissions.

Environmentalist opposition to nuclear power played a major role in Europe and the United States rapidly constructing coal plants during the 1970s and 1980s. Those coal plants were by far the biggest reason for increased carbon emissions in the West over the last 50 years.

And the biggest reason for coal's victory was the environmental movement. That is right. The very same movement that today says that carbon emissions are a threat to human existence favored high-emissions coal over zero-emissions nuclear. Think about that for a minute.

If the environmentalist movement had been as pro-nuclear in the 1970s as they are pro-renewable today, government policy under Democratic administrations would have subsidized nuclear power instead of strangling it with regulations. The nuclear industry might have scaled up much faster, so that it could reduce production costs. These high production costs were created, not by technology, which almost always gets cheaper, but by government regulation. These regulations were put in place due to fears promoted by environmentalists.

I know that most Greens, like most people involved in politics, are just repeating what they have heard other people say, but at some point, they need to focus on practical solutions that might require them to change their policy stances. We instead need to focus on results. The results of Green opposition to nuclear power greatly increased global carbon emissions.

Green Opposition to Hydro Power

Nor is nuclear power the only carbon-free energy source that is opposed by environmentalists. Environmentalists are also opposed to the construction of new hydroelectric dams. Many environmentalists also campaign to decommission existing hydroelectric dams. If one truly believes that we face a climate catastrophe, this makes no sense whatsoever.

Hydroelectric dams are by far the most widespread renewable energy sources. After decades of subsidies for wind and solar, they are still far behind hydropower in total global electricity generation.

Of the eight nations who have more than 30% of their total energy source coming from renewables, every single one of them has hydroelectric power as their primary source (Iceland, Norway, Sweden, Switzerland, New Zealand, Brazil, Canada and Austria). And yet you almost never hear about this accomplishment (Our World in Data).

Disadvantages of Renewable Energy

There are unfortunately many disadvantages of renewable energy sources compared to fossil fuels, and these are simply ignored by Greens. The most important is that renewable energy sources only generate electricity, and electricity accounts for only 18% of global carbon emissions. This alone shows the futility of focusing on solar, wind and biomass (Our World in Data).

Even if the entire electrical grid goes renewable (which I argue is impossible while maintaining human progress), this ignores 82% of global carbon emissions. Worse, if you focus exclusively on the electrical grid in Western nations, you have not even dealt effectively with the majority of emissions of that 18%, which come from Asia.

Solar Power

Before I go on to discuss the disadvantages of renewable energy, I first want to discuss their advantages. Contrary to what one might think, I have been a fan of solar power (and other renewables) for decades. In fact, I was a strong supporter back in the 1980s when no one had even heard of climate change. I recognize that solar power has many advantages:

1.   No pollution or carbon emissions, except during construction.

2.   Deployable on rooftops, so in many cases no land is removed from housing, agriculture or wild habitat.

3.   Rapidly declining costs over the last few decades, at least until 2018 when the trend starting reversing.

4.   Technological innovations constantly improve the efficiency of converting sunlight into electricity.

5.   The electricity produced is somewhat timed to cover peak electricity usage, particularly summer afternoons and early evenings when air conditioning is most often run.

6.   Solar is extremely useful for off-grid housing, off-grid facilities, and small devices.

Given all of these advantages, it is not difficult to see why solar power has so many fans and why there is widespread popular support for subsidizing the technology. And there can be no doubt that government subsidies are a big part of the reason why costs have been declining and efficiency has been increasing.

Government subsidies and mandates created a constant demand that has enabled private industry to invest in research and manufacture at scale. Government policy has also forced utilities to purchase electricity from solar power in much greater quantities than they otherwise would.

Despite these advantages, no nation generates a substantial portion of their total energy from solar power. Chile is the world leader at 6.0% with only Vietnam and Australia breaking the 5% threshold. The

European Union average is a mere 2.52%, despite massive government subsidies (Our World in Data 2021).

So, if solar power has so many advantages, why have no nations been able to scale production up so much that they can phase out fossil fuels?

While solar power has many advantages, its disadvantages outweigh them in most circumstances. First and foremost, solar power generates no electricity during the night and limited amounts during the morning and early evening.

Residential roof-top solar is still far more expensive than other energy sources. You have probably heard someone say that solar power is cheaper than fossil fuels. While there is some truth to this statement, it is highly deceptive. By some measurements, utility-scale solar is cheaper than fossil fuels or nuclear. This is far from the case for residential rooftop solar, which is what most people think of when they say solar (Lazard's 2021).

While the most efficient natural gas plants cost between $45 and $74 per MWh, unsubsidized residential roof top solar energy costs about three times as much between $147 and $221 per MWh. Moreover, existing natural gas ($24 per MWh), coal ($42) and nuclear plants ($29) cost even less to keep running, largely because their high construction costs have largely been paid off.

It is important to note that, by the same measure, utility-scale solar and wind are cheaper than coal, competitive with existing nuclear, and only more expensive than existing natural gas.

While this is not technically a disadvantage, the rapidly declining costs of both wind and solar power have fallen off substantially over the last few years. With the global supply chain disrupted by Covid lockdowns, spiking cost of raw materials and the United States attempting to reshore many industries from China, the glory days of declining renewable costs may be over.

Solar power is also highly restricted by geography. To be efficient, solar power stations need to be near the equator, temperatures must not be too hot, have unobstructed views of the sun, and have low humidity in the air. Few regions meet all these conditions.

Most of the world's population lives in the northern temperate latitudes, where the angle of the sun is low, particularly in winter. East Asia and North America are quite far from the equator, while Europe is even further from the equator. This means many of the most densely populated and economically important regions have little solar potential.

Solar power is highly constrained by season. In temperate latitudes, solar power generates far more electricity during the summer, when the sun is visible for longer periods than during the winter. The higher the latitude, the less efficient solar power becomes and the greater the percentage of its electricity generated during the summer.

Solar power is highly constrained by humidity in the air. The greater the amount of water vapor in the atmosphere, the less electricity is generated. Ironically, the very same nations that are close to the equator, where solar power is more efficient, also tend to have high humidity.

Solar power is highly constrained by hot temperatures. The very regions that are most suited for solar power, tropical deserts, typically reach a temperature high enough to greatly degrade the efficiency of solar panels. Many of those deserts also frequently have dust storms that coat solar panels with a thick layer of dust, degrading their performance even more.

Finally, solar power must have an unobstructed view of the sun. Unfortunately, populated areas tend to have lots of trees and buildings. Cloud cover can also create wide variations in output each minute, hour and day. This, of course, does not make solar power impossible, it just either limits the areas that can be used or requires systematic destruction of trees (not exactly Green).

If we take a look at a world map that shows the total levels of average solar radiation per day, we can see widespread geographical variation. There are some regions that are blessed with large amounts of solar radiation (although many of them are very hot and dusty):

- Southwestern United States
- Northern Mexico
- Southeast coast of South America (Chile, Peru, plus parts of Bolivia, Argentina and Brazil)
- The Sahara Desert
- Middle East
- Southern Africa
- Himalayas
- Mongolia
- Most of Australia

Unfortunately, the vast majority of densely populated regions have minimal solar radiation. This does not make solar power impossible, but it does make it an unwise investment in comparison to other energy sources.

Below is a list of densely-populated regions with limited solar radiation:

- The eastern half of the United States (where about 80% of the U.S. population lives)
- Canada
- Europe, except for Spain and Portugal
- East Asia
- South Asia
- Southeast Asia

In total, these regions make up the vast majority of the world's population. Again solar power is not impossible in those regions, but it is so inefficient that other energy sources make more sense.

Wind Power

Wind power has even greater problems than solar power. Only five nations produce more than 10% of their total energy usage from wind power (Denmark with 22.49% is by far the world's leader with only Ireland, Portugal, Sweden and Spain breaking the 10% threshold). The vast majority of nations generate less than 5% of their energy from the wind (Our World in Data 2021).

Wind turbines have higher capacity factors than solar, but the levels are far below fossil fuels, nuclear and hydroelectric. The capacity factor, however, greatly exaggerates the usefulness of wind. Wind tends to blow harder at night and during winter when electricity demands are lower.

While solar power is somewhat predictable over the course of a day, wind power is extremely erratic. The total amount of electricity produced fluctuates wildly throughout the day. For electrical workers who are trying to keep their grid from collapsing as demand changes throughout the day, the wind is a serious problem. It is such a problem that, unless a region is very windy, wind turbines are not worth the investment.

Wind power is also far more restricted by geography than solar is. There are very few regions in the world with strong and consistent winds. The only large regions are the Great Plains of the United States, the parts of Europe bordering the North Sea, Argentina, Somalia, and the Gobi desert in China. Of those regions, only the North Sea region is densely populated.

Other regions have wind, of course, but not in the abundance necessary to make wind turbines cost-effective today. Offshore winds are much more common, but offshore turbines are also much more expensive.

The erratic nature of wind also undermines the performance of fossil fuel or nuclear power plants. To balance out the wind-induced variability, other power plants need to constantly turn on and off and modulate their output. Only hydroelectric and peaker natural gas plants can do this without significantly damaging their equipment. Ironically, doing so also produces more carbon than just letting highly efficient CCGT plants run 24/7.

The combination of wind blowing at the wrong time, in the wrong place, by unpredictable amounts, and the strain placed on other power plants, means that utilities often dump electricity or sell it at a loss. This means that the turbines are spinning, but either the electricity is not entering the grid or the utility is actually paying other customers to buy it. Neither makes economic sense.

Wind turbines also have some highly undesirable characteristics from an environmental standpoint. They require huge amounts of concrete, steel, and other raw materials compared to fossil fuel plants. And while nuclear and fossil fuel-powered plants take up very little land, wind turbines take up huge tracts of land that could otherwise be devoted to agriculture or wild habitat.

Asia Has Few Renewable Resources

A critical fact that few Greens seem to realize is that Asia has few renewable resources. East Asia, South Asia, and Southeast Asia, which together make up more than half of the world's population, have no regions with strong wind, and only the very sparsely populated Gobi desert in China has a sunny climate. This makes Green energy policies almost impossible to achieve at scale in the very region that generates the bulk of global carbon emissions.

The only renewable energy source that Asia has in abundance are rivers that can be dammed to create hydroelectric power. And remember that Greens are opposed to this source of energy as well.

To the best of my knowledge, not one Green has ever acknowledged this critical geographical constraint to their vision. While Green energy policies are deeply expensive and undermining economic growth in wealthy Western countries, in Asia they are physically impossible. Even if Greens convince Asians to invest trillions of dollars (as they have done in the West), they cannot overcome Mother Earth's choice of where to locate solar and wind resources.

So current Green energy policies cannot expand into the region that has seen by far the most significant increase in carbon emissions. For this reason (and many others), Green energy policies will inevitably fail to reduce global carbon emissions. Only natural gas, nuclear and hydroelectric power can do so.

Green Electricity Undermines Electric Vehicles

Another huge weakness of Green energy policy is that it makes an abundant, affordable and secure electrical grid impossible with current technology. This is in turn makes it far more difficult to expand the Third Energy Transition into the transportation sector.

Many advocates of renewable energy also support widespread electrification within the transportation, commercial, residential and industrial sectors. Unfortunately, the more the energy sector is based on electricity, the worse the intermittency issues become.

Scaling up wind, solar and other renewables to generate 100% of electricity would make our electrical grid very unstable. Wind, in particular, generates radically shifting amounts of electricity. And solar generates no electricity at night when consumers typically want to charge their electric vehicles. Adding on the demands of the entire transportation sector will make the situation even worse.

We are already seeing this happen. As I write this book, Switzerland is seriously considering outlawing consumers from recharging their electric cars during the winter of 2022-23 for fear that it will bring down the grid. During the summer of 2022, California asked electric car owners not to charge after 4PM during summer heat waves. Given that neither Switzerland nor California is very far down the Green energy transition, this is probably just a hint of what is to come.

Widespread electrification of transportation is dependent upon a stable, affordable electrical grid. Only fossil fuels, nuclear and hydropower can deliver that. That is one of the many reasons why environmentalists should favor these energy sources, not oppose them.

It order to electrify the transportation sector, consumers and corporations are going to have to see very clear economic benefits for doing so. An affordable and stable electrical grid significantly lowers the long-term operating costs of electric vehicles. An expensive and unstable electrical grid pushes consumers and corporations away from investing in electric vehicles.

Transportation makes up about one-third of the energy sector and that proportion increases as a nation experiences progress. In the United States, for example, the transportation sector made up 37% of CO_2 emissions from energy consumption in 2021 (EIA). This is significantly greater than the amount of carbon emissions that come from electricity. Failing to fully electrify the transportation system fully guarantees that Greens will fail to achieve their goals.

Just imagine a nation with an electrical grid based entirely on solar and wind and a transportation sector based on electricity: all cars, trucks, trains, ships, and airplanes. The typical usage pattern for electrical transportation is to drive during the day and then charge during the night.

We know that solar power will be useless for recharging transportation devices during the night, so now we are entirely dependent upon wind. What if there is little to no wind in any particular night? The entire transportation grid temporarily collapses! People cannot drive to work or do food shopping; buses do not work; trains do not work, entire supply chains are disrupted for the day. At the same time, home electricity, appliances, heating/cooling and industrial production temporarily shuts down.

We already experienced something like that during the Covid lockdowns of 2020 and 2021. Now electricity lockdowns could be a common occurrence, although hopefully far shorter in duration than Covid lockdowns.

But what about batteries? We could vastly over-build our solar and wind production and then store the rest in batteries. And then each night we just transfer the energy into the batteries in electric vehicles. That might work, but as we will see, batteries are highly expensive, their production emits large amounts of carbon, and each transfer leads to losses of electricity.

To make people want to switch from ICE to electric cars, we need three things:

1. Very cheap electricity to make up for the high initial cost of the battery.

2. An extremely stable grid that guarantees that vehicles can recharge every night.

3. Ever-declining cost, size, weight and increasing longevity of electric batteries.

The third is occurring due to rapid technological innovation in the private sector along with government subsidies to guarantee a market. The first and the second items, however, cannot be achieved with Green energy policies. Rather than making electricity abundant, affordable and secure, Green energy policies make electricity expensive, unstable and constrained. This is the opposite of what we need.

Land Use

The single most negative human impact on the natural environment is not climate change, urban sprawl, air pollution, or water pollution. It is land use. When humans develop land, they destroy or at least negatively impact land that could be used for habitat by wild plants and animals. If humans do not develop land, nature will find a way to adapt regardless of the temperature or levels of pollution.

The single biggest land use by humans is agriculture, including rangeland and cropland. Fossil fuels enabled agriculture to become far more productive, so they reduced the amount of land needed to grow food for humanity. As motorized transport replaced horses, this greatly reduced the amount of land needed to grow horse feed. So fossil fuels actually reduced human land use.

Unfortunately, utility-scale solar and wind are both very land-intensive compared to fossil fuels and nuclear power. Nuclear power uses 0.3 square meters of land per MWh of electricity, while natural gas uses only 1 square meter. Large hydroelectric dams use 14 square meters. Coal power plants use relatively little land, but the mining and excavation of raw coal uses 15 square meters (Our World in Data).

Meanwhile, utility-scale solar use 19-22 square meters per MWh of electricity, and onshore wind uses a colossal 99 square meters. That is 100 times the land used by natural gas and 300 times the land used by nuclear!

One can make the case that utility-scale solar and wind are bad for the natural environment because of the amount of potential wild habitat that they destroy compared to other energy sources. At the very least, this should be factored into the question of whether the technologies are good for the environment as Greens claim.

Capacity Matters

As we saw, solar and wind are highly constrained by geography. Worse, even where solar and wind power is possible, its capacity percentage is quite low. Advocates of renewable power often use deceptive terminology to boost their cases. They often talk of the huge amounts of renewable "capacity" being installed each year. It looks impressive until one realizes what capacity actually means.

Capacity is the theoretical amount of electricity that would be generated if the technology were running a peak efficiency 24 hours per day and 365 days per year. But there is a huge difference between capacity and actual generation of electricity, particularly for renewable energy sources.

The capacity factor is the percentage of electricity that is actually generated compared to its theoretical capacity. Most modern energy sources achieve capacity factors at or over 90%: this includes coal, nuclear and natural gas. These power plants essentially run 24-7 and are only turned off for regular maintenance. Hydro-electric dams can theoretically produce power 24-7, but this is rarely the case in practice.

Solar power in the United States has a capacity factor of about 20-25% with very large differences between sites. Wind power capacity factors reach closer to 35%, though there are even bigger differences between sites. Outside the United States, capacity ratings are typically much less. Biomass (59%) and geothermal (71%) are the only renewable energy sources that remotely approach the capacity factors of coal and nuclear (US EIA).

Renewables Require Fossil Fuels

Greens conveniently ignore the fact that you cannot use renewable energy to construct solar and wind infrastructure. You need fossil fuels to mine the raw materials, you need fossil fuels to refine those raw materials into finished materials, and you need fossil fuels to install the generators on site.

Solar and wind use huge amounts of steel, copper, nickel, and zinc, all of which require vast amounts of fossil fuels in their extraction and construction. Solar also requires huge amounts of aluminum, rare-earth elements, cadmium, gallium, and tellurium, which also require vast amounts of fossil fuels to mine, process and transport (McKinsey).

So if we completely phase out fossil fuels, how do we construct solar and wind sites (or any other industrial product for that matter)?

Diminishing Returns

Perhaps the single biggest disadvantage of solar power and other renewable energy sources is that it is subject to diminishing returns. Supporters of renewable energy see constant technological improvement and assume that scaling up those technologies will become easier and easier. In fact, it is the opposite.

As a region constructs solar power facilities, it naturally sites them in the best geographical locations. As more solar power facilities are constructed, they must be located in less and less productive locations. This means solar power capacity declines as the energy source is ramped up, the opposite of what we need.

This is even more of a factor when one takes account of when the solar and other renewable energy sources create electricity. If one constructs a large amount of solar plants, they will all produce power at roughly the same time of day. Any additional electricity comes when it is least needed. And no electricity is produced 50% of the time (i.e. during the night).

At some point, additional solar produces too much electricity on sunny summer afternoons meaning all that additional electricity is worthless. Useful electricity is only generated when solar is less efficient (i.e. mornings, early spring, late fall, etc.). This means solar is locked into ever-diminishing returns. Each new solar facility produces less and less useful electricity per unit. Constant technological improvement will mitigate this problem but never entirely do away with it.

All of these limitations together clearly make solar power a niche source of energy for the foreseeable future. Incremental improvement in the efficiency of solar panels is very unlikely to overcome these disadvantages. And a fundamental breakthrough in solar power is no more likely than for any other energy source.

I do believe that solar power can play a role in our energy future. In highly populated regions with high levels of solar radiance and high enough temperatures, solar power can essentially cancel out the additional electricity needed to run air conditioning.

But with current technology, solar power cannot replace fossil fuels: not by a long shot. And as we will see, the same goes for wind.

Matching Supply and Demand

The amount of electricity generated by wind and solar varies widely minute-to-minute, hour-to-hour, day-to-day, season-to-season and year-to-year. This leads to a fundamental problem. How do you match electricity supply with customer demand minute-to-minute? Failure to match customer demand will make the electrical grid very unstable. Failure to do so in a cost-effective way will make the electrical grid very expensive.

Supporters of renewable power are forced into one or more of the following options:

1. Supplementing wind and solar with fossil fuels, particularly natural gas peakers that turn on when renewable electricity production is lower than demand. This is the most cost-effective solution, so the vast majority of nations choose this option, but it is not considered

Green. Nor does it reduce carbon emissions by more than CCGT already does.

2. Supplement wind and solar with biomass. Biomass would perform the same role as natural gas peakers, but as we will see this is not Green either.

3. Storing the electricity in utility-scale batteries, but as we will see this is not Green either.

4. Building far more wind and solar capacity than is needed, so there is always enough electricity produced at any one time.

5. Using hydroelectric dams to store the excess power in the form of water. This option is only possible in a few geographically unique regions where hydroelectric and wind are cost-effective. Norway/Denmark is one of the few examples. This is unlikely to be a global solution.

The only truly Green option is the fourth option: building far more capacity than is needed. Unfortunately, this option increases the amount of wind and solar that are needed by roughly three to five times. And even then it is not clear that the system can generate enough electricity during non-windy nights, particularly in the winter. This is a particularly bad problem if the transportation sector is electrified.

In addition, what do you do with the excess electricity that is generated? As renewable energy ramps up, this will become more and more of a problem. Some potential solutions are:

1. Dumping the electricity by disconnecting the system from the grid. This is obviously very wasteful of economic resources.

2. Paying other customers to let the electricity into their grid (called negawatts). This drives up the cost of electricity, and it only works if other nations and regions are not also pursuing Green energy policies. If all nations adopt Green energy policies, this is not a viable option at scale.

Biomass and Biofuels

To make up for the intermittency of solar and wind, Greens advocate using biomass power plants. They also advocate using biofuels instead of petroleum.

Biomass and biofuels are not Green energy sources. They are very bad for the environment. Solid biofuels emit between 94 and 110 kg of carbon dioxide per gigajoule of energy, while bituminous coal emits about 95 kg and natural gas about 53 kg. Agricultural byproducts, peat and solid byproducts do even worse. This alone should disqualify biomass biofuels as a Green source of energy (Climate Registry).

Burning wood to generate energy on a small scale is perfectly acceptable. Burning wood left over from sawmills and manufacturing wood products also makes sense; manufacturing biofuels from algae does as well. Unfortunately, biomass has gone way beyond that and the natural environment is suffering.

Every material that mankind can find in nature for food or energy production can also be used by other living species. Driven by evolution, living species find a way to exploit every possible natural resource to survive. Land and trees are particularly valuable natural resources that nature needs.

Trees are tremendously important for thousands of woodland species of plants and animals. Burning wood at scale makes absolutely no economic or environmental sense. It is more expensive and more damaging to the environment than fossil fuels, which no known living species relies on for its survival. In addition, with the exception of open-pit coal mining, fossil fuels use far less of the land that could potentially be used for wild habitat.

Unfortunately, Green energy policies are actively subsidizing burning wood in the name of saving the environment. To avoid using natural gas, Greens support burning wood at times when solar and wind are unavailable.

This practice is particularly egregious in the United Kingdom. In order to pretend to meet their emissions goals, the UK recently started burning wood products in their coal-burning power plants. Because the UK has limited forest stocks, they import wood from the United States. That wood is cut, transported via truck, shipped using fossil fuels, and then burned.

Because the wood is harvested in a foreign country, the emissions do not count towards the UK's national emissions goals. So, in the name of saving the planet, the UK is clear-cutting forests in the United States. It is hard to see this as anything other than a Green accounting fraud.

Biomass and biofuels are worse for the environment than coal and more expensive than natural gas. There is absolutely no reason to support either fuel source.

Batteries Are Not A Solution

Some advocates of renewable energy maintain that widespread usage of energy storage will overcome the intermittency disadvantage of renewable energy. They claim that, with widespread installation of utility-scale batteries, we can store electricity when we produce too much and save it for a time when we do not need it.

Battery storage is one of the key technologies that we need to improve over the next century. Innovation in this domain has been one of the most exciting developments over the last few decades. Every few years, new battery chemistries are invented and production costs keep dropping.

Despite this very positive trend, the cost of storing electricity is still very expensive compared to storing fossil fuels. Storing one barrel of oil costs around $1. Storing the energy equivalent of one barrel of oil in Tesla batteries, however, costs a whopping $200. This cost means that the widespread deployment of utility-scale batteries would dramatically increase the costs of our electrical grid (FEE).

To give one example, to store just 3 days of global electrical usage using Tesla megapacks would cost $590 trillion or six times the world GDP. And if we tried to do so within just a few decades, it would cost significantly more. Worse 3 days storage is far less than is needed to maintain a stable grid throughout the entire year (Epstein).

Even today, batteries make up about one quarter of the cost of an electric car. If you do not believe me, look at the cost of electrical cars compared to identical ICE models. Electric cars typically cost one-third more than their ICE version. That is why the federal government believes that it is necessary to give a $7,500 tax rebate for purchasing an electric car. Now apply those additional costs to our electrical grid, which powers over 300 million people, and you can see the cost issue.

Advocates of battery storage also neglect the fact that battery production involves large amounts of carbon emissions. The mining of raw materials such as lithium, nickel, cobalt and manganese is typically done in developing nations with very lax environmental standards. Transportation and manufacturing of batteries are typically powered by coal. So, to cut carbon emissions, we must produce carbon emissions.

Getting exact carbon emissions is very complicated, but one estimate for the Tesla Model 3 ranges between 3,120 and 15,680 kg carbon. A good ballpark estimate is that the batteries roughly double the carbon emitted during the production process of cars. In other words, the production of the electric vehicles emits roughly double the carbon emissions of a traditional ICE vehicle. And a traditional ICE vehicle is one of the most carbon-intensive products on the market (MIT).

Using the Hornsdale Power Reserve in Australia, the largest utility-scale battery storage in the world, as a model, one author computed that wind plus battery power emits only one-third the amount of carbon that coal does. Unfortunately but not surprisingly, the author of this study neglected to mention that this is almost exactly the savings provided by the most energy-efficient gas turbines. And the gas turbines are much cheaper, so why bother building wind-plus-batteries in the first place (Forbes)?

Advocates of utility-scale batteries also seriously underestimate the scale necessary to keep the electrical grid stable. My guess is that many of them deliberately underestimate the scale, so as not to undermine their cause. In most of the studies that I have seen, they look at the cost of installing only a few hours' worth of battery storage.

A few hours' worth of energy storage would work fine on most summer days, when solar power is reasonably efficient due to geography. One only needs a few hours of electricity to get through each night. But when there is a cloudy day, suddenly you need more storage. And wind power is far more erratic than solar power.

Moreover, battery storage needs ramp up enormously when one factors in declining solar power capacity factors outside of the summer. Solar power generates far less electricity during the winter. It is also very inefficient during the early spring and late fall.

Wind power can pick up some of the slack, but wind is inherently less predictable. So the actual amount of electricity that would need to be stored must be measured in months, not hours.

In addition to daily and seasonal variations, there are also very sizable annual variations. An entire winter with slow wind production and very low solar production is not at all uncommon. To mitigate the damage on the economy, one would need to store months' worth of electricity, not weeks or hours.

While it is conceivable that we could produce that many utility-scale batteries, this would be a massive ramp-up in world battery production. Very little of this capacity consists of utility-scale batteries. To produce enough batteries for the world's electrical grid, production would have to scale up something on the order of 100-fold. That is just not realistic to expect.

Batteries produced annually by the Tesla Gigafactory, the largest battery factory in the world, can store three *minutes* worth of annual U.S. electrical demand. To increase that time to just 2 days, far less than is needed, would require *1000 years* of full-scale production at that plant (FEE).

And remember that we also already need to radically increase battery production to electrify transportation. So realistically materials needed for utility-scale batteries will compete with car batteries. I believe that electrifying transportation should take priority over utility-scale batteries, because CCGT can better fill the gap.

Nor are batteries a one-time purchase. Current batteries wear out after 7-15 years and degrade in capacity during that time, so those batteries will need to be replaced periodically. And all of this leads to massive carbon emissions to manufacture the batteries.

For the foreseeable future, utility-scale batteries produced in enough volume to make a 100% renewable electrical grid are just not viable from an economic or environmental perspective. Only nations with widespread hydroelectric or geothermal resources can hope to achieve that goal within one to three decades.

Geothermal

Before concluding, I want to quickly mention another renewable energy source that I have not yet covered: geothermal. Virtually all renewable energy comes directly or indirectly from the sun. Solar energy directly taps into energy from the sun, as do all plants and animals. Wind, waves, and biomass tap energy that ultimately derives from the sun (as fossil fuels do as well). Nuclear and geothermal, however, tap underground energy, in the form of heat caused by pressure and radioactive decay.

Geothermal has many advantages that other renewable energy sources do not. It produces stable base-load electricity, emits virtually no carbon or pollution, and takes up very little land. Geothermal plants are essentially fossil fuel plants that create electricity from heat rather than chemical energy stored in fossil fuels.

Unfortunately, under current technology, geothermal is even more constrained by geography. Geothermal is currently only cost-effective in hotspots where heat plumes from the mantle reach near the Earth's surface.

For this reason, total global capacity is far below solar, wind, and biomass. Geothermal is currently restricted to the western United States, Iceland, Indonesia, Mexico, New Zealand, Philippines, El Salvador, and Italy. Not surprisingly, all of these areas are known for earthquakes and volcanic activity.

Some scientists have hypothesized that, in the future we could drill into the earth's crust to tap the vast amounts of heat in the mantle. This would require drilling far deeper than under current technology. Doing so would eliminate geographical constraints because every point of the earth's surface is above the mantle, but it is not clear that this method will ever become cost-effective. I am excited about the long-term potential of deep-earth geothermal, but for now, it is only an unproven idea, let alone a cost-effective technology.

Focus on Results

Key metrics for measuring the success of policies to maintain progress while cutting carbon emissions should be:
- Global carbon emissions
- Global carbon emissions per capita
- Global carbon emissions per dollar of GDP
- Carbon emissions from Asia
- Percent of global energy derived from coal or wood
- Percent of Asian energy derived from coal or wood

Conclusion

A Progress-based energy policy based on phasing out coal in favor of natural gas, nuclear and hydroelectric power will be far more cost-effective at lowering global carbon emissions than current Green policies. More importantly, while Green energy policies undermine global economic growth, my policy will at worst maintain it or more likely increase global economic growth.

WHAT INDIVIDUALS CAN DO

S o far in this book series, I have dealt with very large historical forces that seem beyond one's control. My theory of the ultimate causes of progress and how it works should make it clear that progress is an evolutionary process. No individual, no institution, no government, and no God is in control of this process.

Evolutionary processes just happen when the necessary preconditions are met. Those necessary preconditions are the Five Keys to Progress.

Progress just happens, yes, but only if humans take action to solve problems. Individuals matter. Because human actions are such a crucial part of how progress works, rather than an impersonal process, it can also be seen as very personal.

This chapter focuses on advice that I feel comfortable giving people on making life choices. It is particularly targeted at people under 30 years old, who want to make a difference by promoting progress. Many people over 30 are on a career or family path that is not easily changed. Many of those under 30 still have a wider range of options.

Individual Choice

In my first book in this series, *From Poverty to Progress*, I made the claim that progress is an evolutionary progress and that there are two levels to understanding causality within an evolutionary process. Well, I lied... sort of.

I stated that when viewed from a very high level, evolutionary processes require two things:

1. Essential *pre-conditions* (I call these the Five Keys to Progress).

2. Specific mechanics that explain *how* that evolution takes place (I call these How Progress Works).

What I said was true, but there is a third level to progress that I did not address. There is a third level, because progress is an evolutionary process that involves human thinking, decision-making and acting. This level is the one that most of us live in day-to-day.

Progress is the outcome of billions of individual decisions and actions. Given that, there must be something that individuals can do to promote progress.

The third level does not explain the grand causes of progress or how a society that is experiencing progress works. It is about the daily lives of individuals. And you are an individual. Without individuals like you who participate in progress, the vast decentralizing problem-solving network collapses.

Progress is not just something that is "out there." It involves you. It is a process that you can choose to join in on or not. And you choose to do so, not by some grand philosophical consideration – "Should I choose to join progress or not?" – but in the small decisions that you make every day. Particularly when you are younger than 30 years, you are probably still making those choices without realizing it.

You cannot create or undo progress by individual action, but you can choose to enjoy the benefits of the progress that surrounds you by getting a job, learning skills, and being a good parent. In doing so, you help yourself as well as help all the rest of society.

By joining progress, you help to sustain current progress. In addition, you provide role models for others that make it easier for them to make the same decision. Everyone who decides to join progress simultaneously helps themselves and everyone else.

Focus On Contribution, Not Distribution

Far too often we focus on the distribution of the benefits to progress. This is particularly true in politics and the media.

Every person should understand that many people believe in ideas that sound good but lead to dysfunctional outcomes. Most dangerous are those ideological activists who believe society is about one demographic group oppressing other demographic groups. They deny progress, seeing it as being nothing but an illusion. They relentlessly focus on the negative and try to misdirect attention away from obvious progress. They deny that individual decisions and actions can make a real difference in people's lives.

They preach their secular religion that only political activists taking power over the government can lead to progress and happiness. These dark visions have failed for centuries and have sabotaged so many people's lives.

They will inevitably fail again. It is just a question of how many people they hurt while they are failing.

Do not listen to them! They are destroying their own lives and trying to take you down with them. Do not let them.

I would argue that we should be far more concerned about contributions to progress. If we all do our best to contribute to society, then there are far more benefits of progress for everyone. We are all born with differing abilities to contribute to society, but we all need to use those differing abilities for the benefit of society. The primary means through which we do so is in our employed work.

Choose a Career Wisely

Some people believe that, to make the world a better place, you need to join a non-profit or become a caring professional, in fields such as teaching or nursing. Others believe that you need to engage in politics to fight for a better world. Some people think that you should go into academia, the clergy, or donate money to charities. Others believe that you should protect people by joining the police, fire department, or the military. Others say that you need to become a scientist.

While I do not want to undermine the value of those life choices, I would advise youths who want to promote progress to choose a different path.

If you want to promote progress, it is far better to go into professions that are more closely related to the technological and organizational innovations that drive the process. I suggest that if you want to create more progress, you should start a career in one of the following professions:

- Entrepreneurship
- Engineering
- Venture Capital (broadly defined)
- Other highly skilled manual labor

All of these professions directly work on creating new organizations and technology to make the world a better place. Without people doing these jobs, progress would be much slower. Fortunately, these professions are well paid. This is because businesses realize that they desperately need more of the skills used within these professions to be competitive.

Look at the six behaviors that I identify in the "How Progress Works" section in the Introduction. Every single one of them involves one or more of these professions. In your day-to-day work environment, you will be solving intellectually challenging problems and getting paid well to do it.

To a large extent, progress works because of technological and organizational innovation. But technologies and organizations do not invent themselves. Humans do.

Entrepreneurs found new organizations that have a business model that is built around one or more technologies. Typically, new organizations involved in emerging technologies must hire a large number of engineers. Those engineers typically modify one or more existing technologies and combine them with many other existing technologies to form a new product.

If that new organization has a business model that solves problems better than the competition, it has the potential to scale up fast. But to do so requires money. Venture capitalists and other forms of finance invest in promising new businesses in the hope that they will scale up to become very profitable corporations.

Some of those venture capitalists fund individual entrepreneurs that are just starting out, while others focus more on more established companies that need to scale fast. Venture capitalists also help to fill in the missing business skills that more technical entrepreneurs and engineers lack.

And while only a very tiny portion of society invents a new technology, that is not the end point.

Invention is just the starting point. For a new technology to promote progress, it has to go through a long chain of building prototypes, testing them, getting results, and updating the original design. If the product involves hardware, then a growing company needs highly skilled manual laborers to build prototypes, test them, give advice to engineers as to how to modify them, and teach themselves all the skills involved in manufacturing them at scale. In some cases, they even invent new technology or start a new business.

Even when the initial design and manufacturing are worked out through trial and error, someone has to test updated versions of the new final product, produce it, package it, distribute it, transport it, market it, and sell it. Someone also has to acquire the necessary raw materials, process them, transport them and make critical sub-components.

We All Can Contribute

All of the four professions that I listed earlier are intimately connected to the innovations that drive progress in the real world.

But not everyone has the intelligence, aptitude, and desire for a career in one of those four professions. Does that mean that everyone else is just a spectator?

No!

Supporting the four professions working on the leading edge of technological innovation are a huge number of workers and managers who make all the critical infrastructures of modern societies function. Our society needs electric grids, highway systems, sanitation facilities, water distribution facilities, trucking, airports, railroads, container ports, internet infrastructures, and computers. The list just keeps going on, and they all involve people like you.

And all of those people working on critical infrastructure need food, clothing, housing, education, and health care. And they deserve to have fun once in a while with movies, video games, or sports.

And every one of those people needs a father and mother that love them, care for them, and give them life advice.

We all matter to progress. We all matter because we are part of the vast, decentralized problem-solving network that is a modern society.

And every one of those people needs skills to play their role. We are not born with those skills. We need to learn those skills, and many of them take decades to master.

Learning skills is hard. We learn some of them from family, friends, and education. We learn even more by starting a job and then learning how to do that job well. If you do that job long enough, you will find that you are constantly having to update those skills, based on new technologies and business processes.

Learning skills is a key part of choosing to join the progress that surrounds you and contributing to it to the best of your abilities. Without skills, it is impossible to contribute to yourselves or the rest of society.

Your Job Is Not About You

Contrary to what many people say, **your job is not about you; your job is about other people.** As long as you live in a society with the Five Keys to Progress, working contributes to progress.

At its most fundamental, a job is about voluntarily working together with your co-workers to solve other people's (i.e. your customers') problems at scale. All potential customers choose between all the various solutions presented by companies and then decide which one best solves the problems that they most care about.

If you and your fellow employees do a good job, those customers then reward your employer by giving them money. Your employer rewards you with a portion of it as compensation for your work. And that portion is probably far higher than you think. Wages plus benefits are a much larger part of the economy than corporate profits.

And, more importantly, if you work hard, cooperate well with others and take the initiative to learn valuable new skills, you can earn much more money in the future. There are no such things as a dead-end job. They all involve learning.

If your employer does not want to pay you more money, find another one who does. If you cannot find another that does, you probably need to learn more skills. Or perhaps you need to relocate to a different area with more jobs.

After a hard day's work contributing to society, you can go home and focus on yourself. You can have fun, doing whatever you love. You can use that money that you earned solving other people's problems for whatever you want. Obviously, most of the money will be spent on necessities, but those "necessities" are luxuries that previous generations could not even dream of. That is a really good thing.

You Do Not Have To Do What You Love

Rather than "doing what you love", I would suggest to young people that you figure out a way to match your skills and interests to a career that is highly valued in the marketplace, learning new skills to make up the gap, moving to locations where those careers are located, and then working at a career for decades to get good at it.

Once you get really good at your job, you will enjoy the status, fulfillment, and autonomy that you gain from being good at what you do. Do not, however, expect to love your job immediately. Instead, try to feel proud of your slowly increasing contributions to the rest of society.

Feel proud of the very real contributions that you make to progress.

Those people who say they love their job are not being fully honest. My response is always "Really? So if your employer stopped paying you, you would keep working for free? If not, then it does not sound like you love your job very much." Inevitably, they look at me with surprise and sheepishly retract their statement.

If you love your job, that is great! But it is one thing to love your job (or more accurately like it better than most other jobs) and another to believe that doing so is a necessity in a career.

We need to be careful about the consequences of using happy slogans without really thinking about their consequences to other people. Many young people interpret the phrase as meaning that, if they do not love their job right now, then they are on the wrong career path.

The reality is that most young people do not know which career path best fits their talents, and they have unrealistic standards for knowing when they are on the right path.

Do not reject a career just because you do not love it immediately. Do not reject a career, just because other people do not give it high social status. Do not reject a career because some people think that it is less moral to choose a career path that pays well instead of a caring profession or politics.

This is not to glorify greed, as much as to recognize the importance of "contribution." At its most basic level, I believe that anyone who has a job or is a good parent is contributing to progress. While most acknowledge that some can contribute more than others because they have a greater inborn aptitude, we all can feel proud of the contributions that we make.

We all matter.

Care At Scale

Far too many people, particularly young people who are thinking about career choices, overestimate the importance of the caring professions and politics that I first listed and denigrate the innovation-oriented professions as "just being in it for the money." Those jobs are high-paying exactly because they solve so many people's problems.

And solving other people's problems is a really good thing. It is caring at scale.

While those in the caring profession tend to focus on one person or a small group of people face-to-face, higher-paying professions typically solve problems of people that they cannot see. But just because you cannot see a person does not mean you do not care. It is easy to assume that these professions are less caring, but they are actually caring at scale.

And many of those who denigrate entrepreneurs and engineers as being greedy also denigrate the contributions made by working-class people who staff critical infrastructures and people who are working in low-paying jobs in the service industry. In their mind, caring professionals are morally better than others, but it is not true. These other professions are just caring at scale.

Caring professions and highly-paid professionals are not better people; they just contribute in different ways. And perhaps they are born with greater abilities to do that, but what matters is if you are contributing to society as much as you can.

We all matter. We all contribute to the vast, decentralizing problem-solving network. And we should each contribute to it to the best of our abilities.

So we have to be careful about elevating a career in a caring profession because we believe that it is morally superior to those professions more involved in innovation. We also have to stop putting down other people because they keep working in jobs that they do not love.

Your job is not about you; it is about other people. And we all have different abilities.

Fortunately, the decisions and actions that promote individual success and happiness also align with those that promote societal progress. Living in a modern society is not a zero-sum game, where one progresses at the expense of others.

And parenting really matters. With every generation, society must reproduce itself. Just like plants and animals, humans need to reproduce themselves biologically. Because we live in complex societies that rely on technologies, skills, and social organizations to survive and prosper, humans must also teach their children how to function within those societies in a way that benefits them and others.

By doing so, we are effectively helping youths to make choices that enable them to enjoy the benefits of progress. The results will increase their chances of success and happiness. If we are unable to pass on skills, habits, and values to the next generation, our children are unlikely to benefit from past, present, and future progress.

My Advice to Youths

You can make choices that optimize your chances of enjoying the benefits of progress by doing the following:

1.   Copy the successful. It does not matter what field you have chosen, you can learn by copying what the most successful people do. Figuring out exactly what to copy is not so easy, but if you copy a large number of successful people in your field, you can narrow down the possibilities of what works. Most of all, do not waste your time resenting the successful. It only robs you of your own chances of success and happiness.

2.   Graduate from high school. A basic education that teaches literacy, numeracy, and how to cooperate with others is critical to success.

3.   Learn skills needed in the job market. Skills are fundamental to both individual success and societal progress. Using those skills to build

a better life for yourself is also fundamental to achieving success and happiness. Skills also give one a feeling of confidence and individual identity. For some, this means going to college and getting a technical degree. For others, it means acquiring a certification.

4.   If you do not live in an area that provides economic opportunity, move to an area that does. We have seen that geography places critical constraints on societies. Those constraints are just as important for individuals. By living close to where jobs are located, one can maximize one's chance of leading a successful and happy life. Progress will not come to you. You have to go to it.

5.   Work full-time in a job or found a business. This will not only pay the bills, but it will also help you to improve your skills far beyond anything that is taught in schools. This will also make you a more desirable mate. Most importantly, work is the primary venue where humans learn to cooperate with large groups of strangers.

6.   If you have children, get married and stay married. The two-parent family is the most fundamental social organization. It is by far the best means yet invented to pass on values, habits, and skills to our children, enabling them to benefit from the progress in society. It also promotes happiness for all family members. The benefit of two-parent families to children compared to other family structures is one of the most validated effects in social science. And particularly for men, it gives one motivation to follow all the other rules listed above.

7.   Tell every child and young adult you interact with, particularly your own children, about these principles. Many people, particularly college-educated people in the West, have followed these principles and implicitly teach them to their children. Unfortunately, those same people feel uncomfortable talking about them with others. But success and happiness are something to be shared, not hoarded.

8.   Be proud of your contributions. Try not to get so wound up with daily problems or other people's criticisms that you forget that you are contributing to the most amazing process on the planet: progress. When you step back from focusing on your own personal problems and look at your contributions to humanity, then the weight on your

shoulders gets a little lighter.

So there you have it: my principles for achieving success and happiness.

I strongly believe that progress does exist and individuals can take actions that drastically increase their chances of benefitting from the progress that surrounds them. And, by doing so, individuals accelerate progress to the benefit of everyone else.

Life is not zero-sum. We all can be successful and happy.

Believing that progress exists and following the principles outlined above does not guarantee success and happiness, but doing so will significantly increase the chances of achieving them.

If a large group of people follows these principles, they will come out significantly better than another large group that does not do so. Which group do you choose to be part of?

There will always be good and bad luck that affects individual outcomes. Some people are born with serious mental or physical disabilities and others acquire them later in life. Some are born into ethnic, religious, or racial groups that view progress as something that only other groups can be part of. Others grow up in such dysfunctional families or communities that they cannot even imagine leading a successful and happy life. Many pessimists sabotage their chances of success and happiness by not believing that they are possible.

I understand that some young people have a more difficult time joining progress than others, through no fault of their own. I also realize that the American government is not doing a good job of helping young people realize the importance of the actions that I suggest. Nor is it doing a good job of giving young people the incentive to follow that path.

In my next book in this series, *Upward Mobility: A Radical New Agenda to Uplift the Poor and Working Class,* I will outline ideas for restructuring social programs in the United States to promote upward mobility. While current policies seek to help the poor live more comfortably in a state of near poverty, policies based on promoting upward mobility would encourage lower-income youths to join in with the progress that the rest of society is experiencing.

I believe that by encouraging young people, particularly those from lower-income families, to make choices based upon a few key principles, we can help them to achieve better results and enable them to live more satisfying lives.

Choose the path to progress.

CONCLUSION

Throughout my *From Poverty to Progress* book series, I have argued for a Progress-based perspective that can be summarized in the following statements:

1. Humanity is better off now materially than it has ever been.

2. The progress that humanity has experienced, particularly over the last 30 years, is the single most important fact of our time.

3. This progress is very widespread. It can be seen in metrics of economic growth, freedom, poverty, agricultural production, literacy, diet, sanitation, life expectancy, neonatal mortality, education, housing, violence, and happiness (to name just a few), and in virtually every nation.

4. Acknowledging the existence of progress is not the same as optimism toward the future. It is an empirical observation about the material conditions of today compared to the material conditions of the past. Progress in the past does not guarantee future progress, though it does make it seem likely.

5. While today's problems seem insurmountable, we must never forget that our ancestors solved far bigger problems with far fewer resources.

6. If we combine an awareness of the progress that previous generations have passed down to us, a feeling of gratitude for benefitting from their efforts, and a willingness to learn how they achieved that progress, we are in a much better position to solve the problems of today.

7. We need to study history to understand the necessary preconditions for progress and how progress works. To maintain

progress we need to preserve and expand those things.

8. The Five Keys to Progress and an understanding of How Progress Works are critical to understanding progress. When a society acquires a sufficient amount of each of these keys, the society transforms into a vast, decentralized problem-solving network that generates progress.

9. The bulk of human history has been a desperate struggle for survival. Our material prosperity was limited by fundamental geographical constraints, particularly on food.

10. We are very fortunate that a handful of societies learned how to overcome those geographical constraints to create widespread progress. Progress started in the medieval city/states of Northern Italy and flowed to modern-day Belgium, Netherlands, Britain, and the United States. Now it has expanded to most of the rest of the world.

11. Our negative perceptions of the present state of the world come not from reality, but from a feedback loop among the fields of psychology, politics, ideology, the media, and social media. These people and institutions have built business models crafted around the narrative that "things are bad, they are getting worse, and those other people are to blame." This is the opposite of the Progress-based perspective. They deliberately trigger our worst psychological instincts for their own benefit. They believe that doing so will lead to a more just world, but it only breeds worry, anger, resentment, and resignation.

12. Progress comes from society, not from the government, but bad government policies can do a great deal to undermine progress (and unfortunately they have).

13. We must build a Progress movement to:

• Promote an awareness and understanding of progress. This will sweep away many of the negative perceptions caused by politics, ideology, the media, and social media.

• Research our history to identify policies and practices that promote progress.

• Build a political movement to sweep away government policies that undermine progress.

The American political process is polarized between liberal Democrats who are either hostile to progress or believe that it can only come from increased government spending and regulation, and conservative Republicans who are skeptical of progress and look back fondly on a past that never existed. The United States desperately needs a third perspective that is based on the concept of progress. That third perspective must be based on the concept and reality of progress.

In this book, I formulated a concrete Progress-based reform agenda focused on the following principles:

1. Promoting long-term economic growth.
2. Focusing relentlessly on results.
3. Reforming the political process to make all the above possible.

In my forthcoming book, *Upward Mobility: A Radical New Agenda to Uplift the Working Class and Poor*, I will add more proposals to:

4. Create a prosperous working class in wealthy nations.
5. Promote a clear pathway that enables youths from low-income families to enter the prosperous working class.

In combination, this Progress-based reform agenda is a radical departure from the platforms typically presented by liberal Democrats and conservative Republicans. The agenda focuses on rolling back bad government policies that undermine material progress. The agenda focuses on policy domains that are part of the Five Keys to Progress and How Progress Works, including affordable energy, affordable housing, affordable universities, decentralization, transparency, political competition, technological innovation, merit-based institutions, skills-based immigration, experimentation, and building export industries in developing nations.

The Left is opposed to the concept of progress and the policies in my proposed agenda because supporting them would force them to admit that society generates progress, and expanding government often undercuts that progress. The Right is opposed to the concept of progress and my proposed agenda because it would force them to admit that our material circumstances are much better than in the past.

To promote progress, we need to construct a new ideological Center between the Left and Right. That Center cannot be based on bipartisan compromise or mild reforms. It must be a Progress-based perspective that focuses on radical reforms of our political process and policies to roll back government policies that undermine progress and upward mobility. It must be both Radical and Centrist.

Supporters of progress should work from the ideological Center outwards. We should cooperate with Democrats, Republicans, Independents, and third parties to the extent that they agree with our agenda.

I believe that there is a critical nucleus of potential supporters who are alienated from both major parties. In particular, this nucleus is composed of working-class voters who do not subscribe to the ideological politics of activists and just want a growing economy with expanded opportunities for themselves, their family, and their community.

I also believe that there are pragmatic liberals and conservatives who see more in common with this ideological Center than the ideological agendas of the two major parties. A political coalition of independent centrists with pragmatic liberals and conservatives would be a potent force in American politics. This coalition should first focus on reforming the electoral process via state-level initiatives. Then, when a critical nucleus of independents is elected, they should reform the legislative process to break the power of party leaders.

With a fundamental reform of the electoral process and the legislative process, I believe that the ability of the two major parties to monopolize American politics would collapse. They would no longer just need to appeal to party primary voters in non-competitive districts and states. They would then be forced to appeal to the entire electorate.

Political reforms would force both major parties to radically change their policy agendas to appeal to the majority of the American people. It is quite possible that one or both major parties would see the benefits of adopting a Progress-based reform agenda. We should encourage such a change but demand results.

If neither major party is willing to adopt a Progress-based reform agenda, then supporters of progress should form a third party that competes on the federal, state, and local levels. While this would likely be quixotic today, after a fundamental reform of the electoral and legislative process, it is far more likely to succeed. It would be possible to achieve results via a third party based on the reform agenda outlined in this book. Let's call it the Progress party.

A reformist Progress party would likely be competitive across the nation. It would probably form the ideological Right in large metro areas of the Pacific coast and Northeast, and it would probably form the ideological Left in the rest of the nation. Without the ideological baggage of the two major parties, a Progress party would be relevant in all regions.

While, in our current political spectrum, a Progress-based reform agenda would be at the political Center, our long-term goal should be to completely replace the current Left. We must transform the political Left from an ideology that undermines progress to a pragmatic movement that promotes progress, upward mobility and achievable results.

One might call this a "New New Left."

Support for conservative parties is to a large extent based on anxieties created by the creative destruction of progress. Giving voters a choice between a progress-based Left and a progress-skeptical Right would enable voters to modulate the rate of progress that best suits them.

Progress should be the long-term goal, but the most desirable rate of progress and the creative destruction that goes along with that progress is not so clear. Some may want faster rates of progress than others.

The choice of the rate of progress should be left up to democratic governance. Unfortunately, our current situation, where the Left either is hostile to progress or unintentionally implements policies that undermine progress, makes this choice impossible. No matter whether voters support the Left or the Right, progress will be undermined by the victor.

As I see it, all current ideologies on the Left have played out and have been shown to not be as transformative as their supporters claim. With each failure, the Left doubles down, assuming that all we need is more passion, greater courage, and less willingness to compromise.

The result is always the same: failure. And each round of failure leaves behind a residue of failed government programs that cannot be rolled back, despite their lack of success.

Ideologies of the Left are very good at channeling the desire of people, particularly young people, towards creating a more just world. Unfortunately, the ideologues of the Left are very bad at implementing policies that achieve positive results. Far too often, their policies fail to deliver the desired results.

For decades the Left has been caught in the endless cycle of ideological enthusiasm, followed by failure in terms of results. This failure is never acknowledged because acknowledging that good intentions can lead to bad outcomes is just too painful. So the Left is incapable of learning and improving. The fundamental problem is that the Left is focused on good intentions, not progress and results.

All ideologies of the Left either reject the concept of progress or are fatally dependent upon economic growth to expand their social programs. The Left mistakenly seeks to transform a society that is operating far better than they realize.

We do not need to transform society. We need to transform key government policies that are undermining the foundations of progress and upward mobility.

Implementing a Progress-based reform agenda will not be easy. It will probably take decades to accomplish, but even the longest journey begins with one step.

I hope that this book series is the first step.

Website for Book Series

If you enjoyed this book, you should visit the companion website at:
frompovertytoprogress.com

> With a **free** subscription to this website, you get:
> - **Large discounts** on audiobooks and e-books
> - Free book samples (E-book and audiobook)
> - Access to videos about related content
> - Plus more.

Credits

Editor: Hugh Barker (can be contacted via Reedsy.com)
Special thanks to Tyler Cowen and Emergent Ventures for generously paying the production costs for this book.

Bibliography

To keep the price of this book as affordable as possible, the bibliography has been moved to the author's website at:
frompovertytoprogress.com

APPENDIX: REFORMING THE LEGISLATIVE PROCESS

Below is a proposed reform of the legislative process of the U.S. House and Senate. Similar reforms can also be implemented in state legislatures and city councils for major metropolitan areas. These reforms are inspired by the processes of the Nebraska state legislature, the only non-partisan legislature in the United States. Unless specifically mentioned, the procedures for the House and the Senate are identical.

Goals for these reforms

1. Reduce partisanship in the legislative process.
2. Transfer power from party leaders, who represent only the majority of the majority party, to committees that are representative of the entire body.
3. Empower committees to focus on legislation.
4. Preserve a balance between a focused agenda and checks-and-balances by individual representatives.

Leadership positions

The following leadership positions shall be abolished in both the House and the Senate:

- Majority Leader
- Minority Leader
- Majority Whip
- Minority Whip
- Deputy Whips

All of the powers of the above leaders shall be transferred to the Committee of Committees and the Executive Board.

Speaker of the House

A position of Speaker of the Senate shall be created. The position shall be identical in every way to the Speaker of the House, as explained below.

The Speaker of the House shall have no powers other than those given by the Committee on Committees and the Executive Board.

At the beginning of each legislative session, any member of the legislature may declare themselves a candidate for Speaker. Voting for the Speaker shall consist of two rounds. In the first round, each legislator shall rank up to five candidates in a secret ballot. The candidates with the five highest ranked-choice votes shall go onto the final round of voting. In the final round, each legislator shall rank the remaining five candidates based upon their preference in a secret ballot. The Speaker shall be the first candidate to receive a majority of the vote after the candidates with least votes are eliminated.

The Speaker of the House may not serve on any committee other than the Committee of Committees or the Executive Board.

The Speaker of the House shall serve for a single two-year term starting at the beginning of the legislative session. Each Speaker may serve no more than one term every ten years. The Speaker may not serve on the Committee of Committees or the Executive Board during that ten-year period.

Committee of Committees

The Committee of Committees shall have the sole power of selecting the members of congressional committees at the beginning of each session. It shall have no other power. No member of the Committee on Committees in the House may serve on any other committee.

Each member of the legislature may declare interest to the Committee of Committees in serving on up to five policy committees and rank those choices. The Committee of Committees shall make a good faith effort to accommodate the declared interests of each member.

Because of the small number of Senators relative to the number of committees, Senators on the Committee of Committees may serve on other committees, but they may not vote for themselves nor select members of the committees that they declare an interest in serving on.

The Committee on Committees shall consist of:

- The Speaker of the House
- Eight members elected by the membership

The members of the Committee of Committees shall serve for a single two-year term starting at the beginning of the legislative session. Each member may serve no more than one term every ten years.

At the beginning of the legislative session, any member of the legislature may declare themselves candidate for the Committee on Committees. From the list of candidates, the full membership shall rank up to 8 candidates in a secret ballot. The 8 candidates with the most votes based upon ranked-choice vote shall be elected to the committee.

The Committee on Committees shall create a report recommending the membership of all committees to the legislature. The legislature may approve the report with a three-fifths vote or reject it, but may not amend the report. If the report is rejected, the Committee on Committee must start over and create a new report until the legislature approves the report with a three-fifths vote.

Executive Board

The Executive Board shall determine:

- Assignment of bills to committee
- Legislative agenda
- Whether amendments to bill are appropriate for consideration by the full membership

The Executive Board shall serve for a single 2-year term starting at the beginning of the legislative session. Each member may serve no more than one term every ten years.

The Executive Board shall consist of:

- The Speaker of the House
- Eight members elected by the membership

The Executive Board shall be selected in exactly the same manner as the Committee on Committees. No member of the Executive Board may serve on any other committee.

Committee Chairpersons

Each committee shall have a Chairperson. After committee assignments have been approved, any member of that committee may nominate themselves to run for committee chairperson.

Voting for the Chairperson shall consist of one vote each in a secret ballot among the committee members. Each legislator shall rank the candidates based upon their preference in a secret ballot. The Chairperson of each committee shall be selected based upon ranked-choice vote.

Each Committee Chairperson shall hold the position for a single 2-year term starting at the beginning of the legislative session. Each Committee Chairperson may serve no more than one term every ten years.

Legislative Process

1. One or more members write a bill.
2. The bill is assigned to the relevant committee.

3.   The committee can write a new bill or edit the bill as desired. They may also refer it to a sub-committee.

4.   The bill is reviewed by the Congressional Budget Office and the Congressional Economic Impact Office.

5.   The bill is moved to the full membership. Debate takes place and amendments are considered.

6.   Final vote is made by the full membership.

7.   Reconciliation of differences between the House bill and the Senate bill.

Assigning Bills to Committees

Any member may propose a bill. The bill can be assigned to a specific committee by majority vote of either:

- the committee itself, or:
- the Executive Board. In case of multiple committees wanting a bill, the Executive Board shall decide.

Any member of the legislature may object to the assignment and attempt to reassign the bill to a different committee based on a majority vote by the full membership.

A bill cannot be voted on by the full membership until after it has been assigned to a committee and then moved from a committee.

Powers of Committees

Committees and sub-committees are the main domain for discussion and amendments on all proposed bills. All bills voted on by the full membership must start in a committee relevant to its content. Committee members may write or edit bills in their policy domain as they so choose.

Committees may assign bills to sub-committees for further review and amendment by majority vote. Sub-committees can be created, changed and dissolved as desired by majority vote of the committee. Sub-committee members must also be members of the parent committee. Sub-committee membership is to be determined in a manner identical to the way the Committee of Committees makes committee assignments.

Leaving Committee

If it has been in committee for at least 60 days while Congress is in session, a bill can move to a vote by the full membership by a majority vote in any one of the following:
- the committee that has been assigned the legislation
- the full membership of the legislature, or
- the Executive Board

The 60-day period may be overridden by two-thirds vote of the full membership.

Review Process

Before a vote by the full membership, a bill must be reviewed by:
- The Congressional Budget Office (CBO) to determine its impact on the budget and revenues.
- The Congressional Economic Impact Office (CEIO) to determine its impact on the American economy.

Before a bill can come up for a vote of the full membership, it must be revenue-neutral or lessen projected deficits. If a bill is not, it will be referred to a committee whose domain is raising revenue for writing a bill, to raise enough revenue to make it revenue-neutral or lessen project deficits.

Debate

Once a bill has been reviewed by the OMB and the CEIO, the membership can open debate by majority vote. The debating period must be at least one week. The one-week debating period may be overridden by two-thirds vote of the full membership.

Once all amendments have been considered (as detailed below), debate can be closed by a majority vote. The filibuster is abolished.

Amendments

During the debate period, any member may propose an amendment to a bill that is before the membership. Before it can be voted on, the amendment must be:

- Directly relevant to the domain of the original bill, as determined by separate majority votes by the Executive Board and its original committee.
- Revenue-neutral or lessen projected deficits (as determined by the CBO).
- Not have a negative economic impact of over $100 million on the American economy (as determined by the CEIO).

The amendment must pass a three-fifths vote by the full membership to become part of the bill.

Voting on the Bill

Once debate has been closed and all amendments have been considered, a bill may be voted on, as long as it remains revenue-neutral or lessen projected deficits as determined by the OMB. The bill must pass by majority vote by the full membership.

Reconciliation

Any bill passed by the full House and the full Senate that address similar policy domains but do not match in exact wording must go to reconciliation. Reconciliation of the bill is conducted via a joint session of the House and Senate committees that originally had the bills. Reconciliation may not change the wording on any part of the bill that matches the bills that came from both chambers.

Reconciliation is passed with a majority vote by:

1. The House committee.
2. The Senate committee, and
3. Both committees combined.

After the bill has been reconciled, it must pass a majority vote in both the House and the Senate.

ABOUT THE AUTHOR

Michael Magoon received a BA in History from University of California at Berkeley and a PhD in Political Science & Public Policy from Brown University. He taught university courses for the following three years. Feeling restless with the staid academic life, Magoon decided to make a career change and entered the rapidly growing field of digital technology.

Starting as a Technical Writer and then as a User Experience Designer, Magoon has worked for some of the biggest and most innovative technology companies in the world, including Microsoft, Apple, Intel, Oracle and Verizon. While working in the technology field, he continued reading books about a wide variety of topics including science, geography, technology, culture and history.

Magoon's background in both academia and technology corporations has given him a unique viewpoint on progress and how it affects our lives.

www.ingramcontent.com/pod-product-compliance
Lightning Source LLC
Chambersburg PA
CBHW070152310326
41914CB00089B/857